From Rugs to Riches

From Rugs to Riches

Housework, Consumption and Modernity in Germany

Jennifer A. Loehlin

BERG

Oxford • New York

First published in 1999 by
Berg
Editorial offices:
150 Cowley Road, Oxford OX4 1JJ, UK
70 Washington Square South, New York NY 10012, USA

© Jennifer A. Loehlin 1999

Berg is the imprint of Oxford International Publishers Ltd.

Library of Congress Cataloging-in-Publication Data

A catalogue record for this book is available from the Library of Congress.

British Library Cataloguing-in-Publication Data

A catalogue record for this book is available from the British Library.

ISBN 1 85973 284 4 (Cloth)

Typeset by JS Typesetting, Wellingborough, Northants.
Printed in the United Kingdom by WBC Book Manufacturers, Bridgend,
Mid Glamorgan.

for my parents

Contents

Acknowledgements

This book has been a long time in the making and I have incurred many debts along the way. Above all, I would like to thank the women who shared their stories with me. Thanks also to the people who helped arrange some of the interviews, especially Frau Christa Hidasi-Wilke. I am also grateful to the archivists at the Bibliothek für Publizistik in Berlin-Lankwitz and the Universitätsbibliothek in Freiburg, who carried many arm-loads of heavy magazines for me.

For permission to reprint illustrations, my thanks to the aforementioned libraries as well as Bauknecht Hausgeräte GmbH/Whirlpool Europe, Bayer Faser GmbH, BSH Bosch und Siemens Hausgeräte GmbH, Constructa-Neff Vertriebs-GmbH, Fakir-Werk GmbH & Co., Henkel KGaA, Lever Fabergé Deutschland GmbH, Linde AG, Miele & Cie. GmbH & Co., Musterring International/Josef Höner GmbH & Co. KG, Temagin Arzneimittel GmbH & Co. KG, Thompson GmbH and J. Weck GmbH & Co. It was not possible to trace all possible copyright holders for all of the illustrations, and I apologize for any omissions.

Many people helped me in many ways during the research phase of the project. My thanks in particular to Kit Belgum, Walburga Geiselmann, Lisa Heineman, Sibylle Meyer, Kathy Pence, Eva Schulze, Patty Stokes and Bernd Weber. Patty and Bernd also provided invaluable assistance in Germany while I was revising the manuscript in Texas. Without the persistence of Gerry Sherayko and Joan Clinefelter, this book would probably never have been published. My editor at Berg, Maike Bohn, has been very patient and supportive, as has my boss at the Texas Higher Education Coordinating Board, Gloria White. This book originated as my dissertation at the University of Texas at Austin, and I would like to thank the members of my committee and my adviser, David F. Crew, for their advice and support. The research was supported in part by a grant from the Department of History.

–1–

Introduction

The 1950s and 1960s were a period of almost alarming economic growth in West Germany. From 1950 to 1965, annual growth in GNP averaged 5.6 per cent. Initially, unemployment was relatively high, due to economic disruption and a large influx of refugees, but, from 1957 through 1970, both inflation and unemployment remained below 4 per cent; in a few years, they were both under 2 per cent, an unemployment level well below what economists consider full employment and almost unimaginable in Germany today.[1] At the time, the growing prosperity stood out against the devastation caused by Germany's defeat in the Second World War. Streets of rubble were replaced by box-like apartment buildings and tidy gardens. In the ruined centres of cities, modern office buildings shot up. The drawn faces of the immediate postwar years gave way to the customary rosy cheeks.

The *Wirtschaftswunder*, or economic miracle, provided a convenient focus for national pride after a disastrous military defeat. Relief from the poverty of the immediate postwar years and hope for a more prosperous future provided the new Federal Republic of Germany with an important base of legitimacy. As an avowedly provisional state, the product of external forces rather than internal choice, the republic faced certain problems on this score. At the international level, the standard of living was an area of competition between East and West in the Cold War. Domestically, economic progress helped the Christian Democrats, who claimed the credit, to maintain political predominance until the *Wirtschaftswunder* started to fizzle out in the late 1960s.

This was also a period of strong emphasis on home and family life. The new constitution of the Federal Republic guaranteed the state's protection of marriage and the family. Adenauer's 1953 cabinet included a Family Minister, who kept up a high public profile, despite the weakness of his office in terms of staff and financing. To restore stability to German families meant to move beyond the chaos of the years in which family members had been separated and strangers thrown together by war, flight and a serious shortage of housing.

Supporting the family was also seen as a break with National Socialism, which had interfered in parents' control of their children's upbringing and sent fathers off to war. Whereas the Nazis had preached the subordination of the individual, and the family, to the needs of the *Volk*, the postwar consensus in West Germany was for a strong family, supported but not violated by the state, as the basic building-block of society. A strong family unit represented a safe path between the collectivism of the East and the consumerism of the West. (In practice, West Germany's resistance to the former was much stronger than to the latter.) The key to the family's success was its 'heart', the stay-at-home mother selflessly devoted to the well-being of her husband and children. In retrospect, the *Wirtschafts- wunder* seems like an island of calm domesticity between the chaos of the war and the economic and social changes of the 1970s.

None the less, the *Wirtschaftswunder* did not leave the household and domestic life unaffected – indeed, it was precisely in everyday life that the economic changes were experienced most directly. This study focuses on the *Wirtschaftswunder* at home, with particular emphasis on the spread of major household appliances. The boundary between luxuries and necessities, between products that would inevitably always be limited to a fortunate few and products essential to a decent standard of living for an ordinary household, moved a long way during this period, not without generating worries about excessive materialism and its consequences.

Changing material conditions in the home, from the construction of new, modern apartments to the proliferation of cleaning products and convenience foods, affected the day-to-day shape of housework. This development took place in a political and social climate in which sharply differentiated gender roles coexisted with formal recognition of the equality of men and women. Housework was defined as women's work; paid employment for married women, and especially mothers, remained controversial. Family law proclaimed that the husband's and wife's contributions to the support of the family – his through wage work, hers through housework – were equal, but housework did not earn concrete recognition in the form of wages or benefits.

The political goals of economic growth and stable, traditional families could come into conflict. Careful budgeting by economical housewives helped to make the *Wirtschaftswunder* happen, but, as time went on, higher disposable incomes and readily available, inexpensive consumer goods diminished the importance of thrift. With cash income valuable and work readily available in a tight labour market, the temptation for married women to work outside the home increased. The use of modern appliances and housekeeping products tended to reinforce the notion that housework was not really work, not deserving of social recognition.

There was a tension between the very notions of modernity and the home. Machines and chemicals were elements of the male, outside world – they clashed with the concept of women as creatures of nature, instinct and emotion. Could this tension be resolved to create a model of housework, and housewives, that was modern and yet traditional, that offered the advantages of labour- and time-saving technology without encouraging women to apply that labour and time to work outside the home?

Boundaries of the Study

Chronological

Given that the spread of household appliances is a central subject of this study, the period under consideration extends through the 1960s. There was a great deal of discussion of household appliances in the 1950s, but their real transformation into commonplace household possessions did not begin until late in that decade and took place largely in the 1960s. In the West German government statistical office's first survey of ownership of durable consumer goods, in 1962–63, 68.9 per cent of the refrigerators had been purchased since 1957 and 67 per cent of the automatic washing-machines since 1959. More than half the households with three or more persons had refrigerators, while about half had washing-machines, generally not automatic ones.[2] By the second survey, in 1969, refrigerators were virtually universal and over half of the families with children had automatic washing-machines, 80 per cent of them purchased since 1961. At that time, 47 per cent of families of white-collar workers and 43 per cent of families of blue-collar workers had automatic washing-machines.[3]

This study is thus in the middle ground between shorter- and longer-term studies of the postwar period. Tracing developments up to the present day has been the concern especially of sociologists, such as Sibylle Meyer and Eva Schulze.[4] Many historical studies, on the other hand, concentrate either on the years during and immediately after the war or on the 1950s. The former period has attracted the attention of historians of women because of women's numerical dominance and the public visibility of traditionally female concerns, such as obtaining food for their families.[5]

Other authors, such as Michael Wildt, focus primarily on the 1950s. Wildt's attention is directed primarily to food consumption, though he also discusses household appliances, principally food processors and refrigerators, in this context. He argues that the improvement in the living conditions of ordinary working-class West Germans set in later than is often realized and was less dramatic than the term *Wirtschaftswunder* suggests. I do not dispute his findings, but see the glass as half full rather than half empty. Indeed, I would argue that the length of time for which growth was sustained makes the development all the more remarkable.

Much of the existing historical work on household technology focuses on earlier periods, particularly the nineteenth century, when key technological developments were made. The period of the 1950s and 1960s is, indeed, not one in which there were a great many crucial technological discoveries – most of the significant mechanical inventions had been made, and the electronic ones were yet to come. Rather, it is the period in which major household appliances became common consumer goods in Western Europe, a development which in the United States was well under way in the interwar period.

Geographical

This study does not cover the late German Democratic Republic. While a comparative study of the two Germanys would be interesting, this would present methodological difficulties because the source materials available for the two countries are not comparable. The East German women's magazine *Für Dich* operated under different constraints from its Western counterparts, and views of East German women of their past seem likely to be coloured in a different way from West German women's views by the ultimate fate of the society in which they lived for four decades and by the problems of the present. None the less, I hope that this work will also contribute to a better understanding of the conditions under which the East German state operated. The issue of the standard of living of ordinary working people played a central role over the years in the propaganda war between the two countries. Ultimately, the East German government's failure to provide a 'world class' standard of living for its people was crucial in undermining its legitimacy.

While the magazines used as sources had national circulations, the interviews were all conducted in south-western Germany, all but one in and around Freiburg im Breisgau. This was intended to counterbalance the tendency of existing studies to concentrate on northern Germany. As it turned out, however, several of the women interviewed had moved to Freiburg from northern and eastern Germany, so the sample was more geographically diverse than originally expected.

Demographic

The focus of the study on domestic roles and the spread of household appliances also limits its demographic focus. This study deals primarily, although not exclusively, with what were termed 'complete families', i.e. those containing two parents of opposite sex and their children.[6] The focus is also on those who were neither so wealthy that they had already achieved fully-equipped mechanized households in the interwar period nor so poor that they did not participate in this development in the first postwar decades. This was the 'normal' family addressed by political rhetoric and the target market addressed by advertisements for household appliances. If the image of the modern housewife promoted in women's magazines was to become a reality anywhere in West German society, then it was here.

Certainly, there were many women for whom this image was completely divorced from reality. Many women of the war generation lost their partners, whether to death or to the strains which long separations and changed circumstances imposed on relationships, and many of them stayed single, whether out of choice or out of inability to find a partner who suited them.[7] In the 1960s, the rate of divorce was also rising, though far below today's levels.[8] Some women, both single and married, lived in such straitened circumstances that participation in the consumer culture through such high-end purchases as washing-machines and refrigerators was out of the question during this period. Some women pursued careers and did not think of themselves primarily as housewives. Some women were lesbians, although the popular press and the politics of the day generally ignored their existence.

None the less, most women did marry and take on the responsibility for housekeeping and child care, usually without full-time work outside the home. The 1950s and 1960s saw the peak of the 'housewife marriage' in West Germany. Before the war, many women had worked to help support their families. The war increased the number of women working outside the home and decreased the number of intact families and the number of intact homes. From the 1970s, rising divorce rates and increased numbers of out-of-wedlock births decreased the number of traditional families, and more and more married women stayed in the labour force.

The primary focus is on families with children of school age or younger, and thus on women from roughly their mid-twenties to their mid-forties. Given the chronological focus on the 1950s and 1960s, this means women born from about the decade before the First World War to the end of the Second. Most of the women interviewed were born in the 1920s or 1930s.

Sources and Methodology

While the changes affecting and promising (or threatening) to affect the West German home in the 1950s and 1960s were significant, they attracted little attention in the Bundestag or the newspapers. The personal was the personal and the political the political, a narrowly defined and masculine area. More information can be found in the magazines whose audience was defined as 'women'. Here there were articles discussing such topics as appliances, housework and gender roles directly, as well as numerous advertisements for the proliferating variety of household products. A sampling of these magazines, chosen with an eye to both relevant content and wide circulation, constitutes one of the principal sources of information used in this study. The particular magazines chosen and the methods used will be discussed in more detail below.

Given that the period under study is relatively recent, it has been possible to supplement this information with interviews with women who experienced the changes firsthand. The two types of source material complement each other. The interviews provide direct input from the people whose history is the subject of the study, but relatively brief glimpses from a small number of viewpoints, and refracted through the subsequent history of the individuals and their society. The magazines reached a national audience, demonstrating their broad appeal and potential influence, and have been changed little by the intervening years.

Interviews

Of the twelve women interviewed, seven were members of a local housewives' organization, four were acquaintances (or mothers of acquaintances) of the author, and one responded to a handbill posted in a neighbourhood shopping centre. [9] Both women who married before 1950 and women who married in the 1960s were included, in order to give a greater sense of the change in circumstances over time. The sample included women from a variety of social backgrounds. One woman had been widowed in 1947 and lived in a household with her children and, until their deaths in the 1960s, her parents, and one woman was married but did not have children; otherwise, all of the interviewees spent at least part of the period 1950–1970 living with husbands and children. Their formal education ranged from the legal minimum (for that generation,

-6-

eight years of school) to a medical degree, and their and their husbands' occupations from blue-collar to professional. Brief biographies of the women interviewed are contained in an appendix. Because some of the women were promised anonymity, I have used initials rather than names in referring to them and have omitted the names of very small towns.

The women from the housewives' group were interviewed, individually, in a separate room during the group's regular meetings. These interviews varied in length but were in general much shorter than the other interviews, which were mostly around ninety minutes. There were also two group discussions, which, however, could not be tape-recorded due to the overall noise level. The interview with Frau Sch. and the interviews with acquaintances were conducted in the interviewees' homes. In most cases only interviewer and interviewee were present; in the case of Frau M., Herr M. was on hand for most of the interview and, in the case of Frau Ge., her younger son was present. The interviews were recorded on audiotape, using a rather primitive tape recorder. Most of them were later transcribed; in two cases, notes rather than full transcripts were used. In all the interviews, a short list of topics was used, but the interviewees were given considerable freedom to tell their stories in their own way.

The national and generational differences between interviewer and interviewees may be presumed to have had some impact on the interviews; for one thing, all interviewees made at least some effort to speak *Hochdeutsch* rather than dialect. Based on my age and status as an unmarried student, I suspect they assumed I was a sloppy housekeeper myself, though they did not have evidence to confirm this. The idea of a historian being interested in housework was strange to most of them.

Magazines

The main criteria for the selection of magazines were subject-matter (focus on women, with substantial attention to domestic roles) and circulation. Most of the magazines used in the study (*Stimme der Frau/Für Sie, Constanze, Brigitte, Ihre Freundin* [10]) were what I will call general-interest women's magazines, featuring entertainment, fashion, recipes and advice on various topics, analogous to US magazines like *Glamour* and *Redbook*. The other magazine used, *Ratgeber für Haus und Familie*, focused more heavily on housekeeping topics. It had a smaller format than the others (15 cm x 21 cm, about 5.75" x 8", while *Constanze*'s 1961 dimensions of 26.5 cm x 35.5 cm, roughly 10.5" x 14", were typical for the general-interest women's magazines) and was a monthly rather than a fortnightly.

Introduction

Most of the magazines were founded in the last years of the 1940s. Some were successor publications to earlier magazines. *Das Blatt der Hausfrau*, which changed its name to *Brigitte* in 1952, dated back to 1886. Its publication was interrupted from 1944 to 1949. *Ratgeber für Haus und Familie*, published under that title since 1950, was the successor to the Weck bottling-jar firm's company paper *Die Frischhaltung*, published from 1901 until the first year of the war and resumed in 1947. Even with the other magazines, there were elements of continuity, as staff members had gained their experience working on prewar publications. The genre of general-interest women's magazines was more typical of postwar West Germany than of prewar Germany, where the principal categories of magazines aimed at women had been needlework magazines, housewives' magazines and relatively low-circulation but influential fashion and society magazines. To some extent, the general-interest women's magazines took over the function of the prewar family magazines. They initially had a substantial number of male readers, but the proportion declined over time (for *Stimme der Frau/Für Sie*, for instance, from 32.6 per cent male readers in 1954 to 22.0 per cent in 1959 and 17.6 per cent in 1968).[11]

Several categories of publications aimed at a primarily female audience were not included in the study. These include magazines devoted to sewing or knitting patterns, magazines produced for women with particular organizational, political or religious affiliations, and inexpensive celebrity-gossip-orientated weeklies, such as *Frau im Spiegel*. The selection of magazines to include was made on the basis of the amount of relevant material and availability. Given the focus of the study on middle-class housewives, the degree of class bias introduced in the source material by excluding the down-market publications was deemed acceptable. It would certainly be interesting, however, to compare their images of gender roles and housework with those presented in the magazines studied here.

Some use was made of the news magazine *Der Spiegel* and of newspapers, principally the Freiburg local newspaper, the *Badische Zeitung*. These sources, however, had little directly relevant content and played a subordinate role. For the most part, except when there was a relevant law being debated in the Bundestag, it was in magazines aimed at a primarily female audience that housework and gender roles were discussed.

All of the magazines used had large circulations. This both increased their potential influence and indicated that they were succeeding in attracting readers. Circulations were, on the whole, increasing through the 1950s and 1960s. *Constanze* dominated the market in the 1950s, having already passed the 300,000-copy mark in 1949. Its circulation levelled off in the early 1960s and generally remained between 500,000 and 600,000 copies thereafter. Both *Brigitte* and *Für Sie* had circulations of around 175,000 as of 1957 but were on their way up. For almost the entire decade of the 1960s, *Für Sie* was the leader among the women's magazines, passing the one-million-copy mark in 1967. *Brigitte* also grew rapidly, overtaking *Constanze* for the number-two spot by 1963. At the end of 1969, *Constanze* was discontinued in favour of its more successful sister publication *Brigitte*, which jumped to above 1,400,000 copies. *Ratgeber* experienced rapid circulation growth in the mid-1950s and then levelled off at around 400,000 copies. The circulation of *Freundin* grew steadily but not very dramatically from a level of just over 200,000 copies in 1954 to around half a million copies by the mid-1960s.[12]

These magazines were doing reasonably well by West German standards. They were not in the same league as the TV and radio programme guide *Hör zu*, which was selling over three million copies per issue as of 1960, at a time when only *Constanze* among the women's magazines exceeded half a million. The tabloid *Stern* had a circulation of well over a million. On the other hand, the news magazine *Der Spiegel* sold just over 350,000 copies per issue, only slightly ahead of *Ihre Freundin*. The per capita circulation of women's magazines in general was slightly lower in West Germany than in France and considerably lower than in the United States and Britain.[13]

Although single women were somewhat overrepresented among the readers of general-interest women's magazines relative to their proportion in the total population, most readers were married. For example, according to one survey, 58.1 per cent of *Brigitte*'s female readers in 1963 were married. For the somewhat more conservative *Für Sie*, the figure was 64.9 per cent. Magazine readers were somewhat more likely to be employed outside the home than the female population as a whole, and those who were employed were somewhat more likely to be in white-collar jobs.[14]

Stimme der Frau (from 1957 *Für Sie*) was a little more sedate than the others and in the 1960s rather up-market, with many advertisements for expensive luxury products. Its readership was slightly older than that of the other general-interest women's magazines. In 1963, 30 per cent of its readers were aged eighteen to twenty-nine, while the corresponding figure for *Brigitte* was 36.6 per cent.[15] The differences among *Brigitte*, *Constanze* and *Ihre Freundin* were rather subtle matters of 'personality', except for *Brigitte*'s rather staid pre-1957 period and *Constanze*'s image shifts in the 1960s.

Introduction

Ratgeber's intended audience was older, more rural (there are articles on gardening and the care of small livestock, especially in the 1950s) and more conservative than the audience envisioned by the publishers of the other magazines. *Ratgeber* did not include articles on the use of make-up until the 1960s and remained virtually free of sex right through the 'sexual revolution' of the 1960s. It was in general less open to the development of consumer culture than the other women's magazines, frequently editorializing on the dangers of living beyond one's means and the importance of non-material values, such as maternal love and neighbourliness.

In part, this reflected its different economic situation. *Ratgeber* was less expensively produced, with a small editorial staff, monthly appearance, relatively few illustrations and smaller size. In addition, it was produced not by a commercial publishing house but by Weck, a bottling-jar firm which founded the magazine to promote proper bottling as well as sound modern housekeeping processes in general. Thus thrift and a tendency to substitute one's own labour for commercial production were beneficial rather than potentially damaging to the publisher's interests.

While *Ratgeber* was a monthly and was sold almost exclusively by subscription, the others were generally published every other week and sold at news-stands, by subscription and to the services which provided beauty shops and other establishments with reading material for their customers.[16] These 'reading circles' increased the number of readers per issue. A 1949 study indicated that a quarter of the West German population read *Constanze* at least occasionally. As of 1956, it was the third most widely read magazine in the country, close behind *Hör Zu* and *Stern*. Even in 1966, well past its prime, it was reaching 9.1 per cent of the adult population with each issue, although it now fell behind *Für Sie*'s 10 per cent.[17] *Ratgeber* probably had a lower number of readers per issue than the other magazines but was also likely to be kept longer.

In the early to mid-1950s, the general-interest women's magazines contained a large proportion of general entertainment, such as fiction, light verse and photographs of cute children and animals. For instance, in a sample of 1956 issues of *Brigitte*, the proportion of editorial content categorized as entertainment (including fiction and discussions of films) ranged from 52 per cent to 59 per cent.[18] Otherwise, fashion was usually the largest single section and tended to be placed near the front. Recipes and articles on cooking were a regular feature, generally with inexpensive dishes featured.

There was more attention to politics at the beginning of the 1950s than there would be again until the late 1960s. One 1951 issue of *Constanze*, for example, featured a story on whether widows' pensions might be cut (a subject of more interest to young women at the time than later) and another on a woman's quest for a doctor willing to perform an abortion (on medical grounds). The decline in coverage of political issues apparently represented a victory of consumer tastes over the interest in political re-education which existed to some extent among editors and especially among the occupation authorities, who had been responsible for issuing the first licences for new publications before the establishment of the West German state. [19]

For *Ratgeber*, the section on cooking was consistently the largest single section in the magazine. *Ratgeber* typically devoted about twice as many pages to cooking as to fiction and other entertainment. It provided considerably more coverage of washing, cleaning and other household tasks than did the other women's magazines.[20] While it included some puzzles and games for children and, at times, a men's page, it was primarily aimed at married women. A 1954 editorial statement of the magazine's purpose saw the 'wish to be a good housewife' as the unifying characteristic of the magazine's readers.[21]

In the early 1950s, hard times were still in evidence. At the beginning of the 1950s, the cover photos were generally not in colour, though colour was used to emphasize the titles. Inside the magazines as well, black and white predominated through the mid-1950s, though with increasing use of single-colour headings. The usual size for *Ihre Freundin* in 1951 was thirty-two pages, including covers, and it was temporarily forced to drop below that due to a paper shortage, but by 1957 it was up to seventy pages.[22] Prices were rising slowly; *Ihre Freundin* cost sixty pfennigs in 1950, increasing to seventy in September 1955 and to eighty at the end of 1960. The prices of its competitors were similar.

Ratgeber covers from the 1950s frequently had pastoral illustrations. They often featured young women, sometimes farmers at work, sometimes simply landscapes. The 1951 cover shown in Figure 1.1 used a black-and-white photograph. The colour of the frame changed every few months. The illustration features a seasonal theme from the agricultural year, harvest. It also highlights a church spire. It could express either a pride in or a nostalgic longing for the wholesome rural life. The other magazines, in contrast, generally featured fashionably dressed young women on their covers, both in the early 1950s and later.

Advertisements at the beginning of the 1950s still reflected an economy of scarcity. Advertisements for products which were inexpensive and hard to do without, such as laundry soap, predominated. An advertisement for

Figure 1.1 *Ratgeber* cover, August 1951.

Sunlicht soap could, except for minor matters of style, have dated from the late nineteenth century rather than from 1951. It showed a woman gleefully doing her wash with the most basic equipment – a wooden washtub and soap. It aimed to prevent housewives from economizing still further by buying another brand of soap. The advertisement pointed

Figure 1.2 Advertisement for Sunlicht soap, *Constanze* 9 (25 April) 1951, p. 37.

to a current paper shortage, indicating that the soap was being sold without a wrapper.

Another type of argument was shown in an advertisement for Fewa, a detergent for delicate fabrics. Lest anyone think that the purchase of such a product was a luxury, the advertisement threatened that sweaters washed with other products would mat to the extent that they would only be good for dust rags. Emphasis on the ability of a particular product to preserve valuable property was quite popular in advertisements for cleaning products and also for appliances such as washing-machines.[23]

Another approach used in the Fewa advertisement, also popular in advertisements for cleaning products in the 1950s, was that of versatility. Fewa was not only good for washing sweaters, but for cleaning painted furniture, doors and windows. Thus, even a fairly specialized product was advertised as being versatile. This presents a sharp contrast to the later proliferation of one-use products, such as toilet-bowl cleaners or cleaners for the burners of electric stoves.

Even cosmetic products weren't to be identified as luxuries. One 1950 advertisement proclaimed quite specifically, 'Body powder has nothing to do with luxury, quite the contrary: anyone who wishes to avoid the expense of perfume finds an ideal solution: Dr Dralle's Body Powder is intensely scented.' The powder was now packaged in a proper tin again instead of in cardboard, but this container was 'practical' and 'durable'.[24]

In the early 1950s, there was a certain tension evident in the general-interest women's magazines between the glamour they portrayed and the realities of readers' lives. Particularly in fashion and interior design, magazines frequently showed products which were out of reach of most of their readers. This is of course still true of high-fashion and interior-design magazines today, but in the early 1950s it attracted resentment from embittered would-be consumers. A piece in *Constanze* on Paris fashions (which the magazine played a highly visible role in promoting) began with a sort of disclaimer, reminding readers that the expensive garments were often bought by fashion houses to copy, rather than by spoiled rich women.

And to transform the sometimes exaggerated ideas of a fashion artist into something practical and wearable is a lovely task for any woman. After all, the little Parisiennes don't do anything else when they sew their new spring dresses out of cheap fabric, the colour and the style modelled on the *haute couture*. [25]

This defensiveness was evidently motivated by complaints from readers. One letter quoted in the same issue attacked *Constanze*'s promotion of Dior's extravagant New Look:

Do we have to dance to this tune, we in our poor, defeated country with its millions of unemployed and displaced people, must we try to imitate this monstrous extravagance, which is not based on any real need? [26]

Ihre Freundin provided readers with hints for altering clothes to fit the spring 1950 fashions. Perhaps it wasn't necessary to buy a new dress; a new hat, a pair of gloves or a handbag might be sufficient to provide that fashionable touch. A 1954 *Ratgeber* article promoted the comforting idea that elegance was more a matter of taste than budget. 'The real lady – and there are still ladies, even today – looks elegant in the simplest of dresses.' Most important was elegance of movement, which did not cost money. [27]

In the late 1950s and early 1960s, the general-interest women's magazines usually featured colour photographs of smiling, fashionably dressed young women on their covers, rather similar to today's covers except for stylistic differences (e.g. more formal poses, and many more gloves and hats). This type of cover, also typical for women's magazines in other countries, personified the magazine's image as a 'girlfriend', further emphasized by the popular use of women's names as titles. One magazine was called simply *Freundin*.

Ratgeber covers commonly featured photographs of cute children and/ or animals. Photographs of young women, though occasionally used, were much less common than with the other women's magazines and the models wore less make-up. *Ratgeber*'s cover was essentially part of the entertainment section of the magazine. Since *Ratgeber* was sold mainly by subscription rather than at the news-stand, its cover did not need to play the same role in projecting the magazine's image and attracting potential buyers as did the covers of other women's magazines.

In the 1960s, the magazines commonly had over 100 pages, while particularly thick issues (there were strong seasonal fluctuations) had over 200 pages. Some issues of *Brigitte* in 1970, after the fusion with *Constanze*, had over 300 pages. The increase in thickness was due in considerable part to an increase in the number and size of advertisements. *Ratgeber* also gained in thickness, though not to the same extent; it was typically around 150 pages in 1969.

Advertisements now increasingly featured expensive products, such as appliances and automobiles. Luxury became a common selling point even in advertisements for inexpensive items. One 1965 hairspray advertisement showed a woman trying on an expensive-looking necklace. The text indicated that 'demanding women' knew how to judge hairspray, too. '*Anspruchsvoll*' was a popular term in advertisements, practically always used in a positive sense. A *Ratgeber* advertisement for stockings proclaimed that 'cultivated women' wore real jewellery rather than costume jewellery because 'more and more women' could tell the difference, and applied this principle to stockings as well: 'more and more women recognize a too-cheap stocking immediately'.[28]

Brigitte and *Constanze* devoted fewer pages to entertainment in the 1960s than in the 1950s, except for *Constanze* in 1969, while *Für Sie* had somewhat more. Fashion and hairstyles played a greater role, especially for *Brigitte*. Marriage and relationships received more attention than they had in the 1950s, as did interior design.

The 1969 *Ratgeber* cover shown in Figure 1.3, like the 1951 cover shown earlier (Figure 1.1), is from an August issue. It also features a seasonal theme – but the season is seen in terms of vacation rather than harvest. The transformation of the cover over time suggests an attempt to project a more 'up-to-date' and less rural image. The content of the magazine underwent analogous changes. Still, *Ratgeber* was clearly not inclined to go as far as the other magazines in keeping up with the times.

In the late 1960s, both cover photographs and content of the general-interest women's magazines became more provocative. Political stories returned in greater numbers. There was more experimentation in cover photography. One 1967 *Constanze* cover, for instance, featured a young woman wearing fashionable tights, period.[29] The hats and gloves were

Figure 1.3 *Rategeber* cover, August 1969.

passé. The stories mentioned on the cover also included provocative topics: one story on unwed mothers, another on 'the angry young girls' (women students involved in the student movement). At this time, *Constanze*, which had lost the dominant position it had held in the 1950s, was trying hard to appeal to a younger audience. After a further editorial change, the 1969 issue was more or less an ordinary tabloid, with stories about such topics as the Manson family and Chappaquiddick. In December 1969 it was discontinued in favour of, or merged with, *Brigitte*, which was published by the same company.[30] This magazine, whose cover price increased from DM 1.20 to DM 1.50 in the course of 1970, continued the type of content which had become standard for the general-interest women's magazines, with fashion, advice and an increasing attention to both careers and relationships.

In this study, a primarily qualitative approach was used, though some quantitative data were also collected. [31] A sample of issues from each magazine from the years 1950, 1955, 1960, 1965 and 1970 (or the nearest available [32]) was examined page by page, while the other issues were skimmed. The samples were evenly distributed, rather than random, to avoid effects from the marked seasonal fluctuations in size and content. *Constanze* and *Ratgeber* were then examined for all odd-numbered years, to give more continuous chronological coverage. Some *Ratgeber* issues from even-numbered years and issues of *Ihre Freundin* from the years 1951–1961 were examined more informally.

Both the editorial portion of the magazines and their advertisements were used. Except for the very beginning of the 1950s, advertisements occupied a substantial amount of space in all of these magazines (somewhat less in *Ratgeber* than in the others). Advertisements for appliances and other housekeeping products were one of the major places where such products were discussed. Except in *Ratgeber*, there were many more pages of advertising than of editorial content devoted to housekeeping and household appliances.

Did the images presented in women's magazines and the advertisements they contained influence the beliefs and behaviour of actual readers? The notion that the media have influence is intuitively appealing. Attempting to demonstrate that influence is none the less difficult, as has been shown in the question of the effect of television and film violence on children. Part of the problem is methodological: observing actual media consumption changes it, while analysing the content of the media themselves can show how influence might occur but not conclusively demonstrate it.

Precisely due to the difficulty of getting at the actual experiences of real audiences, a theoretical debate has developed in media studies between audience-research and textual-analysis approaches. [33] For the historian, there is rarely much of a choice, contemporary source material on audience responses being much rarer than media texts. This study is ultimately concerned with the housewives of the 1950s and 1960s rather than the magazine or advertising industries or their products, but the question of how women interpreted the magazines and advertisements can only be approached indirectly, through an analysis of the texts themselves in light of what we know about the experiences and background knowledge readers brought to them.

To some extent, background knowledge can be inferred from the texts themselves, although this needs to be supported with some other information about the culture in which they were produced and read. Much work on the media, and on print advertising in particular, has focused on making visible the unconscious work done by the reader in making sense of a particular image or text. Roland Barthes analysed an advertisement for pasta and related products, exploring the meanings which can be read from a rather simple visual image with very little text.[34] Judith Williamson has focused even more on what she terms 'advertising work' in reference to Freud's concept of 'dream work'.[35] There is always a danger of overinterpretation, of finding meanings in advertisements which would not register on the ordinary observer even subconsciously. This approach does, however, emphasize two significant points: that the relationship between the advertisement and the reader is complex, and that an advertisement's effectiveness depends on the reader's possession of the 'common-sense' knowledge required to interpret it 'properly', in other words as its producers intend.

The reader doesn't actually have to agree with the intended interpretation; negotiated and oppositional readings are also possible, to use Stuart Hall's terminology.[36] Some authors, such as Michel de Certeau, emphasize the independent role of the reader in the construction of meaning and the possibilities of creating alternative readings which contradict the intent of the author.[37] Others, like Angela McRobbie, emphasize the ideological intent of the creators of texts and the ways in which these shape, or attempt to shape, the readers' perceptions of the world.[38] Writing of the British case, Janice Winship questions the extent to which oppositional readings of women's magazines were possible in the 1950s:

> What I want to draw attention to here is the possibility that in the 1950s, although the reader of women's magazines can be regarded as active in her meaning-making, available discourse registers did not offer alternative ideologies to allow the reflexivity Frazer points to. There *was* a dominant ideology of femininity, and the women's weeklies were contributors to the cultural processes by which hegemonic consent around women's position was strived for, if never finally won.[39]

It can be argued that there was a dominant ideology of femininity in West Germany in the 1950s and 1960s, but I would argue that the fact that it was not an internally consistent ideology offered possibilities of resistance to particular aspects. In addition, in the area of housework, women had their own experience as a point of reference. Advertisements

-18-

which portrayed housework as non-existent could hardly have been perceived as literally accurate; however, they could very well have reinforced views of housework as unimportant, which certainly existed in West German culture in the 1950s and 1960s.

While oppositional readings were certainly possible, especially in the case of advertisements, there were also circumstances which tended to support magazines' influence on their readers. Women's magazines dispensed not only entertainment, but also advice. This was particularly true of *Ratgeber*, which was intended as a professional journal for housewives. Covers into which the issues for a given year could be bound with paper clips were available from the publisher. The pages were numbered by year rather than issue and articles often contained references to earlier treatments of the same topic. Frau Ge. has shelves full of *Ratgeber* neatly bound in the red covers.

A 1957 study commissioned by the publishers of *Constanze,* a more entertainment-orientated publication than *Ratgeber,* found that 91 per cent of the magazine's readers had made use of its advice in matters of housekeeping, rather more than the 71 per cent who followed its advice in matters of make-up. Although only 39 per cent of female readers and 29 per cent of male readers admitted having bought products on the basis of advertisements they had seen in *Constanze,* 95 per cent of the women and 79 per cent of the men said they remembered seeing at least one of the four ads published in the previous year which were shown to them as part of the study, and 81 per cent of the women and 66 per cent of the men said they enjoyed the ads which appeared in the magazine. [40]

Additionally, it is reasonable to suppose that the influence of contemporary sources such as magazines increases in periods of rapid change. [41] Much of what a woman of 25 in 1960 had learned about housework from her mother in the 1940s would have had no direct relevance to the conditions under which the daughter found herself living.

Thus, though it would not be possible to prove that magazines and their advertisements influenced readers' thinking on matters of housework, household appliances and gender roles, it is certainly plausible. In any event, the creators of both magazines and advertisements intended them to appeal to the reader. The magazines in this study, except for *Constanze* in the 1960s, all managed to at least maintain stable circulations, while *Constanze* in the 1950s and *Brigitte* and *Für Sie* slightly later recorded dramatic gains. This suggests that their creators' assumptions about what advice would be useful, what stories entertaining, what information relevant to their readers were reasonably accurate.

Modernity, Gender and the Home, 1920–1950

Modernity and Women's Roles in the Weimar Republic

The developments of the 1950s and 1960s were striking but not wholly novel. Technologically, economically and socially, the changes at work in the West German household of the postwar decades had their roots in developments in the nineteenth century and the first half of the twentieth. The term 'modernity' is sometimes used to describe the complex of developments that separate the society in which we live from earlier times. This is in many ways an unsatisfactory term – it tends to turn the 'premodern' world into a homogeneous lump, it is often used (particularly in the study of German history) to suggest that there is one normal path of modernization which all societies ought to have followed, and taking the word 'modern' from its usual, chronologically shifting sense of 'now' and nailing it down to one particular point in the past creates the problem of what to call what comes later.

Nevertheless, the concept can be useful, at any rate in looking at Western European and North American developments, the regions in which it was developed. Detlev Peukert's definition, from his study of the Weimar Republic, can serve as a starting-point:

Let us . . . take the term 'modernity' to refer to the form of fully fledged industrialized society that has been with us from the turn of the century until the present day. In an economic sense, modernity is characterized by highly rationalized industrial production, complex technological infrastructures and a substantial degree of bureaucratized administrative and service activity; food production is carried out by an increasingly small, but productive, agricultural sector. Socially speaking, its typical features include the division of labour, wage and salary discipline, an urbanized environment, extensive educational opportunities and a demand for skills and training. As far as culture is concerned, media products dominate . . . In intellectual terms, modernity marks the triumph of western rationality, whether in social planning, the expansion of the sciences or the self-replicating dynamism of technology, although this optimism is accompanied by sceptical doubts from social thinkers and cultural critics.[1]

This is a definition without reference to gender, focusing on the public sphere. What did modernity mean specifically for women and for household life? What changes had already taken place, or were well under way, in the interwar years which would set the stage for the developments of the 1950s and 1960s?

Women's Employment

'Bureaucratized administrative and service activity' meant many white-collar (or 'pink-collar') jobs for women, for instance as typists and saleswomen. The percentage of employed women who were civil servants and white-collar workers increased from 3.9 per cent in 1907 to 12.6 per cent in 1925 and 16 per cent in 1939, a much smaller percentage than those employed in family businesses or blue-collar jobs but highly visible and clearly growing.[2] The number of women employed in domestic service was declining; many women from the countryside initially moved to the city to work in households, but they were increasingly likely to move on to other options.[3]

The percentage of women employed in farm labour was beginning to decline, but this was due to the increase in employment in other sectors; the trend away from agricultural employment had by the time of the Second World War affected men much more than women. The percentage of employed men who were employed in agriculture had fallen from 43 per cent in 1882 to 28 per cent in 1907, while the figure for women was still 43 per cent in 1925 and was falling only slowly.[4] Much garden work or seasonal labour done by women who were officially not economically active would not appear in employment statistics.

Women had moved into many industrial jobs during the First World War. Most of them lost their jobs to returning men or to the postwar economic troubles, but as the economy picked up again in the latter half of the 1920s more and more women were employed as unskilled workers in expanding industries, including those producing increasingly popular consumer goods, such as cosmetics and light-bulbs. The perception that, through greater rationalization of production, cheap female labour could displace male workers led to strong hostility towards the employment of women, especially once the Depression hit and male unemployment began to sky-rocket.[5]

The extensive educational opportunities and demand for skills and training that Peukert declares characteristic of modernity applied much more to men than to women. None the less, in the 1920s it was becoming increasingly usual for middle-class young women to spend a few years working before they married, rather than staying at home learning housekeeping skills after they finished school. They would not receive the extensive professional training their brothers did, as a rule, but neither would they go into completely unskilled work. One woman interviewed in an oral-history study expressed it thus:

> but already back then everybody had to have a profession, you couldn't necessarily count on getting married, it was the First World War, you know, people had learned from that . . . There was no telling what might happen, maybe you'd need it, maybe it would be useful.[6]

Some working-class women saw business-school training and the white-collar work it opened up as a path to social advancement.[7] Some middle-class women had more extensive professional training, but the number was still quite small. German universities had only been opened to women during the first decade of the century, so the women students of the interwar period were unlikely to be following in their mothers' footsteps. The proportion of entering students who were female reached a peak of 18.9 per cent in the winter semester of 1931/32, at a time when the total number of students was also relatively high.[8] Women won the right to practise medicine in 1899, and law in the early Weimar years. As of 1929 there were two women full professors at German universities and 2,231 women doctors.[9]

An increase in the number of women working outside the home was one of the most striking characteristics of the Weimar period, in the eyes of contemporaries. The media image of the 'New Woman', glamorous or threatening depending on one's point of view, presented a distorted picture of the reality, however.[10] For the most part, the ideal was that a woman would quit her job when she got married, if her husband earned enough to support a family (often not the case in the working class, and sometimes not in the middle class, given the economic turbulence of the period). But one characteristic of modernity was the use of wages as a measure of the value of work. The more men were involved in a wage labour system, and the more women themselves experienced being paid for their work before marriage, the more difficult it became to classify women's housework as work in a theoretical sense, though scrubbing laundry and beating rugs were obviously work in a practical sense.

Demographics

Another feature of modernity was a fall in birth and death rates. The birth rate in Germany had been declining since around the turn of the century, having been generally between 35 and 40 births per year per thousand inhabitants of the German Empire in the years since its foundation. It had fallen below 30 by the beginning of the war, and rebounded only to around 25 in 1920/21 after the drastic drop during the war (13.9 in 1917). It then started falling again, but the death rate was no longer falling as much as in the prewar years.[11] The threat of population decline loomed. Despite laws on the books banning abortion except for medical reasons and severely restricting the distribution of information on contraception, people were finding ways of limiting family size, aided by sex reformers and sympathetic doctors. Couples who married in the early 1920s had an average of only 2.27 children, while for those who married in the second half of the decade the average was only 1.98. Feelings ran high on reproductive issues during the Depression, as some worried about the impending decline of the German *Volk* and others protested against laws they saw as forcing poor women to bear children they could not afford to raise.[12]

Women and Politics

Women's greater visibility in public life extended to politics as well as the world of work. German women won the right to participate in political organizations in 1908 and the right to vote in 1919. The National Assembly (constitutional convention) elected in 1919, immediately after women gained the right to vote and stand for office, had 10 per cent women members, a figure not reached again in the Bundestag until 1983. The first Reichstag elected in the Weimar Republic had 8 per cent women members, a figure which was exceeded by only two of the Bundestags elected from 1949 to 1980 (the 1953 and 1957 Bundestags had 9 per cent). In contrast, Sweden in the 1920s had up to five women in the lower house of the Riksdag, or 2 per cent, and exactly one in the upper house. French women didn't get the vote until 1944.[13]

The constitution of the Weimar Republic guaranteed women equal political rights. The Civil Code, on the other hand, which had come into effect at the beginning of the century, enshrined the husband as head of the household. If the couple could not agree on matters like place of residence or education of the children, he had the final say. A husband could also terminate a contract of employment undertaken by his wife if he felt it conflicted with her obligations to him and the family.

As in other countries, the inclusion of women in the electorate did not result in any sudden political leap towards more practical equality. Women voters were quickly integrated into the existing political parties, all of which continued to be dominated by men. Only the Social Democrats had officially called for the extension of the franchise to women before the war, but the more conservative parties, which glorified women's traditional roles as wives and mothers and promised order and stability, benefited more from women's votes.[14]

The women's movement had been fragmented along class and political lines before the war. With the vote achieved, there was a lack of consensus on future goals. On the whole, the organized women's movement in interwar Germany was dominated by members of the older generation. Relatively conservative forces seeking greater recognition for housewives, more and better-trained servants and a role for women in social welfare as an outgrowth of their traditional maternal concerns tended to predominate. There were also organizations of professional women, but they were a small group, whose interests did not necessarily coincide with those of the majority of employed women.[15]

The increase in importance of housewives' groups led to an increased focus within the women's movement on issues relating to housework. Both within and outside the women's movement, the question of how modernization would affect the home was a subject of discussion in the 1920s. The impact of industrialization was quite visible by that time in the form of household utilities, factory-produced consumer goods and early appliances. The process was particularly advanced in the United States, which Germans treated as a sort of window to the future. Even under the less prosperous conditions prevailing in Germany, however, there was a movement to apply the teachings, as well as the products, of modern factories to domestic life.

Visions of the Modern Home

Utilities, Technology and the Household

The complex technological infrastructures of modernity reached into the home; the presence of utilities such as electricity and running water in the home is one of the most obvious differences between modern and premodern housework. The urbanized environment facilitated the spread of utilities and the provision of services, such as laundry or food service, outside the home. As of 1925, 26.8 per cent of the German population lived in cities of over 100,000, with an additional 13.7 per cent in cities of between 20,000 and 100,000. Housing construction was strongest in the large cities as the urban population continued to grow.[16]

Long before electrically powered appliances became widespread in Europe, technological developments had brought about major changes in housework and domestic life and laid the groundwork for more.[17] Municipal piped water-supplies trace their history in modern Europe from the mid-nineteenth century, when concern about epidemics of diseases such as cholera in the expanding cities and a growing understanding of the nature of their transmission led city governments to intervene. The first German city to establish a centrally run water and waste-water system was Hamburg, in 1848.[18] The connection of households to water and waste-water networks eliminated a particularly labourious household task, carrying water. This in itself greatly reduced the amount of work involved in doing laundry.

Gas was initially used for lighting and heat. Towards the end of the nineteenth century, as electricity became a serious threat to the lighting part of the business, the gas companies became more interested in the potential for other household applications. Gas irons had been produced in Germany as early as 1858, but this particular application proved somewhat hazardous in practice. Gas stoves came into use in about the 1880s. Gas was not available in all areas, but the supply to urban households gradually improved.[19]

Then came the spread of electricity. Like gas, it was first used for street lighting, the first experiment being made in London in 1807. In the late nineteenth century, it was used for trams and underground railways. The first domestic application was lighting. Electric light and the more advanced varieties of gaslight not only lengthened the working day (especially in the winter) but also helped keep homes cleaner because they produced less soot than oil-lamps and candles. On the other hand, dirt was more visible in a brightly lighted room.

The domestic use of electricity remained rare in Germany in the years before the First World War but increased rapidly in the 1920s. Fifty-three per cent of German dwellings had electric lighting by 1925 and 75 per cent by 1930; the figure increased to 87 per cent by 1936.[20] Early electric appliances included electric irons and electric kettles. The earliest models tended to be very expensive and subject to frequent and occasionally dangerous technical problems.

Many small manually powered devices for use in the kitchen, such as hand-cranked mixers and apple peelers, were being mass-produced by the end of the nineteenth century in Germany and elsewhere. There were also some non-electrically powered major appliances for the home, such as iceboxes and hand-cranked washing-machines. The most important was the manual sewing-machine, a product sold for both home and commercial use. It was often used for commercial sewing in the home.

The sewing-machine had the advantage of not actually requiring much power, so that a great improvement in speed over hand-sewing was possible without any source of energy other than the treadle. The hand-cranked washing-machine was less competitive. On an industrial scale, though, there were many new technologies which would later be applied in the household. Ice for iceboxes could be manufactured rather than harvested from frozen lakes in the winter. Refrigeration technology was also used in the brewing of beer and in the long-distance transportation of meat. The household washing-machine has its ancestors among the machines developed for the textile industry and commercial laundries. The first vacuum cleaners were large units which could be installed in the basement (of particularly well-appointed buildings) or pulled from door to door by horses.[21]

Around the time of the First World War came a technological break-through. Small electric motors were developed which, though far from trouble-free, were reliable enough to be of practical use. They were applied to various existing household devices. One motor produced in the US from 1912 primarily to power sewing-machines also featured attachments for other tasks, including what may have been the world's first electric mixer.[22] Small electric motors also made possible the electric portable vacuum cleaner (various mechanical bellows models were already in existence). Washing-machines presented a greater technical challenge due to the necessity of keeping the water and the electricity separated, but working models of several types were developed and commercially produced before the Second World War.

Electricity companies promoted the use of electrical appliances in order to increase daytime consumption of electricity. Power companies some-times aided customers in the purchase of electrical equipment by means of instalment plans, with the payment for the appliance added to the electricity bill. Gas companies also promoted the purchase and use of gas appliances.

Despite these efforts, major appliances remained out of reach of the average European consumer. Not only were they expensive to purchase, but the cost of electricity was high relative to other fuels. Appliances which drew much current might also require the installation of additional wiring. Items such as refrigerators and washing-machines were therefore luxury goods. Only in wealthy households did such major appliances play much of a role. They helped to improve both efficiency and working conditions for domestic servants, who were becoming harder to find and to retain as more alternative jobs became available to women.[23]

Many housewives were introduced to modern technology through electric lighting and electric irons. Electric irons had major advantages over most other electric appliances. They were not very expensive, and they provided a number of obvious advantages over their non-electric competitors. An electric iron could be used without heating the stove, which made ironing cooler work in the summertime. It was cleaner than a flat-iron heated on the stove, and it could be used more or less constantly (though early models tended to overheat) rather than using several irons in relay. In addition, an electric iron did not present the same fire dangers as gas or alcohol-fuelled models. Outlets designed to screw into an overhead light socket allowed the use of irons even in homes wired only for lighting, with no wall outlets.[24] One study conducted in the early 1930s in rural Württemberg indicated that most households had electric irons. There was some variation according to social class, but even in working-class households the figure was 58 per cent.[25]

The economic policy of the National Socialist regime in Germany was geared primarily to preparation for war rather than to promoting consumerism. The regime was quite interested in the propagation of certain household electrical devices, however. The '*Volksempfänger*', a cheap radio for the masses, provided households with a tangible benefit from the new regime and facilitated the dissemination of political propaganda. Household electricity rates were generally lowered, and a new rate was introduced for refrigerators.[26] A more widespread use of refrigerators would help avoid waste of food, helping to achieve the goal of German economic self-sufficiency. Efforts to develop a '*Volkskühlschrank*' (People's Refrigerator) were not, however, successful in the 1930s and were put on ice with the coming of the war.[27]

The spread of household technology in Germany was on the whole equal to or ahead of that in other leading European countries. For instance, in Britain only 65 per cent of households had electricity in 1938 and the distribution of electrical household appliances was probably lower than in Germany (except for the peculiarly British 'electric fire'). The establishment of a national grid with standardized voltage occurred earlier in Britain, however. Innovations such as the penny-in-the-slot gas meter and the rental of appliances by the gas companies aided the spread of gas appliances in Britain. In France, only 69 per cent of dwellings in towns of 30,000 or more had both electricity and running water by 1940. As in Britain and Germany, there were few major appliances before the war, though electric irons were common and some households used gas or electric stoves. During the war, the solid-fuel-burning stove, with its independence from gas and electricity supply, had distinct advantages. In urban Sweden, gas and later electric cookers became relatively common, found in roughly half the households by 1940, but most of the population lived in the countryside, where wood-burning stoves continued to predominate. The great breakthrough for household appliances in Northern and Western Europe would come in the postwar period.[28]

The Rationalization of Housework and Housing in the Interwar Period

Even though the use of modern technology in the household remained limited, there were those who sought to introduce modern management techniques and more efficient ways of carrying out household tasks. This was part of a larger international trend. Beginning before the First World War, home economists such as Christine Frederick and Lillian Gilbreth in the United States sought to apply the ideas of Frederick Taylor to the daily work of housewives. In doing so, they carried forward a push for greater household efficiency associated with the nineteenth-century American home economist Catherine Beecher, who sought to redesign kitchens and houses to enable housewives to do without servants. These ideas spread to Europe as well, promoted by authors such as Irene Witte (who translated Frederick's book *The New Housekeeping* into German) and Erna Meyer in Germany and Paulette Bernège in France. Erna Meyer's book *Der neue Haushalt* was published in 1926; by 1929 it was in its thirty-seventh printing.[29] In Germany, household rationalization was promoted in the 1920s by industrialists and bourgeois feminists and viewed with favour by the Social Democrats as well.[30]

In Germany, advocates of household efficiency aimed their efforts particularly at working-class housewives, though the language of their appeals often suggested a classless society. Under the economic conditions of the 1920s, widespread mechanization of German kitchens was not a realistic expectation. Consequently, experts emphasized the importance of proper arrangement of furniture and energy-saving ways of performing household tasks with minimal mechanical help – the best way to hang up laundry to dry, the desirability of ironing or peeling vegetables in a sitting rather than a standing position, and so on.

Reformers also promoted changes in kitchen design. For example, cabinet tops along the walls were preferred as worktops to a kitchen table in the centre of the room because walking around the table cost extra steps. Designers planned continuous work surfaces with cupboards above and below, preferably built-in. This type of design would become predominant after the Second World War, although the central table in the form of a kitchen 'island' would reappear in the 1980s.[31]

The efficient kitchen could be smaller in size, an advantage in planning economical housing. The most famous example of German kitchen design, the Frankfurt kitchen designed in the 1920s by Grete Schütte-Lihotzky, was an attempt both to save space (it measured 1.9 by 3.44 metres) and to maximize efficiency in housework. Between 1926 and 1930, 10,000 flats in Frankfurt were equipped with this kitchen.[32]

Increased interest in hygiene, as well as overall design trends, also influenced ideas about kitchen design. Kitchen furniture was to be painted white, so that even traces of dust would show up and, it was hoped, be immediately removed. Blue was sometimes recommended as a colour for kitchen walls because it was believed to repel flies. In the design of appliances, there was a movement away from the furniture look towards a white, streamlined appearance. Smooth enamel surfaces were easy to clean.

A central idea in the new kitchen design was that activities not directly related to the preparation of food should be performed elsewhere. This built on the concept of the kitchen in the design of blocks of flats and houses for the bourgeoisie. Here the kitchen, being the province of the servants, was traditionally segregated, often located at the back of the building and sometimes quite inadequately provided with light and ventilation. While these shortcomings were to be overcome, the kitchen was still to be used exclusively for food preparation.

Reserving the kitchen for cooking and designing it to be as efficient and hygienic as possible was all well and good if one had the money to redo the kitchen and did not want to use it as a living-room. For many people, particularly among the urban working classes and the rural population, efficiency as well as tradition favoured using the kitchen, heated by its wood- or coal-burning stove, as the main living area. Not all families even had another heated room, and some who did preferred to have a parlour reserved for special occasions. People who used the kitchen for living space did not want a sterile, hospital-like environment. They preferred comfortably upholstered sofas and a big, dark sideboard ornamented with carvings. Embroidered wall hangings and covers for the towel rack with inspirational sayings, decorative canisters and other dust-catching objects remained popular as well, to the dismay of the hygienists.

During the interwar period, economic conditions restricted new housing construction. The reformers' ideas were tried out here and there, for instance in the Frankfurt development, but most households continued to live in housing built before 1914, at a time when servants were common and electric lighting high tech. The Second World War would make extensive construction of new housing unavoidable, giving the new kitchen design a much better opportunity.

Appliances in America

Modernization brought a proliferation of consumer goods, but in interwar Germany it was generally only inexpensive products which could achieve wide distribution, while high-priced durable goods like automobiles and appliances were created in small numbers for the wealthy. In the United States, manufacturers began producing consumer durables for a broad household market earlier. Washing-machines and refrigerators were in over 40 per cent of US homes by the outbreak of the Second World War, a figure which rose rapidly with the return to peacetime production.[33]

Wages were generally higher in the United States than in Europe and there were fewer servants. Door-to-door salesmen and mail-order catalogues helped to promote products. In the case of the refrigerator, the warmer climate increased demand. The availability of consumer credit also aided the spread of appliances in the United States. People desiring to purchase household appliances could do so without waiting until they had saved up the purchase price; sometimes they didn't even have to make a down payment.[34] In the US as in Europe there were traditional prejudices against buying on credit, both because it was seen as irresponsible to spend money which one did not have and because credit purchases were traditionally associated with the poor, desperately trying to get by from one pay-day to the next. By the 1920s, however, these prejudices were being eroded in the United States as some firms gambled that a mass market could be found for consumer durables such as cars. Instalment buying gradually won wide social acceptance.[35] In Germany and elsewhere in Europe, on the other hand, the aversion to credit persisted.

During the interwar period (and subsequently), Germans looked with interest to the United States, both for its own sake and, more importantly, as a model of what Germany's future might be like. Different authors highlighted different aspects, but most were impressed with America's economic success, so important to the Allied victory in the First World

War. The term '*Wirtschaftswunder*', which would be applied to West Germany in the 1950s, was coined by the German author Julius Hirsch in reference to the United States of the 1920s. The image of well-paid workers in Ford's automobile factories driving to work and shopping in their own cars played an important role in German perceptions, however little it accurately represented the lifestyle of most American workers.[36] 'Fordism' had its critics, both on the right and on the left, but its supporters saw in it the promise of a peaceful and prosperous future, without class struggles. Few thought American ideas could be directly applied in Europe, however. Ideological questions aside, the economic starting-point was much less favourable. In Germany, much of the postwar period was characterized by severe economic difficulties: the postwar slump, the hyperinflation of 1923, the Depression. This was not an auspicious time for the development of a mass consumer culture. Under these circumstances, bread was more important than toasters.

Henry Ford's admirers in Germany included the National Socialists, who were interested in his production methods as well as his anti-Semitism.[37] Their regime played on people's desires for consumer goods, most famously in the Volkswagen programme, in which people who gave the government money in the present were promised cars in the future. During the war years, as in other industrialized countries, hopes for greater prosperity in peacetime were nurtured and consumer dreams kept alive. One author wrote of how the enlarged market created by German victories would make possible increased production and the satisfaction of the 'demand for automobiles, tractors, refrigerators, bathtubs, and other ... consumer goods'.[38] It would not, fortunately, be up to the Nazis to make good on such promises.

Women under National Socialism

The central question in looking at modernity in Germany in the first half of the twentieth century is where the National Socialists fit into the picture. With their enthusiasm for technology and efficiency and their determination to present even their racism as 'scientific', they do not fit well into a concept of the right wing as backward-looking.[39] On the other hand, they also glorified the peasant lifestyle and reinvented pagan traditions. Their policies towards women were, not surprisingly, contradictory.

The older housewives in the 1950s were adults by the time the National Socialists came to power in 1933, but many of the women born in the early 1920s would have participated in the National Socialist girls' organization, the *Bund Deutscher Mädel* (BDM), at least briefly (it became mandatory at the end of 1936), with those born in the late 1920s most likely to have been influenced by it. These women would also have been exposed to extensive propaganda in the schools. This was especially true for middle-class women, who generally stayed in school longer and had more of an incentive to conform to teachers' expectations, since their school performance was more relevant to their later opportunities than was the case for working-class women. The young housewives of the 1960s would generally not have been old enough to participate even in the *Jungmädelbund*, the group for ten- to fourteen-year-olds.[40]

The basic underlying tension in the National Socialist policy towards women was between the desire to make maximum use of 'Aryan' women's reproductive capacity and the need for their labour power as men were withdrawn from the civilian labour force by military expansion. In theory, the Nazis favoured sharply delineated gender roles, but in practice they exhibited considerable flexibility in defining women's proper roles, depending on the immediate needs of the state.

Active political roles for women were not foreseen; for the National Socialists, who were by no means in the minority in this belief, politics was fundamentally men's business. The male leadership saw to it that the party's women's organizations could not become any kind of independent power base for women. The former independent women's organizations were disbanded. None the less, the belief in the separation of the sexes meant that girls' and women's organizations provided leadership opportunities for girls and women, both as volunteers and in paid positions.[41]

Theoretically, the National Socialists, who tended to be anti-intellectual in general, opposed education for women which was not directed at their future role as wives and, especially, mothers. The number of women students at universities was initially limited, and measures were taken to reduce the number of women studying 'inappropriate' subjects such as science and law. Much more serious were the discriminatory measures against Jewish students, which included a sizeable minority of women students (7.1 per cent in 1929/30, although Jews were less than 1 per cent of the overall population). Some universities stopped admitting Jews altogether. Many women professionals were also affected by anti-Jewish discrimination; as of 1933, 13.4 per cent of the female doctors were Jewish, and 12.7 per cent of the tiny number of female lawyers.[42] It became essentially impossible for them to practise their professions; those who chose exile in response were fortunate.

In National Socialist policy toward 'Aryan' women, in contrast to that towards Jews, practical considerations tended to win out over ideology.

By the end of the 1930s, with military expansion producing a labour shortage, women were being recruited even into technical careers. It was even possible for propaganda to suggest that women might be bored with the life of the housewife and mother and long for fulfilment through work.[43] Voluntary measures did not have the hoped-for success in inducing women to work, however; indeed, some women quit work once they began receiving the allowances paid to wives of soldiers. Conscription measures were mainly limited to young unmarried women and were carried out in a less than efficient manner. Although women's employment did not increase to the degree that it did in other countries involved in the war, there was a marked decrease in the number of women who quit work immediately upon marriage, particularly middle-class women.[44]

National Socialist policy saw women first and foremost as mothers – provided that they were 'Aryan'. Motherhood was celebrated, with much attention given to Mother's Day (a holiday imported from the United States during the Weimar years, largely at the instigation of florists) and decorations given to mothers with particularly large families (provided that racial and behavioural qualifications were met). Medals for prolific mothers had been awarded in France since 1920 (and continued to be awarded after the war). The Nazi peculiarity was the explicit focus on 'race' and supposed genetic health as determining whose motherhood was to be celebrated. References to the Mother's Cross as the 'rabbit medal' suggest that there were those who saw large families in general as undesirable, however ethnically pure. During the war, the production and distribution of contraceptives were banned and penalties for abortion increased (if the continuation of the pregnancy was seen as desirable from a racial standpoint). The Nazis did not succeed in producing a baby boom, but the decline in the birth rate during the Second World War was not nearly as severe as during the first.[45]

While National Socialists tended to see men's authority in the family as natural, they undercut the authority of both fathers and mothers by emphasizing extrafamilial organizations for young people. The BDM provided some girls with a welcome excuse to escape from household chores. If parents were not loyal to the regime, their children were encouraged to report this to the proper authorities. The National Socialists also liberalized divorce laws, reasoning that unhappy couples were unlikely to be fertile, and some advocated support for those women who were making their contributions to the German population outside wedlock. Here, they ran into considerable resistance, especially from the Catholic Church.

Impact of the Second World War

National Socialist political propaganda probably had some effect, especially when it reinforced views which already had widespread social support. Except for those who found themselves targets of ethnic or political persecution, however, the greatest impact of the Nazis was through the war they unleashed. This was not the plan; the Nazis, aware that the previous war had ended in a revolution, sought to protect the German civilian population from the worst effects. There was much better planning this time; the first ration cards were issued even before the war was started. There were more captured territories to loot, too, while the disinclination to provide decent rations for 'racially inferior' workers and prisoners of war reduced demands on the food supply. There were war-related inconveniences for German civilians – fat and sugar were in short supply, for instance – but nothing like the hunger experienced during the First World War.[46]

Aerial bombardment, on the other hand, had been a relatively minor problem in the First World War but now assumed catastrophic proportions. Large numbers of people were evacuated or fled from the cities, and many others died. The population of Berlin decreased by over a quarter between March 1943 and March 1944; Würzburg had only slightly more than half as many inhabitants in 1945 as it had in 1939. The party leadership estimated at the end of 1944 that 8.9 million people had been 'relocated'.[47] Among the women interviewed, Frau Ga. and Frau R. lost their homes in the one major air raid suffered by Freiburg, in 1944. Frau S. and her family moved from Berlin to rural south Germany when the firm for which her husband worked was relocated. Housing was scarce with the influx of people into the region; the family of four had one room in a farmhouse. After the Polish prisoner of war who was working on the farm left to return to his homeland, six months after the end of the war, they also got his (unheated) bedroom.[48]

While the foreign labourers, who, with the end of the war, became 'displaced persons', were mostly repatriated quickly, the end of the war brought an influx of ethnic Germans from the lost eastern territories. The initial population gain for West Germany was almost eight million people, and some of those who initially settled in East Germany and Austria later moved farther west. Frau T., then a nine-year-old girl, was among the refugees.[49]

The population of both East and West Germany increased above prewar levels because there was now less Germany than before, but overall there were also fewer Germans. Figures on military losses vary, owing in part to the impact of the war on record-keeping, but three million appears a reasonable estimate. Frau R.'s husband was killed in 1941, while Frau Ge.'s died in 1947 of an illness contracted during the war. Civilian losses, which affected women and children as well as men, were also considerable, but the war resulted in a gender imbalance among young adults. Among those born in 1921 and still living in 1950, there were 319,289 men and 432,226 women. The shortage of men was substantial among people born as late as 1926. Since most people married in their twenties, men typically around ages twenty-three to twenty-six, there was still some gender imbalance among the people of an age most likely to be marrying in the early 1950s.[50]

The first years after the war were characterized by pervasive shortages of food, fuel and housing and gave most of the population a taste of poverty. Until the currency reform, economic life required a good deal of improvisation. Herr S. and his colleagues, temporarily out of work after the French dismantled the factory, made curling-irons and potato graters out of aeroplane parts they had hidden under the floorboards and traded them to the local farmers for food. Like other evacuees, the family also had a garden allotted to them by the village authorities. Frau S. worked for the farmers planting and harvesting potatoes.[51]

The disruptions and insecurities of the postwar years were of course not only of a material nature. Many women and children made it through the difficult war and postwar years without their husbands and fathers. Many men did not return, either because they died in the war or because they found other partners during the separation. Some returned only to find that their wives had found other men. There were delays in the release of prisoners of war, especially those held in the Soviet Union, and the work of tracking down other family members could be difficult. Many couples had married in haste during the war and now found themselves almost total strangers, with no shared history to look back on. Couples reunited after years of separation often found that they had grown apart. Many children barely knew their fathers. The divorce rate reached levels not known again until the 1970s. The stability of the family came to be a source of great concern by the end of the decade.[52]

Under the circumstances, many women wanted nothing more than a return to a 'normal' family life. They worried about their children growing up with too little supervision and, in the cities, exposed to the physical danger of playing in the rubble.[53] They wanted to help their husbands reintegrate into the families. Men wanted the self-respect which came with regular work and the ability to provide for their families.

While the war divided men and women, it also divided generations.

Many housewives of the 1950s had experienced the 1940s as wives and mothers, carrying heavy family responsibilities in difficult times. Almost all were old enough to have strong memories of the first years after the war and the still-modest standard of living of the early 1950s. By the end of the 1950s, young wives' memories of the war were likely to be childhood memories, and by the end of the 1960s many brides had been born after the war and experienced the early 1950s only as children. For them, the *Wirtschaftswunder* was normal.[54]

The *Wirtschaftswunder* in the Home

Although at the end of the Second World War the economic situation of most of Europe was bleak, the decades following the war saw not merely a return to the status quo ante but, for the more industrialized countries west of the 'Iron Curtain', a change in standard of living remarkable in both its scope and its magnitude. If the 'American way of life' had been out of reach in the 1920s, it seemed much less so by the 1970s. The routine availability of food and clothing well beyond physical needs, the individual mobility provided by motor cycles and cars, the comforts of modern flats with indoor plumbing and with electricity to power more and more devices for housekeeping and entertainment – all this became not only widespread but taken for granted. This transition included the spread of household appliances, still luxury goods in the early 1950s, to an unprecedented number of households. For West Germany, the 'economic miracle' promised not only more comfortable lives, but a new, improved national identity focused on the future, not the past.

While the change was celebrated, contemporaries also pointed to negative side-effects – overwork, risky use of credit, health problems from overeating, a focus on the material at the expense of family and spiritual values. Gender was central to this debate. Women were highly visible as consumers, but were they thrifty housewives or profligate victims of seductive advertising? Would they neglect family responsibilities in favour of working outside the home in pursuit of a higher standard of living?

West Germany's Economic Miracle

The term '*Wirtschaftswunder*' became popular in the early 1950s, but steady and remarkable economic growth continued through the 1960s, though interrupted by a mild recession in 1966/67. After an economic crisis in the late 1940s involving problems with transportation and the balance of payments, prewar levels of production in industry were reached by about 1950. Until the recession of 1966/67, growth was remarkably steady. From 1950 to 1965, annual growth in GNP averaged 5.6 per cent.[1]

The last period of sustained, steady economic growth in Germany had been before the First World War. Most Germans in 1950 had no personal memory of periods of even relative economic stability lasting more than five years, and those in their twenties had known nothing but war and hard times in their adult lives.

In view of this fact and the enormous destruction caused by the war, it is no surprise that West Germany's postwar recovery appeared miraculous to many contemporaries. In fact, however, a surprising amount of Germany's productive capacity had survived the war in reparable condition. The United States, wanting a bulwark against the much-feared spread of communism, provided substantial assistance, rather than requiring reparations. West Germany also had valuable natural resources and a skilled workforce.

While there was high unemployment in the first years after the war, as prisoners of war returned home and almost eight million persons displaced from the formerly German territories in the east entered the country, by the late 1950s it had fallen to unusually low levels, despite continuing immigration from East Germany until the border was sealed in 1961 (over three million people total, more than half after 1950). In the 1960s, foreign workers were recruited on a large scale, going from 1.3 per cent of the labour force in 1960 to 6.1 per cent in 1966 and 10 per cent in 1971.[2] Fewer and fewer ethnic German males held unskilled jobs. The average real income of employed persons, already near prewar levels at the beginning of the 1950s, rose about 76 per cent in the course of the decade.[3]

The 1960s represented the peak in the percentage of the labour force employed in industry, before the service sector became predominant in the 1970s. There was a steady shift of workers from agriculture to industry. The number of farms declined dramatically and their average size increased (though they remained tiny by American standards).

In part as a response to the consequences of the war, the postwar decades saw a major expansion in social spending. While the most generous expansion came in the period 1969–74, there were already significant gains in the 1950s. Even in 1952, West Germany was making more payments than the Weimar Republic, with its larger population, had in the Depression. In 1957, a pension reform increased payments and tied pensions to the cost of living. This aided elderly people, war widows and other pensioners and provided the large (and expanding) section of the population covered by pension plans with an assurance that they would receive significant financial assistance in old age. Poverty involving physical hunger and cold, widely experienced in the hard years after the war even by the social classes for which it was not a familiar threat, became an exceptional situation of a few unfortunate people. Social policy did not aim at a major redistribution of income, however. Even the payments made to 'equalize the burdens' of the war were made over a long enough period for them to be paid for mainly out of overall economic growth.[4]

Households in which the primary wage earner was a woman tended to be among the last to benefit from the economic upswing, as women's wages were generally lower than men's. As a result of the war, the number of such families was relatively high in the 1950s. Women in paid employment did, however, accumulate pension claims in their own right, while housewives did not.[5]

Frau T.'s description of her family's lifestyle in the late 1950s illustrates both the material progress that many families were achieving at the time and the pockets of poverty which remained. Her father was a village schoolteacher, hardly a wealthy man, but the family was able to acquire a washing-machine, a rug, a telephone and a record-player in 1958 and a refrigerator in 1959. She described these new possessions as

> no luxuries or anything, absolutely not. But compared for instance with my girlfriend, we were doing well. As a place to live, they got what had been a barn for hogs, sheep and chickens. There were the four children and the mother, in two rooms.[6]

Frau P. remembered a different kind of inequality:

> A businessman always made a lot of money. Always. Already back then. In the whole economic upswing. They always got money a lot faster than somebody who gets so-and-so much per quarter-hour. [Somebody like that] can't ever get rich. That will always be just enough to get by on.[7]

Both of these statements reflect the coincidence of rising standards of living and rising expectations. Especially in the early 1950s, talk of a 'miracle' probably clashed with many people's own perceptions of their standards of living. Certainly from a 1990s perspective life in the 1950s and even in the 1960s looks modest.

But, if the man who earned 'so-and-so much per quarter-hour' did not get rich, what constituted 'just getting by' changed remarkably. While it is important not to forget that the *Wirtschaftswunder* affected different groups at different times and a few hardly at all, this should not make us lose sight of the magnitude of the overall changes.

Households were generally spending less of their income on necessities, although rents started rising in the 1960s as controls were relaxed. In 1950, the four-member families of employees with moderate incomes surveyed by the statisticians used 46.4 per cent of their total monthly expenditures on food, similar to the proportion spent by working-class families in the Depression. By 1960, the figure had fallen to 38.2 per cent and by 1970 to 30 per cent, while the foods being purchased were fancier. The percentage spent on household furnishings rose from 4.7 per cent in 1950 to 7.7 per cent five years later, climbing to 10 per cent by 1965 and jumping to 17.7 per cent in 1970.[8]

Prosperity and the Nation

The *Wirtschaftswunder* played a central role in the development of a West German national identity and the recovery from the trauma of the war. Germany had been one of the great powers since the late nineteenth century and had briefly achieved a rather impressive position of hegemony in Europe. Its position had always been based on economic as well as military power. This made the postwar picture of rubble, short rations and power cuts particularly depressing. The return to more or less normal conditions and then to a growing prosperity with a speed that attracted widespread attention and admiration was naturally satisfying, perhaps particularly so for people who considered industriousness to be one of their leading national characteristics.[9] Contemporary magazines sometimes used the expression '*deutsches Wirtschaftswunder*' or simply '*deutsches Wunder*' even if they were not comparing Germany's economic performance with that of other countries.

West Germany's 'miracle' offered new self-esteem to the millions of men who had as soldiers experienced Germany's defeat firsthand. Veterans of the First World War had at least had the option of believing that their cause had been just and their army 'undefeated in the field', beliefs which enjoyed a reasonable degree of popular support during the Weimar period and were encouraged by the Nazis. After the Second World War, the repression of overt expressions of support for the National Socialist regime and publicity about the atrocities committed by Germans during the war made the political environment less congenial to a glorification of the 'lost cause'. Furthermore, there was no escaping the reality of the defeat. The men had ultimately failed as soldiers even in the task of defending their own country. The war experience was interpreted not in terms of heroism and glory, but in terms of suffering and, at best, comradeship.[10] Against this background, civilian life looked good, not boring or stifling.

The men received a chance to succeed in another male role, that of workers and breadwinners.

The focus on physical and economic reconstruction emphasized peaceful economic power and made the war appear like a natural disaster such as an earthquake or hurricane – it had caused a lot of destruction but now it was over and time to rebuild. The Germans, in this picture, were victims (hence innocent), but they did not have to be passive. There was a task at hand into which they could throw their energies. This labour would be richly rewarded. Later, the perception that West Germany's economic success and the prosperity of individual families was due solely to individual hard work (discounting other factors) would contribute to resentment against East Germans and foreigners, who were seen as unjustly benefiting from it.

The standard of living in Germany immediately after the war was abnormally low by the standards of twentieth-century industrialized countries. Increased levels of consumption as well as production were needed to reassure Germans that they lived in a civilized country. A few advertisements made explicit use of the contrast between 'civilized' and 'primitive' lifestyles. In one advertisement, a blonde 'Frau Müller' was presented as saying people without radios lived 'like Negroes', who were depicted in the background, lightly and bizarrely clothed, under a palm tree.[11] Another advertisement presented the refrigerator as the civilized way of enjoying fresh food, an alternative to the raw grasshoppers and grilled crocodile of '*Naturmenschen*'. Again, the '*Naturmenschen*' were caricatured in such a manner that one is a little surprised not to see stewed missionary on their menu.[12]

As conditions improved in the course of the 1950s, West Germany's performance could be compared favourably with that of East Germany and the rest of Eastern Europe. This type of comparison was a popular Cold War tactic in the United States, with its very high standard of living. In the famous 'kitchen debate' of 1959, Vice-President Richard Nixon promoted peaceful competition in consumer goods, an area in which the United States had a decisive advantage over the Soviet Union, in place of military competition, where the outcome was less clear. Visiting the model suburban home featured at the American National Exhibition in Moscow, with which the Americans were then attempting to convince the Soviets of the superiority of the American way of life, Nixon explained to Nikita Khrushchev the connections between freedom and appliances:

> To us, diversity, the right to choose . . . is the most important thing. We don't have one decision made at the top by one government official . . . We have

many different manufacturers and many different kinds of washing-machines so that the housewives have a choice . . . Would it not be better to compete in the relative merits of washing-machines than in the strength of rockets?[13]

In West Germany, too, the standard of living was an issue in the Cold War, though the competition in the 1950s and 1960s took place more at the level of the shopping basket than the entire kitchen. West Germans were urged to send packages to their 'brothers and sisters' in the East. This helped to keep the political goal of reunification alive, reminded West Germans of the benefits they received from living in the West (and, implicitly, from living under a Christian Democratic government) and encouraged the Easterners to see the West in a positive light. It also allowed West Germans, themselves recipients of (Cooperative for American Relief to Everywhere) CARE packages and other aid, to play the more prestigious and powerful role of donors.

Accounts of life in the East emphasized food shortages. 'It's no fun to be a housewife in Leipzig,' one 1963 article stated.

Her day is spent in shopping, or rather 'organizing', and cooking. And when her husband comes home from work in the evening and sits down at the table which has been set more with imagination than with good things, his wife is exhausted from all the trivial errands.[14]

'*Organisieren*' was a slang expression, popular in the late 1940s, for obtaining goods by irregular means. These were conditions which most West German housewives could remember, at least from their childhood years, but with which they no longer had to cope on a daily basis.

With East Germany, a position of superiority could be established early, especially since that country's leaders were initially much more interested in developing heavy industry than consumer goods. In another competition, that with the United States, even a position of equality seemed a long way off in the 1950s. America appeared as a sort of consumer paradise. One girl who worked as an au pair for an evidently wealthy family wrote in 1958, 'You can't imagine how high the ordinary standard of living in the USA is.'[15] The high value of the dollar relative to the German mark meant that American soldiers in Germany were conspicuously well-off. One article in a women's magazine suspected ulterior motives behind the importation of flashy American cars into Germany. The author informed readers that most people in America drove used cars rather than the shiny 'street cruisers' seen in the US occupation zone: 'Because over there, the automobile is not a propagandistic demonstration of the prosperity of a free economy, but a utility vehicle.'[16]

Cars were a symbol of American prosperity, but also of American vulgarity and extravagance. The influential news magazine *Der Spiegel*, aimed at a well-off and predominantly male audience, followed the progress of European small cars on the American market. An advertisement for motor cycles, mopeds and scooters appearing in the magazine in 1960 claimed that big cars, which it mentioned in the same sentence with monocles, had become less important as status symbols. 'A more sensible perspective goes hand in hand with a healthier way of life. What the European small car now is for the American, the elegant scooter, the practical moped or the sporty motor cycle is for the German driver.'[17] On the one hand, this advertisement made a virtue of necessity, asserting that the traditionally American status symbol of the flashy car was not important. On the other, however, the American's acceptance of the European small car as an economical second car did matter.

A 1955 advertisement assured German women that they were up to international standards. It told the story of Mary Hope, an American woman travelling to Germany who stocked up on nail polish and lipstick before she left home but was pleasantly surprised to discover that German women, too, were well-groomed and could buy Cutex nail polish and lipstick in their shops, including her favourite colours.[18]

While Germans generally chose to rely primarily on cultural evidence of their superiority over Americans, they were not going to give up on economic competition. Speaking to an audience of manufacturers in 1955, Ludwig Erhard expressed the view that a refrigerator was just as much a part of the essential household equipment as an iron, a gas or electric stove or a vacuum cleaner, and that it was a sign of backwardness if only every twentieth West German household had one, compared with every second US or Swiss household. Manufacturers and consumers should overcome this backwardness by producing and buying more consumer goods.[19]

Ludwig Erhard began functioning as Economics Minister of West Germany even before the state was actually created. He continued in the post until he became chancellor in October 1963 and served in that office until 1966. The success of the economy, beginning with the currency reform of 1948 and his daring decision to remove rationing and price controls on most products at the same time, made Erhard's political career. It also helped to gain support for his party, the Christian Democratic Union (with their Bavarian sister party, the Christian Social Union). The dominant position of the Christian Democrats lasted as long as the *Wirtschaftswunder;* as the economic situation began to deteriorate in the mid-1960s the issue of how to balance the budget became a source of disagreement with the junior coalition partners, the Free Democrats, leading to the fall of Erhard's government in 1966. The Christian Democrats then had to share power with the Social Democrats in a 'grand coalition', but the latter had long since abandoned its rhetoric of opposition to the capitalist system.

The *Wirtschaftswunder* in the Home

Changes in production figures were politically important, but the impact of West Germany's economic growth was experienced directly in daily household life. Increases in household income and in international trade affected the daily menu. New construction gradually eased the acute housing shortage which existed at the end of the war. Household appliances, as well as other expensive consumer goods, became much more widely distributed. Housewives' day-to-day savings helped families get through the difficult years of the late 1940s and the 1950s and to save up money to purchase new consumer goods, but the new prosperity threatened to make their contribution to the household economy appear less important.

The Wirtschaftswunder *on the Table*

At the end of the war and in the first postwar years, the damage which the war had caused European agriculture and the transportation system made itself felt. The period between the end of the war and the currency reform is vividly remembered as a time of hunger. In conversations about the years following the war, talk frequently turns to the subject of food. More than forty years later, Frau P. remembered with bitterness:

> My mother always made sauerkraut . . . For us. And the French found out about it, that we had sauerkraut in the cellar. And they took it all. Although they could have eaten anything. They had everything to eat, the occupation forces, the officers. And we didn't have anything, and they took it anyway.[20]

Frau Ge. recalled her brother's tales of his experiences in a POW camp in Czechoslovakia at the end of the war. He spoke of having boiled nettles in an old tin can along with old bread crusts he picked up off the ground. When people from the city came to the countryside to beg or barter for food, he told his sister not to turn them away empty-handed.[21] Frau T., who was a girl at the end of the war, found that her family's situation worsened once they were all together again and her father had a teaching job in a village. She remembered begging her mother for bread. On the family's flight from Lodz to Lower Saxony in 1945, there had been lice and danger (they passed through Dresden two days before the great air raid there) but at least there had been soup from the Red Cross. 'After the war it was actually worse than before.'[22]

A certain nervousness lingered even after the crisis had passed. World events could trigger panic buying, as a reporter travelling in West Germany in the summer of 1950 noted:

> As I left Hamburg, the housewives were on the hunt for sugar. Their cheeks glowing with Korea fever, with drawn shopping bags they stalked through the grocery shops. They captured not only sugar, but also rice, oil and barley. The men occupied themselves with the Far East in a less strenuous manner: they discussed the latest reports from the war.
>
> 'Coffee is the best currency,' confided one heated Amazon to me. 'I'm the mother of three children. You have no idea what worries I have when I think about Korea.'[23]

A 1952 article extolled the security of having a good supply of potatoes properly stored in the cellar. 'After all, potatoes are our main food in the winter – despite all improvements in the food supply, they are the safe foundation for the family.' The Suez crisis in 1956 led to some panic buying. In the spring of 1962, *Ratgeber* advocated keeping a two-week supply of staples on hand, with vague references to potential emergencies.[24]

Just as hunger is a common feature of discussions about the immediate postwar years, overindulgence in food is a stereotype in discussions of the 1950s. There is a good deal of evidence for an increase in both the quantity and quality of food consumed, a phenomenon popularly known as the *Freßwelle*. This term cannot really be translated into English, but suggests both a uniform, mass movement (a 'wave') and a certain vulgarity ('feeding' like animals). Some also discern a subsequent fad for 'higher-class' foods (*Edelfreßwelle*).

In his re-examination of the *Wirtschaftswunder*, Michael Wildt has questioned this idea.[25] The household budgets he has studied show that many people were certainly not participating in any nationwide 'pig-out' in the early 1950s but rather continued to live as ordinary people had before the war, scrimping so as to be able to afford a little something special on Sundays and holidays. Instead of a sudden increase in consumption, there was a gradual increase in the consumption of such luxuries as real coffee. Wildt also correctly points out the individual variations in

From Rugs to Riches

tastes and priorities which are hidden in the statistics of overall consumption levels. Expenditures in one area required savings in another. From the late 1950s, however, families had more financial room to manoeuvre, more ability to satisfy desires in several areas at once.

Still, even if changes in diet were less uniform and in many cases took place later than has often been assumed, changes did occur, especially from the late 1950s onward. Per capita consumption of both beef and pork approximately doubled from the low 1950/51 levels over the following twenty years, while consumption of potatoes and grain products fell. Beer consumption grew from a most un-German 1.66 litres per household per month in 1950 to 4.47 litres in 1955 and 7.99 in 1960.[26]

Consumption of tropical fruits was at 7.8 kilos annually per capita in 1950/51, already higher than the prewar peak in 1930, though prices were high enough for one magazine to give advice on preserving orange rind so as to get the fullest possible use of the fruit. A common image in narratives emphasizing the hard times of the immediate postwar years is the orange as sole or main Christmas present for a child. In the course of the 1950s, oranges went from being a rare treat to being simply a good source of vitamin C. Bananas were another symbol of prosperity and a return to normal world trade. The West German government, which seems to have seen low banana prices as an important goal, exempted the popular fruit from tariffs. Per capita consumption of tropical fruit in West Germany rose rapidly in the 1950s and remained more or less stable at about 20 kilos from the end of the 1950s through the 1960s. Total fruit consumption doubled.[27]

The *Wirtschaftswunder* expanded many people's culinary horizons. New vegetables became popular, such as bell peppers. There were many articles on how to cook them, generally including the reassurance that they really weren't hot if you were careful to remove the seeds. 'Do you like the sweet-bitter taste of mild peppers, or have you never dared to try preparing them?' asked a 1970 article in *Brigitte*. 'In the past years, the green, yellow and red vegetable has caught on even in North Germany. Here we give you tips for preparation and selection, along with recipes which are suitable even for sensitive tongues.'[28] Zucchini was also new. Frau P., who grew up in the town of Ihringen near Freiburg, recalled:

They didn't have bell peppers. They didn't even know what they were. Once in a fairy tale there was something about fennel. I asked my mother what it was. She didn't know. In the country, there was red cabbage, white cabbage, peas, beans, just the most basic things.

Different styles of cooking and greater variety of dishes were objectives that some women, including Frau P., strove for.

> For instance, I only now and then cook something that my mother used to make. Mostly Alsatian dishes. Those I've kept. But I cook differently, the modern way. Not the old stuff . . . I don't think anybody wants to eat that any more [laughter].

She broadened her knowledge by working in a hotel and by eating out. If she liked something, she asked how it was made. 'But the simple things, like my mother cooked, I'd never make that.' Her childhood memories are of *Grießbrei* (a type of porridge) made so thick you could cut it with a knife, and rhubarb or apple compote. This is in part a transition from rural to urban cooking. But Frau P. doubted whether anybody still cooked like her mother used to. 'Maybe there are still a few eighty-year-olds who do.'[29]

Food was closely related to another sign of the good times, vacations in foreign lands. Foreign dishes could be a substitute for actual travel or a souvenir of it. *Ihre Freundin* offered readers photos and stories about Italy coupled with recipes. It suggested trying out the recipes at home while playing the hit single 'Fishermen of Capri' as a way to enjoy fantasies of Italy. New prepared foods such as canned ravioli also reflected the trend. *Ratgeber* warned its readers of the culinary risks involved in actual travel, however. An article in April 1961 suggested that travellers planning to head south should prepare their stomachs by practising with foods cooked with oil at home. In 1969, travellers were cautioned that in Spain, Italy, Yugoslavia, Greece and Turkey what hotels offered as 'German food' might in reality be difficult to digest and prepared with a great deal of olive oil.[30]

The magazines featured increasing numbers of 'exotic' recipes. For the most part, these required only conventional ingredients, but featured foreign names and in some cases combinations of flavours unusual in German cuisine. In the course of 1955, *Ihre Freundin* provided recipes for Russian sauerkraut soup, Roman meat patties, French omelettes, 'false chicken' (rabbit) on curried rice, Turkish rice, an Arabian meat dish and an Indonesian rice dish. Except for the roasted soybeans in the Indonesian dish, the exotic ingredients didn't go much past curry powder. In 1960, on the other hand, one piece in the same magazine featured such exotica as artichokes and squid, while another, evidently assuming an urban readership, indicated that the necessary ingredients for the Indonesian recipes discussed were available in specialized shops. The degree to which eating habits actually changed depended on the individual housewife and on her family's tastes, but the *Wirtschaftswunder* offered more options and more financial room to manoeuvre.[31]

New Flats and Modern Furniture

Along with increased quantity and quality of food consumption, new housing construction was one of the most visible effects of the *Wirtschaftswunder* on daily life. The war rendered approximately 20 per cent of the housing which had existed in Germany in 1939 uninhabitable, and there had already been a housing shortage. The damage was greatest in the cities, especially in the western industrial areas and in Berlin. Rural areas were largely spared, but faced streams of evacuees from the cities, and later refugees from Eastern Europe and East Germany. The first years after the war saw rising marriage and divorce rates, which added to the number of households seeking housing. The occupation forces also requisitioned housing, reducing the amount available to Germans. In 1950, an estimated 16 million households sought shelter in 10.7 million dwellings.[32] Families and the housing authorities coped with the situation as best they could, but many people were living in quite cramped quarters.

Overall, the war years tended to reduce the disparities between rich and poor in urban housing. Some of the wealthy lost their homes, whether to enemy action, to confiscation by the occupation forces or because they happened to be located in the wrong part of the country. Those who were more fortunate were compelled to share. One 1870s villa in a Hamburg suburb, previously home to one wealthy widow, was divided into three flats. Her grandson's wife, who had come over from East Germany with her two children, wrote to her former classmates:

> On the ground floor, we were the so-called primary tenants, but besides us there were eight additional people in the flat. So there were fourteen people waiting for the 'facility'. If I don't count the big kitchen, which we all had to share, we had 35 square metres of living space in one and a half rooms. When little Christoph was born in 1951, his crib had to go out in the hall, there wasn't any other place for it.[33]

New construction gradually replaced the housing damaged in the war and made it possible for more families to get homes of their own. In West Germany, construction began in earnest after the currency reform, with considerable state support. In 1950, only 18 per cent of new construction was done exclusively with private funds. Public support was linked to certain minimum and maximum standards and to rent controls, in order to promote the construction of small, affordable flats for families. From 1953 until the early 1970s, over half a million units were completed per year, while in three-quarters of the interwar years the figure had been under 300,000 for a larger geographical area. By 1960, 34 per cent of West German flats were in buildings which had been built since the currency reform, a figure which rose to over half by 1968.[34] After 1960, government efforts were directed increasingly at promoting home owner- ship rather than the construction of flats for rent, but by 1972 the percentage of households owning their homes had only increased to 34 per cent, from a 1950 level of 27 per cent.[35]

New construction was concentrated in the cities, which had sustained most of the damage from the war and where the need was most pressing. The population in rural areas tended to decrease over time as evacuees moved back to the cities. Even as late as 1978, over half of farmers and farm labourers were living in homes built before the First World War.[36] While conditions in the 1950s tended to reduce differences in housing conditions among urban dwellers, the difference between urban and rural conditions was exacerbated.

Rent controls on prewar housing were relaxed in the course of the 1960s. For the 'four-person employee household' of the government statistics, rent decreased from 9.8 per cent of net income in 1950 to remain relatively stable at about 9 per cent for the rest of the decade, climbing to 9.9 per cent by 1964 and to 13.8 per cent in 1969. The percentage of households spending more than 20 per cent of their net income on rent was 6.0 in 1956, 8.5 in 1960, 13.0 in 1965 and 20.6 in 1972.[37]

For most people, then, rents were not unaffordable during this period. The real difficulty, particularly in the 1950s, was finding a flat. Builders of privately funded housing often sought to transfer their costs to their future tenants by means of what was known as a *Baukostenzuschuß*, a contribution towards the building costs. Often this would be credited against the rent, but coming up with the large lump sum in advance could be very difficult. Dr S., who lived with her husband in a single room (the library), which they rented from a tubercular widow (which made them less inclined to use their kitchen privileges), reported:

> the only way to get something was through a so-called *Baukostenzuschuß*, and my father made the money available to us . . . it was five thousand marks . . . That was an enormous sum . . . And of course the building was only half-finished, I believe it was three times altogether we moved into half-finished buildings where the water was running down the walls.[38]

In her survey of employed mothers, the sociologist Elisabeth Pfeil found that saving in order to build a house or to pay a *Baukostenzuschuß* was a common reason why mothers worked, particularly among working-class women. In some cases, the decision to build a house was made because the couple simply could not find a flat.[39] Those whose employers arranged housing for them were fortunate. In 1952, Frau S. moved with her family from the two rooms in a farmhouse where they had been living since the war into a flat provided by her husband's employer: 'I felt like I was in heaven.' As a bride in 1963, Frau P. moved with her husband into a two-room flat supplied by his employer. It featured central heating and a bathroom, unlike the flat where she had been living with her parents. She found it delightful.[40] Under the circumstances, people naturally attached a great deal of importance to having their 'own four walls'.

The housing shortage continued to be an issue; *Brigitte*'s special issue for brides-to-be in 1960 included a section on getting a flat. Still, by the 1960s the situation was not nearly as serious as it had been in the first years after the war. Of a sample of sixty-nine mostly working-class Oldenburg couples who married in 1949–51, only half had been able to establish an independent household as soon as they married, while nearly half lived with relatives and a few lived separately. Among couples who married in 1969–71, three-quarters were able to move into their own flat when they married (in some cases, even before, which had not been an option in the 1950s). The older couples overwhelmingly named the housing shortage as the main reason for continuing to live with relatives, whereas the younger couples cited financial reasons.[41]

Over time, the overcrowding of housing became less widespread, due both to new construction and to the decline in the number of large families. In 1950, the statistical average number of rooms per person (counting the kitchen) was 0.63, while in 1968 it was 1.04. The portion of the population living in severely overcrowded conditions, with more than two persons per room, was 14.9 per cent in 1950 but declined to 3.7 per cent by 1956 and 0.8 per cent by 1968.[42]

Whether sharing flats with others or living in their own small flats, many people in the 1950s were faced with the problem of how to furnish small spaces. Women's magazines were ready with advice. For instance, in a two-room flat, the bedroom could be furnished in such a way as to allow it to be used as a living area during the day.[43] Folding beds, sofa beds and day-beds were popular, especially for people living in single rooms.[44] One company offered a shower with a base which folded up against the wall, for the small bathroom.[45] The arrival of children could make a previously adequate flat suddenly too small, and there was advice on how to cope with the situation.[46]

Ratgeber in 1954 gave advice for improvised washing arrangements for the bathroomless and noted that one firm manufactured a bath-tub concealed under a folding kitchen sink and draining-board and sharing the same drain. The sink and counter could be folded up against the wall and the pipe connecting the sink drain to the bath removed ('easily', according to the article) in order to use the bath.[47]

Improvisation was not limited to practical matters. The magazines also offered advice to those seeking to update the style of their flats and furniture. For those who really wanted a new, modern flat with new, modern furniture, it could be frustrating to be stuck with old-fashioned quarters.

Magazine articles with advice on modernizing pieces of furniture were common in the 1950s. One woman wrote to *Constanze* of an old marble-top washstand she wanted to use in a room she rented out. Such a piece of furniture could evidently not even be inflicted on a tenant. The magazine gave her detailed advice on how to fix it up:

> Saw off the clumsy feet and replace them with a plain moulding. Remove the old paint or finish and repaint the whole thing: in a colour which goes with the rented room, or even in two colours . . . Take off the mirror and cover the marble top with plastic film. Now put two or three bookshelves over it, which can also be painted to match, and you'll see: the 'old-timer' is rescued![48]

Other articles gave similar advice. The usual changes were the removal of mouldings and other ornaments and the replacement of 'feet' on dressers or desks by a plain base. As a final step, the piece was refinished. The reasons given for the changes were always aesthetic rather than practical. There were, however, also reductions in housework involved: fewer surfaces to dust, less need to sweep under dressers, finishes which were easier to care for.

It was also possible to update the style of a whole flat. New buildings were usually designed with rather low ceilings. For those who would have preferred a flat in a new building, the high ceilings in older buildings seemed unattractive. Decorative details gave further evidence of the building's age. The unhappy occupant of one such flat wrote to an interior-decorating advice column for help:

> I live in an old building where the ceilings are very high. That's unpleasant enough, but even worse are the stucco ornaments. Unfortunately, I don't have the money to have a lower ceiling put in. Can I at least knock the plaster off carefully without damaging the ceiling?

The writer's problem was compounded by a love of long curtains, which might make the ceiling seem even higher. The column suggested painting the ceiling and the top of the walls a dark colour and beginning the curtains at the line between that colour and the lighter colour used on the lower part of the walls. This would kill two birds with one stone: the ceiling would appear lower and the ugly stucco decorations (which, it was warned, could not be knocked off without leaving marks) would be much less visible.[49]

Some readers of women's magazines were evidently quite enthusiastic about expressing their 'modernity' by keeping up with the latest trends, in interior decoration as in clothing. *Stimme der Frau* received a letter in 1955 from a man who was contemplating the purchase of new mattresses. '[A]s progressive people, we'd like to buy something "progressive"; in other words, we're flirting with foam-rubber mattresses.' He was interested in hearing about other readers' experiences with this new type of mattress. On the same page, several readers offered their support to a woman whose letter, published in an earlier issue, complained that her husband wanted to put a display of family photographs in their living-room, which was otherwise decorated in a modern style. 'You're absolutely right,' wrote one reader, 'photos don't belong on the wall of a modern flat.'[50]

There was more at stake here than a simple matter of taste. Buying a foam-rubber mattress or removing the mouldings from a dresser could be a statement of one's own 'modernity'. To embrace 'modern' furniture meant to embrace a whole way of life, or at least its advocates hoped so. One advertisement for Braun, a firm at the forefront of the modern design movement, stated that the firm's radios and televisions fitted the lifestyle of 'progressive-thinking people of today'. The advertisement emphasized the appeal of modern style to young and educated women, citing survey results to the effect that 44 per cent of all women under thirty, 54 per cent of all female white-collar workers and 56 per cent of all women with the *Abitur* wanted to 'live in a manner appropriate for our time'.[51]

Modern style, then, was associated with youth, white-collar social status and education. Another characteristic of 'progressive-thinking people of today' was individuality. Home furnishings were supposed to express one's personality. The practice of buying furniture one piece at a time and mixing styles was one way of getting a more 'individual' look. Even advertisements for mass-produced furniture emphasized 'individuality'.[52]

The 'modern' individual was open to the new (not just in furniture styles, presumably) and not burdened by tradition. Cheerfulness was another characteristic. In one article, a shopper found modern lamps 'like

Das schöne Heim

Figure 3.1 Modern living room furniture as presented in *Rategeber*, December 1953, p. 537.

an image of today's bright, cheerful lifestyle'.[53] This notion of modern life as happy and free had a natural appeal after the difficult times of the recent past. The emphasis on looking forward rather than backward was also, obviously, politically convenient in post-Nazi Germany, both for young people wishing to dissociate themselves from the sins of their elders and for older people not wishing to examine their own pasts. The modern style was international, with a pronounced Scandinavian influence, rather than emphatically German.[54]

Typical attributes of the 'modern' home as depicted in magazine articles and advertisements of the 1950s and 1960s included the presence of light, ideally from large plate-glass windows. Furniture styles were also 'light' – thin, angled legs were very characteristic of the period. Shapes tended to be simple, though sometimes weird: new materials such as foam rubber and particle board made possible new forms. The kidney-shaped coffee-table later came to be considered an icon of 1950s style. It was not, in fact, especially popular at the time, but more modestly 'modern' designs did compete successfully with period styles.

From Rugs to Riches

According to a 1960 study, modern furniture was most popular among young people and in southern Germany. Overall, 31 per cent of those surveyed said they preferred furniture in historical styles, while 37 per cent preferred 'moderately' modern styles and 18 per cent 'emphatically' modern styles. Fourteen per cent preferred to combine old and new styles. Period furniture was preferred by 54 per cent of those over fifty-five and 45 per cent of northern Germans between thirty and fifty-five, but only by 15 per cent of all Germans under thirty. Among this latter group, 43 per cent preferred moderately modern styles and 32 per cent ultra-modern, in southern Germany 50 per cent.[55] The greater openness of southern Germans to modern style may have been related to the fact that, for much of southern Germany, the past meant mainly rural poverty, while more of the people of the north had something to be nostalgic about. The influential design institute Hochschule für Gestaltung was located in south Germany, in Ulm.

Alphons Silbermann's study from the same period suggested a lack of clear preferences for particular styles; asked to choose among eight photographs of living-room furniture, a sample of Cologne residents ranked a semi-modern style first, an eighteenth-century look second and a quite modern Scandinavian style third. The photo which featured a kidney-shaped table was not popular.[56]

On the whole, advice on interior decoration in women's magazines supported the notion that modern furniture was most appropriate for the modern age. One author asked why so many contemporaries wanted old-fashioned furniture, noting:

> One doesn't become like Goethe by using furniture like his. A quill pen doesn't make a classical poet, an Empire desk doesn't make a Napoleon, a carved sideboard doesn't make a bank director. He who wants a relaxing environment must be unburdened and open-minded, must be modern.[57]

The magazines also advocated what was presented as the 'modern' way of buying furniture – buying piece by piece rather than in complete 'suites'. (Furniture produced in series made it possible to combine the economic advantages of the former with the coordinated appearance of the latter, a tactic which was downplayed in the articles but emphasized in furniture advertisements.)

Magazine articles recognized, however, that modern styles weren't to everybody's taste. Occasional articles sang the praises of period reproduction furniture (*Stilmöbel*).[58] Even articles which advocated modern home furnishings could be somewhat defensive. One asked the question, 'Do modern houses have to be cold and plain?' This was apparently a common concern.[59] Another potential criticism, ironically, was a lack of individuality; one article stated, 'One often hears the accusation that flats decorated in the modern style are as alike as eggs.' This was, the article continued, 'at any rate not necessary'.[60]

One critic of modern design compared her friends' flats to 'toys from a modern kindergarten – so hygienic, so shiny, so devoid of imagination'. She continued, 'When one sits down, one feels as though one were sitting in a glossy catalogue which enlightens the dumb masses about how one ought to live.'[61] In the 1950s and 1960s, as earlier, some advocates of modern design were, in fact, filled with a missionary zeal which could render them uncompromising and authoritarian. They ridiculed the taste of those who preferred 'old-fashioned' furniture, the infamous '*Gelsenkirchener Barock*', which was mass-produced in factories but didn't celebrate this fact with efficient, modern industrial design.

Some designers and social planners saw the small size of many new flats as an opportunity. The new flats would force people to live as they ought to, getting rid of pretentious, impractical furniture, having usable living-rooms rather than sterile parlours, restricting the use of the kitchen to functions which actually belonged there. When people none the less resisted the modern-style gospel, critics were furious:

> As a matter of principle, room furnishings are bought in complete 'suites', especially the marital bedroom. The 'completeness' is of particular value. The dimensions of the cabinets and beds are Cyclopean. People risk buying furniture of this size even though they've long since heard that new flats usually have very small rooms. The rest of the decor of the rooms is in keeping with the neo-Wilhelmine style of the furniture.[62]

This criticism of existing taste in furniture concentrated on two issues: the impracticality of large, old-fashioned pieces for small, new flats and the purely aesthetic issue of 'tastelessness'. Both of these arguments were common. Organizations such as the Leistungsgemeinschaft des deutschen Möbelhandels e.V. encouraged furniture shops to educate the taste of consumers rather than simply selling 'badly' designed furniture with the excuse that it was what the customers wanted.[63]

The social issues were obvious as well, with progressive white-collar professional types thinking the working class ought to follow their lead rather than aping the tastes of the stuffy old bourgeoisie, while some workers had their own ideas about how to demonstrate that they had achieved economic success. But other workers did embrace the new fashions.[64] Age, geographical location and personal taste, as well as social class, shaped preferences, and both traditional and modern styles were offered in a range of price classes. Whether their taste was 'good' or 'bad', people in the 1960s were increasingly able to express it, while in the 1950s it had been more necessary to make do with what was available.

The debate over kitchen furniture and the proper uses of the kitchen which had been going on in the 1920s continued in the 1950s. The *bête noire* of advocates of modern kitchen furniture was still the large standing cupboard known as the *Küchenbüffett*.[65] This featured top and bottom cabinets, with a counter in between; the doors of the top cabinet might feature glass panes, sometimes with little curtains behind them. The *Küchenbüffett* offended through its size, its dust-catching decorations and its dust-hiding dark colour. It provoked passionate attacks:

> The traditional sideboard is one of the least practical pieces of furniture: usually expensive, space-stealing, tasteless in form and material, impractical, because the physiologically most useful space is taken up by His Majesty the Breadbox. But despite all the efforts of architects, manufacturers and dealers to create and offer more useful and more attractive kitchen furniture – the sideboard is unbeatable and continues to hold its own, because many housewives are unteachable.[66]

The reformers were, in fact, in the process of winning this particular battle. The traditional *Wohnküche*, kitchen and living space at the same time, fared poorly in 1950s housing design. So did the dining-room, however, and that set up a new debate – was eating in the kitchen acceptable, in the name of efficiency, or unacceptable, because a proper family dinner required a proper setting, in the living-room if necessary? The author of one textbook on interior design expressed reservations:

> In the USA, the kitchen with a dining area is a matter of course and has often assumed the character of a snack bar. Here, few favour the extreme, American solution, which often seems impersonal and cold. Many need a certain comfort and the gathering of the family at a table.[67]

A sociological study of the living habits of coal miners noted with distaste: 'In the new settlements, where the kitchen with built-in furniture was 10 square metres in size, we found that some families ate their lunch lined up at the counter rather than gathered around the table in the dining-room.'[68] Through the restriction of kitchen size, the authors hoped that the use of the kitchen for improper functions could be discouraged. While it might be efficient for the family to eat in the kitchen, this represented too great a sacrifice of proper family life.

If some argued that eating in the kitchen was uncivilized, it was also possible to embrace it as a modern trend. The 'breakfast nook', which had become popular in American kitchens in the 1920s, offered a saving in time and steps over serving meals at a table in the living-room. Some authors strongly advocated German imitation of this model.

> Not only in America and in Scandinavia, where a very conscious effort has been made to spare the housewife all unnecessary work, without giving up living comfort, has the dining area in the kitchen become fashionable (*modern*). Here as well, this solution is being chosen more and more frequently, and, happily, the manufacturers of kitchen furniture have adapted it and offer a great variety of models with the help of which one can solve the problem of the dining area in small or large spaces. All variations are possible, from the 'kitchen bar', where one eats breakfast or snacks, to the *Wohnküche* with a proper dining-table.[69]

Now the old-fashioned *Wohnküche* was modern again, but the argument was based not only on convenience but also on the doctrine that functions should be separated: the living-room should not also be used as a dining-room. The dining-table took up too much space and interfered with the proper focus of the living-room on comfort and relaxation. The photos which illustrated the article were from Scandinavia.

Small kitchens tended to limit the use of household appliances simply due to the lack of space to put them in. Many advertisements for appliances emphasized compactness.[70] Technological innovations such as better insulation for refrigerators helped to reduce size. On the other hand, though, lack of suitable storage space in the form of basements or proper pantries was an argument for the use of the refrigerator.[71]

By the late 1960s, there was a tendency towards larger kitchens, in part in order to make room for more appliances. The number of electrical outlets also increased. Women's magazines carried more and more advertisements for entire new kitchens. The individual appliances faded into the background, hiding below the counter top or hanging from the wall, blending in with the ordinary cupboards. It was the ensemble, its durable plastic-clad surfaces gleaming spotlessly, which was presented as a status symbol.

The number of advertisements for kitchens jumped between 1960 and 1965. By 1970, the emphasis had shifted somewhat away from the labour-saving potential of a well-organized and well-equipped kitchen and towards its value as a status symbol. Kitchens were not merely to be clean and efficient, but also comfortable and attractive. Hygienically minded reformers of the 1920s had demanded white kitchens, so that the smallest speck of dirt could be seen and removed. Decorative objects were dust-catchers to be banished. Now, the requirements of hygiene and decoration were synthesized. Cupboard surfaces were flat and covered with new plastics even easier to keep clean than painted wood, but they no longer had to be white. The firm ALNO praised its kitchens as 'young – modern – chic'. The kitchens were available in various bright colours, including 'Garde-rot, Inter-grün, Pop-lila, Star-orange und Strato-blau', as well as wood grain.[72] The combat against germs was carried on at the invisible microscopic level with specialized cleansers.[73]

As status symbol, the kitchen was not to be seen as a workplace. Its function was partly decorative: one advertisement compared it to a piece of jewellery. Through the use of its high-tech appliances, the lady of the house could effortlessly conjure up gourmet delights for her husband and their guests. Rather than work, cooking was a lady's 'accomplishment' like playing the piano. Though equipped with the latest in technology, the kitchen was no longer compared to a laboratory. In her futuristic kitchen, the housewife was to play the role of a nineteenth-century lady in her salon.

Such an attractive kitchen was no prison for the housewife. One 1970 advertisement for Nobilia kitchen furniture stated:

A woman's place is in the kitchen. False!

A woman has a Nobilia.

It used to be said that a woman's place was in the kitchen. Today, every woman regards her Nobilia as an adornment which, though not everybody has one, everybody can afford. With the purchase of a Nobilia you can demonstrate your good taste to your neighbour. You will be envied because of the contemporary form and the good quality.[74]

This advertisement, like many others, managed both to appeal to the desire for luxury and to present the product as affordable. The general mention of durability had the same effect – the outlay for the new kitchen was worthwhile because it would remain attractive.

From Luxury to Necessity: the Increasing Distribution of Household Appliances

The new appliances finding room in West German kitchens in the 1950s and 1960s constituted another important change in everyday life brought about by the *Wirtschaftswunder*. Major appliances had been luxury goods before the war; two studies conducted in the late 1930s, one in an industrial city and one in a small town, showed that among the households surveyed, fewer than 2 per cent had washing-machines and fewer than 1 per cent had refrigerators.[75] Production of household appliances ceased in the war and resumed only gradually in the late 1940s. Until 1949, electricity was rationed and there were restrictions on how it could be used (for instance, bans on electric hot-water heaters and lighted signs).[76] In the early 1950s, major appliances continued to be regarded as luxury items. There was discussion of applying a luxury tax to refrigerators.[77] They were envied status symbols. One woman recalled:

> Since we were both teachers, we could afford some things somewhat earlier than other families. In 1951, for instance, we were able to buy our first refrigerator. It was a great big one, a Bosch. We were terribly proud. Everyone who visited us was led into the kitchen and shown the refrigerator.[78]

Some advertisements for appliances promoted the products as status symbols. One 1950 advertisement stated simply 'you, too, will be envied when you own the new Juno electric range'.[79] An advertisement for a Linde refrigerator in 1955 showed a picture of an open refrigerator, full of food, superimposed on a sketch of an elegant iron gate with the suggestion of a fine house in the background. The text extolled the elegance and solidity of the house and its furnishings in general terms. Like the illustration, it left the details to the reader's imagination. The Linde refrigerator, 'with its timelessly beautiful form', fitted in with these surroundings.

In 1960, a north German court took the position that a washing-machine did not belong to the category of household equipment necessary to a modest lifestyle which was protected against seizure for debt. The court decided that 'at the present time, a washing-machine is still quite a luxury object for broad sections of the population. If the debtor's wife is unable to do the washing herself for health reasons, the debtor can be expected to send it to a laundry.'[80]

The movement towards greater use of household appliances took place gradually and by several paths. Through improvisation, those with less

Figure 3.2 Advertisement for Linde refrigerators, *Ihre Freundin* 5/1955, p. 82.

money could at least share in some of the benefits of modern consumer culture. Industry cooperated by providing cheap substitutes for big-ticket items. The best-known of these are the quaint and curious mini-cars which proliferated in the 1950s,[81] but there were similar developments in the household. Some types of household products could be promoted as a means of saving money, making them seem less extravagant. Mass production and distribution made it possible for manufacturers to reduce the prices of major appliances over time.

Substitutes. Women's magazines in the early 1950s offered suggestions for those whose fashion or decorating tastes were ahead of their purse. For those who could not afford appliances, too, there were ways of coping. Magazines described methods of keeping foods cool in warm weather, generally based on evaporative cooling. These were now presented as ways to manage without a refrigerator rather than simply how to keep food fresh in warm weather.[82] One 1950 article gave recipes for cakes to be steamed in a pudding mould for women without ovens. 'The crust, which a boiled cake doesn't have, is replaced with a sugar or chocolate glaze, which gives the cake a tasty appearance.'[83]

If there was no money for a washing-machine, a laundry press or a spin-drier could at least eliminate the wringing. One 1960 advertisement showed a small girl standing next to a laundry press, claiming, 'Mummy can afford this! . . . even if there's not enough for a "great big" washing-machine – with the new Frauenlob even the biggest washday is child's play.' The advertisement also praised the product's durability. The Scharpf spin-drier cost DM 198 in 1955, a fair bit of money but far less than an electrically heated AEG washer with wringer for DM 550 or a Zanker Intima-Waschbüfett, which featured a washing-machine and spin-drier side by side and cost DM 1150 in 1956.[84]

Frau P. recalled products advertised in the postwar years to make washing easier. The first was a bell-shaped aluminium plunger called a *Waschglocke* (washing bell), which her mother and many other housewives in the village bought after a demonstration at the local inn in 1949. It cost over twenty marks, 'that was a fortune in those days, that was with the new money, that wasn't the Hitler money'. The plunger, which made it possible to wash without touching the laundry directly (sparing the hands, and eliminating the necessity of waiting until the water had cooled to below scalding), did help, unlike the expensive detergent advertised a couple of years later as 'a washing-machine in a bag'.[85]

One of the more peculiar products was the Bosch *Schallwäscher*, a device which claimed to wash clothes by means of ultrasound waves. Like the *Waschglocke*, it was a hand-held device used in a conventional washtub. It was apparently a spin-off product from the development of an automobile horn. One of several enthusiastic users of the device who wrote letters to *Stimme der Frau* on the subject reported:

> In our [refugee] barracks there's no laundry room. Until recently, I had to send my washing to a commercial laundry. Now that I have the *Schallwaschgerät* [sound washing device] it [the washing] is lily-white and wonderfully clean. In the summer I wash in the garden with the help of an extension cord.[86]

**das kann
sich Mutti leisten!**

. . . denn wenn es auch zu der „ganz großen" Wasch-
maschine nicht reicht – mit der neuen FRAUENLOB
ist auch die größte Wäsche ein Kinderspiel. Die neue
FRAUENLOB-Wäschepresse hat ein großes
Fassungsvermögen und eine sehr hohe Trockenleistung.
Ein modernes, formschönes und dabei besonders preis-
wertes Markengerät aus gutem Hause, das fast keinen
Verschleiß kennt. In jedem Fachgeschäft erhältlich.

Frauenlob

Figure 3.3 Advertisement for Frauenlob laundry press, *Ihre Freundin* 8/1960, p. 84.

A page on helpful household devices in a 1950 issue of *Constanze*
mentioned a water-cooled refrigerator and a small mechanical washing
device called a Waschbaby for DM 18.75.[87]

From Luxury to Necessity. The perception of major appliances as luxury
items presumably contributed to their attractiveness in some sectors, but
it stood in the way of their reaching a mass market. Consequently, some
producers and dealers sought to work against the luxury image through
their advertising. One tactic was simply to deny it, declaring the appliance
in question an inevitable part of modern life. 'In the modern household,
running hot water is indispensable,' proclaimed one 1955 advertisement
for water-heaters, although running hot water was not something most
households actually had. An advertisement for a spin-drier presented a
picture of two women wringing laundry over a washtub as hopelessly
out of date. 'In 1956, it's really not necessary to strain yourself and your
laundry like that. Today, there are modern AEG spin-driers which no
household should be without.' A group of electrical-appliance dealers
headed their page of advertisements in the *Badische Zeitung* in 1960 with
the proclamation that a refrigerator was no longer a luxury item.[88]

One 1955 advertisement portrayed a sewing-machine as a piggy bank. The text read, in part, 'The good Anker helps me save housekeeping money and time. I sew, darn and patch everything myself.'[89] The advertisement also referred to the possibility of doing embroidery on the machine, but the emphasis was on its utilitarian roles. Extending the life of garments and linens through prompt mending mattered during the war and immediate postwar years when production of new articles for civilian use was low. With even yard goods hard to come by, skills in converting partially worn-out clothing to new uses also paid off. These practices continued to be of clear economic importance in the 1950s. Several of the women I interviewed spoke of this, including Frau Ge.:

> For the children, I made almost everything myself. Knitted sweaters, also sewed pants, out of bigger pants that weren't intact any more, from my brother, that was still enough [material] for boys' pants. And they were still always well dressed. I didn't buy much for the children, most of it I made myself.[90]

Ratgeber regularly provided instructions for making children's clothing out of cast-off adult clothes.

A 1958 article in *Ratgeber* gave instructions for extending the life of sheets. For instance, if a sheet was worn thin in the middle but did not yet have holes, it could be cut in half and the outside edges sewn together. The article assumed the use of a reasonably sophisticated sewing-machine and indicated that the buttons used to close pillowcases and comforter covers were standardized so that they could be sewn on by machine, using a special foot.[91]

As late as 1965, the relatively conservative *Ratgeber* was providing instruction in mending. 'A large proportion of our young working girls', it asserted, had not mastered basic mending skills. The series of articles dealt with such matters as sewing on buttons, patching and replacing the collars and cuffs of men's shirts.[92] A series of articles in 1967–68 even suggested that young women sew their own bedlinen.[93] At this time, sewing-machine advertisements and articles on sewing tended to treat it more as a hobby, though, and some advertisements sought to counteract an image of home-made clothing as unfashionable and unattractive, an image reflected in Frau Ge.'s insistence that her children were 'still always well dressed'.

Sewing and mending could be done professionally as well as for one's family. This was emphasized in the slogan, 'Nähe, spare und verdiene mit der Zündapp Nähmaschine' ('Sew, save and earn with the Zündapp sewing-machine').[94] It could be an important source of income, especially for women who preferred to work at home in order to be with their children. One 1950 article in praise of the portable electric sewing-machine told the story of an enterprising refugee woman who had purchased such a machine and then gone into business doing mending for her neighbours in the barracks. One woman wrote to *Ihre Freundin* in 1951 asking if any of the magazine's other readers had a sewing-machine she could use. '[E]ven if it's an old one, as long as it still sews. Then I could earn something in addition to my pension of fifty-eight marks. Who will help me?' In the 1960s, when Herr P.'s income was inadequate to support the family, Frau P. sewed aprons at home for a local firm.[95]

While most appliances weren't a means of earning money, it was not only sewing-machines that were promoted as a means of saving money. The appeal to economy was used particularly in advertising for refrigerators, which preserved perishable groceries and thus reduced waste. The increased use of refrigerators had been advocated by the National Socialist regime as part of its campaign to decrease German dependence on imports. In postwar West Germany, the appeal was generally to the housewife's thrift rather than to her patriotism. One advertisement depicted coins being thrown in the garbage can.[96] In one 1957 issue, *Ratgeber* cooperatively included a short piece decrying waste (and warning of the potential problems of garbage disposal) on the page opposite a refrigerator advertisement.[97] An article on refrigerators in a 1957 newspaper supplement emphasized the importance of food as a component of the household budget.

> Almost half of our income must be spent on food. The sensible and economical use and storage of these groceries is a matter which troubles housewives daily. The refrigerator protects the dear-bought wares from spoilage and helps the housewife, who today works as an 'independent businesswoman', without helping hands, to save time.[98]

Advertisements often praised the housewife's thrift and presented saving money, even small amounts of money, as a goal in itself. The financial logic was open to question – for the price of a refrigerator, one could replace a great deal of sour milk – but it could make this expensive appliance seem like less of a luxury.

Prices. The demotion of refrigerators and washing-machines from the luxury category could not take place through rhetoric alone as long as their prices remained out of reach of the average consumer. In the course of the 1950s and 1960s, prices for major appliances fell in both absolute and relative terms. For some families, payment in instalments helped make appliances seem more affordable, though there was still resistance to this; others took advantage of rebates or connections.

A 1955 advertisement reported a price reduction on Bosch's model 120 S refrigerator from DM 730 to DM 638. Bosch sold 110-litre refrigerators for DM 770 in 1952 and for DM 380 in 1959.[99] The average weekly pay of a male skilled worker, before taxes, was about DM 90 in 1952, DM 130 in 1959.[100] In 1969, an AEG refrigerator with a capacity of 160 litres and a freezer compartment capable of maintaining temperatures under-18° C was available for DM 418 including tax and vegetable bins. In 1955, Bauknecht had offered a refrigerator half that size for DM 475, while one of the same capacity cost DM 860.[101]

Automatic washing-machines, new to the German market, were much more expensive items, starting in the DM 2000 range. The price of the Constructa model K3 was lowered from DM 1780 to DM 1580 in 1958. In 1969, an AEG Lavamat with various special features, such as 'biological' washing programmes, cost DM 1398, but the advertisement stated that AEG automatic washers were available for as little as DM 648. A Constructa advertisement in the same magazine listed models from DM 698 to DM 1068. At that time, the prices for Volkswagens started at DM 4525.[102]

Mass production and increasingly standardized products made possible economies of scale and lower prices. Sometimes, indeed, production exceeded demand and companies were practically forced to lower prices in order to unload their products. The industry became more and more concentrated as smaller producers fell by the wayside or merged with larger firms. In 1963 *Der Spiegel* reported on price wars in the automatic washing-machine business. After the manufacturers stopped fixing retail prices, many dealers gave rebates in order to attract customers.[103]

Appliance dealers also faced increasing competition from other types of distribution networks. There were the commercial travellers, unpopular but not unsuccessful, especially in the vacuum-cleaner business. The rapidly expanding mail-order houses also began selling appliances. There had been a few mail-order firms before the war, mostly in the textile trade, but there was a great boom in the postwar years. Clothing and textiles remained the mainstay of the business, but, as the firms grew, some widened their range of products and sought to overcome the image of catering mainly to poor people, especially refugees.[104] *Ihre Freundin* advised readers in 1961 that now was a good time to buy refrigerators owing to an offer one of the mail-order firms had made, a 110- or

120-litre compressor refrigerator for under DM 300, which was being matched by other firms.[105] In 1969, Quelle, one of the leading firms, held 28 per cent of the West German market for household sewing-machines and 22 per cent for freezers, doing less well but not badly with refrigerators (13 per cent). Opposition from local shops and from many manufacturers led mail-order houses to develop store brands and build up their own repair services.[106]

A few lucky individuals received appliances as gifts or won them as prizes. Frau K.'s mother, impressed by the sales pitch of a door-to-door salesman, bought a washing-machine for DM 500 and gave it to her daughter.[107] The second prize in *Ratgeber*'s fourth 'Wheel of Fortune Lottery' was a washing-machine (first prize was a car, third was DM 1000 worth of furniture, fourth was a television set).[108] More commonly, families were able to purchase appliances more cheaply through employee discounts or connections. Frau T. and her husband, for instance, got a refrigerator 'cheaper, through connections' when they moved to their first flat in 1966.[109] Rebates also seem to have played an important role in appliance sales; one study reported that 23 per cent of the people surveyed who had purchased refrigerators during 1959 had obtained rebates of between 11 and 20 per cent. By buying directly from the manufacturer, as long as retail prices were fixed, buyers could save the dealer's mark-up.[110]

Some help was available from the state, but this was limited. There were subsidies to help rural households acquire hot-water heaters, as part of an effort to improve hygiene. Some state governments built community centres for villages featuring such amenities as laundry rooms and freezer lockers as well as bathing facilities and TV lounges.[111] In 1955, Herta Ilk, a Free Democratic member of the Bundestag, urged Family Minister Wuermeling to work towards making major appliances tax-deductible, like factory equipment.[112] In a letter to the news magazine *Der Spiegel* later that year, Wuermeling defended himself against allegations that he had expressed anti-consumerist views at a Cabinet meeting and insisted that his ministry was working to promote the spread of household appliances. He did in fact promote tax-deductibility for appliances, but was unsuccessful.[113]

Electricity companies supported state efforts to expand the use of electricity in rural areas and promoted the use of household appliances, which in some cases they still sold. *Ihre Freundin* reported in 1957 that the Bavarian Peasants' League planned to make washing-machines and some other appliances available to farm families at discounted prices.[114] For the most part, however, purchasing household appliances was up to individual families without outside assistance.

Payment by Instalment. One way of making expensive durable goods easier to purchase was through consumer credit. Gas and electricity companies continued to help customers finance purchases of appliances, as they had in the interwar period. Dealers might extend credit on their own account or through arrangements with manufacturers or finance companies. After the 1960s it became more usual for the prospective customer to obtain credit directly from a bank, either as a consumer loan, which was then paid back in instalments, or as overdraft credit on a cheque-book account.[115]

It is not clear what proportion of household appliances were purchased on credit. Figures from the 1950s indicate that other forms of credit besides instalment credit played a larger role, and that sales on credit only accounted for about 15 per cent of total business in retail sales of 'Haus- und Küchengeräten', a category which would include but not be limited to appliances. Credit sales were more common in the radio and television business (over 60 per cent from 1952 through 1955) and in the furniture business (over 50 per cent).[116] These figures had declined somewhat by the early 1960s to around 12 per cent for household equipment, just over 40 per cent for radios and televisions and just under 40 per cent for furniture.[117] Since these figures include sales to other than private consumers (for instance, to hotels) and are not strictly limited to household appliances *per se*, they can provide only a rough guide to the prevalence of credit sales of household appliances. One study in Bavaria in 1957 reported that 39 per cent of refrigerators were purchased on the instalment plan, while the remainder of the buyers paid cash and got rebates.[118] A slightly later study in Baden-Württemberg found that nearly half of washing-machines and vacuum cleaners and over 20 per cent of refrigerators, sewing-machines and cookers were purchased by instalment.[119] It seems probable that instalment purchases were most popular in the 1950s, when the purchase of an appliance meant a considerable financial exertion for most families.

Advertisements of the1950s in women's magazines for appliances frequently mentioned the possibility of paying by instalment, usually in general terms. For example, one 1958 advertisement announced, 'The acquisition of a "Lavamat" is nowadays no unfulfillable wish, favourable financing possibilities make the purchase of an AEG automatic washing-machine possible for everyone.' Advertisements in *Der Spiegel*, which was aimed primarily at the better-off, did not as a rule discuss payment plans, though one Westinghouse advertisement did mention a DM 65 cash rebate which could be obtained when paying cash for one of the firm's automatic washing-machines.[120]

The washing-machine manufacturer Constructa announced the establishment of its own financing system in 1957–58. It offered 12-, 18- or 24-month layaway plans with 'only a low finance charge'. Alternatively, one could pay DM 1000 down, either in a lump sum or in instalments, then take delivery and pay off the balance over twelve months with no interest charges.[121]

References in appliance advertising to the possibility of buying on credit peaked in the mid-1950s, becoming rare by 1959 and disappearing altogether in the 1960s.[122] This further supports the interpretation that instalment credit was a means of bridging the gap between expectations and financial resources in the 1950s but that thereafter families had more room to manoeuvre.

Gradually, major appliances became more and more common. In one study, 28 per cent of the couples who married around 1950 had a gas or electric stove at the time they married, 16 per cent of them started married life with a vacuum cleaner and only 4 per cent had a refrigerator, 2 per cent a washing-machine, 6 per cent a car. Of couples who married twenty years later, 93 per cent had a gas or electric stove, 92 per cent a refrigerator, 86 per cent a vacuum cleaner, 58 per cent a washer and 72 per cent a car.[123]

As of 1963, the proportion of West German households with washing-machines, about one-third overall, was comparable to the figures for France and Austria, somewhat lower than in Switzerland and Great Britain (43 per cent and 46 per cent respectively), and only about half that of Belgium and the Netherlands. In Italy, the figure was only 8.2 per cent (ranging from 10 per cent in the north to 4 per cent in the south). West Germany had thus caught up with the level reached in the United States in the mid-1930s. At the same time, 58 per cent of West German households had refrigerators, a level well ahead of Belgium, France, Great Britain, the Netherlands and Italy and comparable to that in Switzerland and to the level reached in the United States in the first years after the war. In vacuum cleaners, the West Germans had achieved a level of 72 per cent, slightly behind Great Britain and well behind the 96 per cent level of the Netherlands, but well ahead of Belgium, Finland, France, Italy and Austria and only slightly behind the 79.1 per cent level of the United States.[124]

Articles in women's magazines on what items a couple needed to have in order to establish their own household offer an indication of changing standards. A 1951 article in *Stimme der Frau* included a small electric or gas stove, preferably with an oven, and an iron, but no other appliances in its list of essential supplies (just under DM 1000 total). 'Naturally, we don't see the vacuum cleaner as the most essential purchase, although it is one of those devices which can make life much easier, especially for the employed housewife.'[125]

A similar list in a 1969 *Constanze* article included not only the vacuum cleaner but also a sewing-machine, refrigerator and hand-held mixer. A washing-machine was optional. The *Constanze* article also reflected a different attitude towards consumption, an expectation that there would be a rapid change in tastes in the future. For instance, it recommended saving money rather than accumulating a 'bottom drawer' of linen, since the patterns or colours which appealed to the teenager might no longer appeal to the bride. Earlier, sheets had been sheets – white and not subject to fashion.[126]

> What belongs in a complete trousseau, and how much – opinions on this matter have changed a great deal in the past years. Because, in our fast-moving times, obsolescence in fashion and technology doesn't stop at the front door. So the things you buy for your first household don't necessarily have to last a lifetime. You'll want to keep up with progress.[127]

In buying things which were expected to last, the bride should try to anticipate future developments – for example, the article recommended buying dishwasher-safe dishes.

When Frau P. married in 1963, she had savings and also received some money from her parents. She was a cosmetician, her husband an engine fitter. 'It was enough. For a Neckermann fridge, an electric range, just the essentials.' A Frankfurt court agreed the following year that a refrigerator was 'essential' due to such factors as shop-closing hours and the lack of suitable cellar storage space. Thus, it belonged to the list of articles which could not be confiscated in case of non-payment of debts.[128]

By 1969, automatic washing-machines could be found in the homes of 54.5 per cent of families with children. Over 80 per cent of these modern machines had been purchased since 1961. Refrigerators and vacuum cleaners were now virtually universal. Most households with children also had a car, very rarely two.[129]

Consumption and Controversy

While the changes in the West German standard of living in the postwar decades were generally seen with pride, there were worries about the negative side effects of the *Wirtschaftswunder*. Concern focused primarily on the social rather than the ecological costs, though this would change in the 1970s. Were West Germans living beyond their means, desperately trying to achieve ever more comfortable lifestyles (and keep up with the neighbours) at the cost of a happy family life, proper child rearing and even physical health? Where was the line between an appropriate standard of living and materialistic excess? Did rampant consumerism threaten its own roots, the economic health of the country?

The Threat of Debt

Particularly in the early 1950s, consumer credit was a source of concern. Not only was it traditionally frowned upon in Germany, but extending credit to consumers had often been a bad business risk in the recent past. Many firms had found their payments interrupted when purchasers were called up for military service in the First World War. Then the hyper-inflation of the early 1920s temporarily put an end to all offers of credit, since there was no way to calculate the amount by which the value of the currency would have sunk by the time payment was made. The Depression caused further problems, and the rearmament drive of the 1930s and then the war kept consumer goods in short supply and demand for consumer credit correspondingly low.

After the currency reform, a new consumer credit business was built up in West Germany essentially from scratch. Due to the dislocations caused by the war and the economic crisis after it, demand was high. The total amount of instalment credit extended by financial institutions expanded strongly in the early 1950s, fuelling concerns that the development was getting out of hand.[130] Concern focused not only on the risk to the individual consumer who might become overextended or unemployed, but also on the economy as a whole. Opponents feared that the use of credit would reduce saving and hence limit the resources available for investment. The experiences of the United States in the 1920s and 1930s were pointed to as evidence that the wide availability of consumer credit acted to exacerbate the ups and downs of the business cycle.

Criticism of consumer debt was based not only on real dangers, but also on a widespread cultural distaste for borrowing. The fact that German uses the same word for 'debt' and 'guilt' probably contributed to the stigma. The economist Wilhelm Röpke prefaced a pamphlet on the subject with a quotation from Goethe on the horrors of being in debt:

> The swine are never fattened now;
> Pawned is the pillow or the bed,
> And to the table comes fore-eaten bread.[131]

Röpke was not alone in his sentiments. Surveys in the 1960s indicated that most Germans disapproved of buying on credit. In this respect they were similar to and possibly more conservative than other residents of western continental Europe and very different from Americans.[132]

Magazine articles in the early 1950s reflected an ambivalent attitude towards the credit system. On the one hand, many indicated that the economy could not function without credit, that it was not inherently evil. One article explicitly stated, 'Obviously, buying on credit is neither shameful nor immoral nowadays.'[133] Evidently this was not so obvious as to go without saying. Magazines sometimes portrayed use of credit as the modern way, sometimes as a necessity in view of the amount people needed to buy to replace wartime losses, but also sometimes as a dangerous temptation to excessive consumption and finally bankruptcy.

A *Ratgeber* article in 1954 implied that people who took on instalment debt ought at least to feel guilty about it. 'With an almost unimaginable matter-of-factness,' the article stated, people in almost all sectors of society, 'even people who are otherwise cautious in their calculations,' included instalment payments in their household budgets and 'rather lose sight of the fact that they are living on borrowed money and have considerable debts'.[134]

If one had slipped into the debt trap, the article advised not taking on new debts before the existing ones were paid off and in fact not making any purchases beyond those necessary for day-to-day life. Money-saving measures suggested including not going out, patching the sheets again instead of replacing them and eating meat or sausage 'instead of three times or two times, just once a week'.[135] Discussion of the dangers of credit in magazines was mainly limited to the early to mid-1950s. As time went on, there was less use of credit for perishable or semi-durable goods, which was the practice most obnoxious to critics. Economic stability and low unemployment also lowered the perception of risk.

Runaway Aspirations? Consumption and Class

Condemnations of consumer credit often betrayed a certain lack of confidence in the financial skills of the working classes. The miners of the Ruhr were singled out repeatedly as bad examples.[136] In a statement introduced in support of one of many attempts to reform the 1894 law which regulated payment by instalment, a Social Democratic member of the Bundestag cited the dangers under the existing law to 'a worker and especially also his wife, who aren't so familiar with economic questions' and who might find themselves under a greater financial burden than they had been led to believe when they signed the contract.[137] In fact, both blue- and white-collar workers were more likely to use credit than other groups. A 1959 study suggested that there was less stigma attached to buying on credit among people with lower incomes. People with higher incomes who had instalment debt were likely to describe themselves as frivolous and carefree, suggesting that they saw their behaviour as somewhat irresponsible.[138]

Regardless of whether consumers paid in instalments or in cash, critics feared that the desire for more and more expensive items would lead to upward pressure on wages. This would siphon off money which could otherwise be invested in repairing and modernizing West Germany's industrial plant and also tend to reduce West Germany's competitive advantage over higher-wage countries like the United States. West Germany's economy was strongly, and increasingly, export-orientated. Germans were also highly sensitive about the risk of inflation, due to the experiences of the 1920s. The years between the end of the war and the currency reform had provided further experience of worthless money. The deutsche mark was very much a symbol of the *Wirtschaftswunder*, of the new regime's ability to provide economic stability and a return to normality.

A foundation associated with the Christian Democratic Party advertised brochures on the wonders of the 'social market economy' with full-page ads in women's magazines. 'Die Waage' took the line that wage increases would just be eaten up by inflation. The wife should remind her husband of the importance of increasing productivity, which would make life better for everybody.[139]

Walter Dirks of the *Frankfurter Hefte* quoted, from a newspaper story, a 'well-known CDU representative' as expressing the view that the tenth commandment should be amended to include the sentence, 'Thou shalt not covet thy neighbour's motor cycle, TV set and refrigerator.' Dirks was inclined to agree that the 'little man' should do without a television. On the matter of refrigerators, he wrote:

> Keeping foods cool is highly recommended; if you don't have a cool basement, see that you get a refrigerator, you need it for your leftover sausage and your milk more urgently than the rich man does for his fancy pickled herring and champagne.[140]

Those who greeted the spread of household appliances to more and more families were concerned that such purchases should not be seen as a sign of rampant materialism. The author of a 1960 dissertation in economics, citing a survey on current appliance ownership and the demand for appliances, stated,

> These tables . . . clearly show that these devices are only acquired when they are absolutely needed; they cannot be regarded as status symbols, and it is incorrect to accuse today's consumer of ostentation, as frequently occurs.[141]

Ludwig Erhard, who as Finance Minister presided over the development of the 'social market economy', made use of similar arguments. Although he regularly called for moderation in union wage demands, he defended the wider distribution of household appliances.

> Do the radio receiver, the vacuum cleaner, the refrigerator and so forth mean something different in the house of a wealthy man than they do in, for instance, the flat of a worker? Are they in one case an expression of civilization and in the other evidence of a materialistic outlook?[142]

Erhard presented increased consumption on the part of the working classes as appropriate to a new, more democratic society. Concerns about materialism he attributed to the desire for the maintenance of social inequality.

By portraying the refrigerator in the worker's flat, Erhard and others could also attempt to shift people's attention away from the existing inequalities in the distribution of wealth. The worker should not be discontented (and tempted to vote for the Social Democrats) because his boss had a house and a refrigerator and a fancy car and he did not. Instead, he should hope that through overall economic growth he would at least acquire a small refrigerator and a motor cycle, perhaps even a Volkswagen, at some time in the future.

Women's Paid Work

The question of what was an acceptable standard of living and what was excessive was linked to the question of work outside the home for married women, since the traditional rationale for this was economic need. A 1956 *Brigitte* article illustrates the defensiveness often found in portrayals of working women. It first emphasized that the majority of employed women were single, then indicated that two-thirds of employed women would prefer to be housewives. Wives who worked usually helped in the husband's business, in order to keep the money in the family, or earned 'extra' money if the husband's earnings were insufficient or to help pay for major purchases or 'luxuries':

No great luxuries by any means. Perhaps a TV set or perhaps an icebox. Things
... which one sees in every shop window, which are close enough to reach
out and touch – and for which one still has to lay a lot of money on the
counter.[143]

Did a TV set or a refrigerator justify a wife's working outside the
home? Opinions on this subject were divided in the 1950s and 1960s.
There was some opposition to married women working even if they did
not have children, and much more if they did. Work for single women,
on the other hand, was now an established norm even for middle-class
women, though there were concerns, as there had been in the 1920s, that
young women were not learning enough housekeeping skills before
marriage.

The number of married women and mothers working outside the home
was rising. The increase in work by married women was associated with
a tendency for women to marry earlier. The average age at first marriage
for women declined from 25.4 in 1950 to 23.7 in 1960, remaining fairly
stable until 1967, when it began to fall noticeably again. In 1970, it was
23.[144]

It was increasingly regarded as normal for couples to marry before
they had the requisite savings to completely furnish a flat in a style in
keeping with their social class, with the expectation that the wife would
continue to work for a little while. The war experience probably played a
role in making early marriage acceptable; at that time, many couples had
gone ahead and married even though they would not be able to set up
house, because they didn't know whether they would be able to if they
put it off, and, while some of these marriages had failed, there were also
many who were glad they had not waited. Being able to furnish a flat
once and for all was beginning to seem like an illusion anyway.

While women's magazines generally portrayed women working
outside the home as young, there was a definite increase in the employment rate among women over thirty, and especially between thirty-five
and fifty-five. For instance, in 1950, 35.4 per cent of all forty- to forty-
five-year-old women were employed, while in 1961 the figure was 45.4
per cent and by 1971 it had risen to 48.5 per cent. (Rates for men of the
same age were over 97 per cent in all of these years.) The increase in
employment by older women, most of whom were married, offset the
decrease in employment for women aged fifteen to twenty, almost all of
whom were single, as the educational system expanded in the 1960s.[145]

In 1950, 53 per cent of employed women were single and 37 per cent
married, with the rest widowed or divorced. By 1961 there were more

married than single women, and by 1968 53 per cent were married and only 34 per cent single.[146] The percentage of employed persons who were female was actually comparable in West Germany in 1950 and 1970 to what it had been in the Weimar Republic in 1925, but more of them were married.[147] In 1950 9.6 per cent of married women were employed, not counting those employed in family businesses, while in 1961 this had risen to 20 per cent and by 1970 to 27.4 per cent.[148]

The trend already seen in the 1920s for more working women to be employed outside family businesses, especially in white-collar work, continued in the 1950s as the number of family businesses and farms continued to decline. Overall, 30.7 per cent of employed women in 1950 had worked in family businesses, while by 1970 it was only 15.8 per cent. The percentage of women workers who worked in white-collar jobs rose from 21.3 per cent in 1950 to 41.6 per cent in 1970, while the number of women in blue-collar jobs sank slightly over the same time period, from 40.4 per cent to 36.6 per cent. The proportion of women who worked in the agricultural sector fell steadily from 33.6 per cent in 1950 to 13 per cent in 1970, the result of the shrinking of the agricultural labour force as a whole (the relationship between the numbers of men and women employed in agriculture remained fairly steady, with a slight predominance of women).[149]

Work outside the home for married women, and especially for mothers, was much less accepted than for single women. In a survey conducted in August 1959, 55 per cent of men and 61 per cent of women favoured a legal prohibition on work outside the home for mothers of children under ten. Indeed, 32 per cent of men and 22 per cent of women opposed employment for married women without children.[150] The differences in responses suggest that women were primarily concerned about the welfare of the children, while men also considered the benefits to themselves of having a full-time housewife at home, or worried that working women would displace men in the labour force.

Once working outside the home became acceptable for young brides, however, it was all but inevitable that there would be more young mothers working as well. It was not only the age at marriage which was declining, but also the age at which women began having children. The birth rate among 21-year-old women was 92.2 per thousand in 1950, 120 per thousand in 1961 and 133.8 per thousand in 1969. In 1969 the birth rate actually started to decline after age 23, whereas in 1950 the peak years for childbirth had been 24 to 28.[151] In 1969, half of all first-born children were born in the first year of marriage, almost 37 per cent of them in the first seven months.[152]

Overall, the birth rate was low. Among women born in the late 1920s and early 1930s and having children in the 1950s and early 1960s, the statistical average of children per woman fluctuated only within the narrow range from two to two and a quarter.[153] This was in contrast to the situation in France, where the average was just under three in the early 1950s as the immediate postwar baby boom tapered off.[154] Among West German couples who married in 1951, 23.9 per cent still had no children twenty years later and 18.6 per cent had only a single child. The situation improved somewhat; among couples who married in 1961, only 17 per cent remained childless and 15.5 per cent had only one child, the difference probably being due to improved economic conditions and greater optimism about the future.[155]

As of 1961, 13.7 per cent of married women with children under six and 15.7 per cent of those with children under fifteen were employed, not counting those who worked in family businesses or were self-employed. In 1970, 22.2 per cent of married women with children under six were employed outside the agricultural sector.[156]

Most married women with children, then, chose not to work outside the home, although the number who did was growing. Frau K. and her husband initially followed traditional gender roles:

> I was brought up that way, and I agreed with it, and I don't think my husband ever would have insisted that I go out to work, if he had stayed healthy. Because he was always of the opinion that he was the breadwinner. That was the attitude in those days. Nowadays opinions are different.[157]

Here the question of whether the wife should work was portrayed as finally the husband's decision, as long as he was capable of fulfilling the male role of breadwinner. Three of the other women interviewed indicated that their husbands strongly preferred them to stay at home; Herr M., who was present during part of the interview with Frau M., expressed this view for himself.[158] Frau K. endorsed the view that the husband ought to support the family. She did go to work when her husband became disabled due to cancer. In describing this decision, she depicted it as her own, based on her experience as a housewife of the difficulty of getting by on her husband's pension, rather than as her husband's. The economic necessity was decisive. In contrast, young women nowadays 'all think they have to earn money', although they are much better off financially than the K.s were in the early years of their marriage.

Some housewives felt quite adequately burdened with housework and resented any suggestion that they ought also to work outside the home, as Walther von Hollander found when he wrote a column in *Constanze* advocating part-time work for married women with older children. He reported receiving many angry letters, though this did not cause him to change his mind.[159]

Even without children, Frau Ma. found a half-time job to be all she could combine with her domestic responsibilities. After five years of full-time housekeeping and hoping in vain for a child, she went to work at a bank, but

> always just half-days . . . so that I could be fair to my marriage, my household . . . That way, you could combine [work and household duties] well. I'd never have wanted to work full-time. Better to save and do a lot yourself than to get into that stress.[160]

The presence of children increased both the domestic workload and the ideological pressure on women to stay at home. Children were believed to need '*Nestwärme*' (the warmth of the nest), which could only be provided by a constantly accessible mother. Presence and emotional openness, rather than any specific knowledge or parenting skills, were emphasized. A magazine article about a bored housewife stated, 'Veronika is not superfluous or useless, because her simple presence protects, now and for the future, her children's emotional balance.'[161] Women's magazines gave little attention to child rearing. (Fathers were apparently expected to regard children primarily as noisy nuisances; keeping the children from bothering the father was the responsibility of the mother.)[162] One symbol for this '*Nestwärme*' was the family dinner at midday. While fewer and fewer fathers were able to eat their midday meal at home, schoolchildren were still expected to.

Ratgeber reported that child psychologists warned that a lack of '*Nestwärme*' could lead to serious emotional damage and often to a tendency towards asociality. 'The warmth should be provided in the first instance by the mother. But how can she do that, if she places this beautiful human responsibility behind another, very material goal, that of earning money?'[163] The article went on to make clear that the criticism did not apply to women who had to work out of financial necessity: 'the reference here is to the other women, whose subsistence is assured, but who still earn extra money to raise their "standard of living", to be able to acquire a television set, a refrigerator, a small car or other amenities'. Here, unlike in the *Brigitte* article cited at the beginning of this section, the TV set or refrigerator was not regarded as an adequate motivation.

In a round-table discussion by men published in *Brigitte* in 1965,[164] the participants generally took the position that mothers should not go out to work, though three of them said that it might be all right in some cases, since some women were not by nature suited to be full-time mothers and would be bored and restless staying at home. They seemed to identify with such women. Another participant took a more conservative position:

It's not so much a matter of the mother's personality as of the child's needs. And the child needs the mother. Personality! – that doesn't matter at that point. The woman is a mother, she brought the child into the world, therefore she has to be there for it.

He was a married lawyer, father of two small children. Another participant, a fifty-four-year old gynaecologist and father of five, also took the position that a child was a profession, opposing even part-time work by women whose children were in school on the grounds that the children would want their dinner when they came home and would want their mother to be able to give them her full attention, without being tired from work. One supposes that he also expressed these views to his patients.

Several of the women interviewed strongly defended their decision to stay at home with their children and criticized young mothers of today for going out to work. 'A mother can raise her children best, not a kindergarten teacher,' proclaimed Frau K. Frau Ma., herself childless, spoke approvingly of her sister's dedication to her children. 'My sister with five children, she never worked, although she completed medical school. She says she has a good conscience, because her children never lacked anything.'[165]

There was great concern about 'latchkey children' (*Schlüsselkinder*), who were without adult supervision after school. They were thought to be at greater risk of becoming juvenile delinquents, another concern in the 1950s. A *Ratgeber* article on women in Finland automatically connected employed mothers, latchkey children and juvenile delinquency: 'Naturally, there are many latchkey children here as well [as in Germany] as a consequence of women working, and there is likewise talk of a youth problem [*Halbstarkenproblem*].'[166] The actual number of unsupervised children was small, as was the number of children who spent the whole day in institutions such as kindergartens or day-care centres; about 70 per cent of the children aged two to six whose mothers worked full-time and 80 per cent of those whose mothers worked half-time were cared for by individuals, usually grandparents or the mother herself. Individuals also provided most after-school care for school-aged children.[167]

In discussing kindergartens, Elisabeth Pfeil emphasized the negative views held by a minority of the women she surveyed. She discounted the more positive assessments of 71 per cent:

> The question: 'What do you think of kindergartens?' – which was asked of all the women, although only one in six had her child there – gave no clear picture, because evidently many mothers were thinking of the kindergarten in its original sense (as a complement to, rather than a substitute for, care by the mother).[168]

Pfeil also presented one quotation in favour of the kindergarten as an argument against it: 'It's a good thing – you can get rid of your kids there.'

The provision of day-care centres and kindergartens was sometimes looked to as a way to make it easier for women to combine work and family. However, one (male) author, considering options such as school meals and increasing the number of kindergartens, found that, on the whole, allowing women to participate fully in the labour market while finding substitutes for them as wives and mothers was not the right approach.[169] He did advocate making more part-time work available, and said that a Swiss employers' journal had found that the productivity loss compared with full-time work was not great, since 'the women can do their housework in the afternoons in peace, get enough sleep, and can do their work in the morning hours more efficiently and happily; in addition, there is less absenteeism'. As of 1969, approximately one West German child in three between the ages of three and six attended kindergarten, usually only for a half-day.[170] Day care would be one of the demands of the women's movement in the 1970s.

Measures to make it easier for women to combine family and work raised associations with the Eastern bloc. *Ratgeber* reported in its news column in 1960 that the German Democratic Republic (which it called the Eastern Zone) planned the introduction of day-care centres where schoolchildren would be required to go in the afternoons after school hours. It credited this decision both to the desire for a more thorough political indoctrination of the children and to the desire to increase the number of women workers. The piece was headed 'First production, then the family', which was clearly not the proper order.[171]

The question of whether a wife should or should not work outside the home could appear very differently depending upon the social and economic circumstances of the couple and on their individual preferences and values. Dr S., who was married to another doctor and worked as a substitute for other doctors who were on vacation, reported that her acquaintances envied and admired her. 'At work, when I got to know people a little, they said, "You're an ideal couple, really modern, and the wife works too, that's really great," and in the first years it really was like that.' Her husband did not help with the housework at all, but they generally had a cleaning woman at least once or twice a week.[172]

Elisabeth Pfeil's study of employed mothers found that 85 per cent of professional women, but only 15 per cent of saleswomen and 5 per cent of unskilled blue-collar workers, indicated that they would certainly continue working even if there were no economic necessity. The results when the women were grouped by educational level were similar, though less dramatic. None the less, 45 per cent of the unskilled workers and 55 per cent of the saleswomen said that they liked working, and 68 per cent of the former group and fully 90 per cent of the latter said that they were satisfied with their present jobs.[173] Unlike in the interwar years, newly married middle-class women were more likely to be employed than working-class brides, although the figures for both groups were rising over time.[174]

Women's magazines did portray women in high-status, professional work (particularly as film actresses), generally positively. This was not the norm, however. The West German labour market remained highly segmented, with most women working in predominantly female (and, not coincidentally, predominantly low-paid) occupations.[175] In the late 1960s, there was a push for increased education, including more education for girls, due to a fear that West Germany was falling behind in this area. Before that, the educational gap between men and women was substantial, education being commonly viewed by parents as wasted on girls because they would just get married. A woman's social status and success in life were expected to depend on her husband's career, not her own. These social expectations dovetailed nicely with the employers' desire for cheap labour.

This meant that married women rarely had the skills to earn as much as or more than their husbands. Frau Pr.'s husband ridiculed her desire to go back to work after the children were old enough to take care of themselves, pointing out that he could earn in an hour what she could earn in an entire day.[176] As of 1971, 77.6 per cent of employed women earned less than DM 800 per month (net), while 70.4 per cent of men earned more than that.[177]

While women in well-paid careers were the exception and married women's income tended to be regarded as supplemental, some women derived substantial pleasure from work outside the home. Frau P., a trained cosmetician, withdrew from paid employment for a time after her children were born and first returned out of necessity, sewing aprons at home for a local factory. But later, after the family moved to a larger town, she found more satisfactory work. Her son was in school by this time; she sent her daughter to a ballet school. When she returned from work, she often found the children sitting in front of the door waiting for her. She said, 'I never wanted to be completely without work. I didn't want to just putter around at home. I never could stand that.' Asked why, she said simply, 'I would feel really stupid.'[178]

Frau P. gave herself most of the credit for her family's comfortable lifestyle. Her husband, a skilled worker, was apparently more easygoing. She spoke of the satisfaction she found in achieving her goals: a house, a swimming-pool, a St Bernard. Although the house and swimming-pool could not have been achieved without help from her parents and brother, she credited the fulfilment of her dreams to her own will-power and energy. 'If you imagine something, and work towards it, and think positively, you can achieve one thing after another . . . But nothing comes by itself. I worked hard for all that.' While Frau P.'s satisfaction came mainly from her own private *Wirtschaftswunder* (though she also enjoyed the human contact she received through her business), Dr S. gave primary emphasis to the emotional satisfaction of working. When she was at home with her two children, she missed her work.

Frau P. and Dr S. had skills and interesting work, and neither of them had had an entirely happy home life growing up – Frau P.'s family lived in difficult circumstances due to her father's ill health, while Dr S.'s father tended to use his position as sole breadwinner to tyrannize the family. It is notable, though, that the women who had worked outside the home tended to emphasize this fact in the interviews, even though the focus of the questions asked was on housework. Dr S. also found that other women shared her views:

Later, when one of my patients, some saleswoman or hairdresser or whatever, told me she had to go back to work, she wanted to go back to work, because she couldn't stand it at home any more, I could understand that. I've always paid attention to that, how other women experience that. And here, too, at the state hospital, I've known a lot of colleagues with children . . . Many of them, I could name at least three off the top of my head, have told me, 'When I don't work, I get depressed.'[179]

Dr S.'s interest in other women's feelings about their work may reflect a trace of insecurity about her own decision, but she found a number of women to ratify her feelings.

Pfeil's study of employed mothers in 1956–57 found relatively few complaints, mostly dealing with low pay, lack of opportunities for advancement and sometimes difficult customers or bureaucracy. White-collar workers, she found, often reported experiencing work as a pleasurable contrast to domestic life. They found it widened their horizons and gave them new impulses. Pfeil found it telling that no blue-collar workers in her sample expressed this view. Blue-collar workers could none the less find satisfaction in creating order or handling pretty things, which Pfeil regarded as a redirection of their maternal instincts.[180] Social contacts were another reward of work outside the home; Frau Ma. continued to socialize with her former colleagues even after her retirement.[181]

Gender and Consumption

In some cases, women helped to earn the family income; in almost all cases, they helped to spend it. Women's highly visible role as consumers made it inevitable that criticism of the consumer culture would be linked with attitudes about women. Women's responsibility for day-to-day household purchases, principally of food, was recognized as being of enormous economic importance. In her discussion of women in West Germany in the 1950s, Erica Carter emphasizes the importance of the role of consumer in the construction of women's place in West German society.[182]

Although women's role as consumers was highly visible, this could bring blame as well as praise. Rising prices could be attributed to women's unwise spending, and overwork by men to their wives' extravagance. The division of gender roles which identified men as rational and women as emotional suggested that women might not manage money well, that they might be easily seduced by fast-talking commercial travellers or by advertising.

Husbands, Wives and Money. As a rule, family income was derived mainly from the husband's earnings. Day-to-day expenditures, however, were made primarily by the wife. Individual families made different decisions about how to manage money, but there were two basic patterns. In some families, the wife received the husband's pay, except perhaps for a personal allowance the husband kept for his own use, and paid the family bills. This was more typical for working-class families. In households where there was more money to administer, the husband tended to take primary responsibility for financial matters, allotting a certain sum to his wife to cover basic housekeeping expenses. Discussion of family finances in magazines was generally based on the middle-class model of a fixed housekeeping allowance.[183]

One complaint aired in magazine articles was that the housekeeping allowance was too small and that men did not pass on financial gains (through raises, for example) to their wives. Some men reportedly kept secret from their wives both the amount of their income and the amount of regular expenses for rent, insurance and so on which they paid. One author wrote of the 'dictatorship of the money earner', stating: 'In a genuine democracy, the income from all sources is publicly known and the budget is voted on. Unfortunately, there are far too few "marriage democracies"'.[184] The role played by money in the functioning of actually existing democracies was not the issue; rather, the ideology was taken at face value and used as a basis for claims on behalf of married women.

One advertisement presented the purchase of a refrigerator as a solution to disagreements over money. The illustration showed an attractive young woman holding a mop like a gun to lend force to a call for more housekeeping money. The drawing hastened to defuse the potential threat from the woman's discontent, however. First of all, the mop handle was not pointed at the viewer, but down. The manner in which it was held also served to draw attention to the woman's breasts. The woman's clothing was both feminine and chaste. Her hair was soft and slightly dishevelled. Although her (lipsticked) mouth had a firm line, her huge eyes and slightly raised eyebrows gave her a vulnerable rather than an angry expression. The advertisement treated the wife's discontent as a bit of a joke and offered a simple solution: buying the refrigerator, which would help her save money.

A 1970 round-table discussion published in *Brigitte* illustrates several of the issues associated with women's financial dependence.[185] The topic of the discussion was how large an allowance a housewife who did not herself earn income should receive for her personal use. Five middle-class housewives, all with small children, participated in the discussion. Their husbands earned from DM 900 to DM 2000 monthly in take-home pay, the housekeeping allowances were mostly between DM 400 and DM 450, and only one received a personal allowance (DM 30 monthly). While this group cannot be seen as representative, the discussion does illustrate some ways in which women experienced financial conflict in marriage at the time.

One of the women managed the family's finances. The others all stated that they were not good at managing money. Their responses to the question of who managed the money were different, but all reflected a lack of confidence in their own financial acumen. In at least two cases,

Mehr Wirtschaftsgeld für die Hausfrau

Figure 3.4 Advertisement for Bosch refrigerator (detail), *Ihre Freundin* 13 (18 June) 1957, p. 38.

this view seems to have been shared by the husbands. Another woman stated that both she and her husband were particularly good at spending money. Still, the arrangement was that he gave her the housekeeping money. (She reported stealing from him on occasion if the housekeeping money ran out: 'He usually doesn't notice, because he never knows exactly how much he has.')

One problem experienced by at least two of the women was that the housekeeping allowance was not increased despite rising prices and additional children. Another problem was disagreement between spouses on how often new clothes were necessary.

> Usually what happens is, he says, 'You got a lovely coat four years ago, it's still in perfectly good shape.' My husband isn't interested in fashion at all. He finds all that completely unnecessary. Besides, he says, I could sew myself, and one can get dresses altered.

Her husband, she reported, had almost to be forced to buy new clothes himself. None of the husbands had a fixed allowance and most did not spend much money on themselves (one bought expensive suits, which he presented as necessary in his position as a bank employee). Here, patriarchal principles worked against the development of a consumer culture.

Two of the women voiced objections to the principle of a fixed allowance. 'I don't want to be a paid housekeeper,' said one. Another stated, 'It seems to me that a woman, with the work she does, contributes just as much to the family as the man does and that therefore she has a right to some of the man's income, too.' These remarks prefigure the wages-for-housework debate of the 1970s. The other women did want some money for which they did not have to account to anyone. Two of them explicitly used the phrase 'Rechenschaft ablegen müssen'. Because the husband earned the money, he was entitled to authority in financial matters.

Women as Consumers: the Value of Thrift.   Day-to-day expenditures for food and household items represented a large portion of total expenditures, particularly in the 1950s, and were largely under the housewife's control. Women's magazines provided advice on buying economically and on budgeting.[186] Some advocated keeping detailed books, as a help to budgeting or in some cases as evidence to persuade the husband to raise the housekeeping allowance. While articles on thrift were more common in the 1950s, an article in *Constanze* in the prosperous year 1965 told the story of a young wife learning to manage on a housekeeping allowance of DM 150 per month. She began by changing the money to five-mark pieces and putting them in thirty envelopes for the days of the month. After she had saved up enough money, she bought an account book to keep her records in. The piece praised her and indicated that her efforts were also appreciated by her husband:

> In the meantime, saving and allocating money well has become so much a part of her that she doesn't need the envelopes. She manages superbly with

her housekeeping money and has achieved a standard of living for her family which appears much higher than that of his colleagues with the same income. That makes Hannerl's husband especially proud, of course.[187]

Here, the family's economic success was credited as much to the wife's thrift as to the husband's earnings.

A 1955 advertisement portrayed men as reluctant to marry because they thought their money would only go half as far for two people. When they did marry, they discovered to their surprise that they were living better than before. 'Sometimes they realize why: because of their wife! . . . Through careful shopping, she obtains the highest value for her husband's mark.' The advertisement included a quiz so that the reader could determine whether she was a wise shopper (one of the requirements was buying brand-name products such as those advertised).[188]

With her cooking skills, the housewife could prepare palatable meals from leftovers and inexpensive ingredients. An article in March 1954 gave recipes for less popular, but cheap, meats such as pigs' ears and calves' feet.[189] The weekly menus given in *Stimme der Frau* generally did not emphasize meat. They were for a range of budgets, with estimated prices for a family of four given.

The degree to which demands for thrift were made on housewives depended on the economic situation. The recession of 1966/67 evidently induced housewives to be more careful with their money. *Der Spiegel* reported that sales of cheap cuts of meat were up. 'Parts of the pig that until recently nobody wanted, such as feet, belly or ears, can be sold again.' One grocery chain reported selling 'fewer rolls, but more bread, less Hungarian salami, but more coarse *Mettwurst*'. Sales of luxury foods, such as goose-liver paté or turtle soup, were down.[190]

In a 1964 survey in which men were asked to select from a list the five qualities they most valued in women, 65 per cent included thrift, making it the most frequently chosen response.[191] It could also be a source of satisfaction for housewives. Frau M., for instance, took pride in her skill in this area. She gave an example of a time when this ability had been of great value:

> When Käthe had the whooping cough, that was at the end of the month, I still remember that today. The prescription cost twenty-seven marks and something. At the end of the month. If I hadn't saved, I wouldn't have been able to get it.

Their health insurance reimbursed them for the medicine, but they had to pay for it initially. In contrast, an acquaintance 'got into debt so badly, she didn't know what to do. Then she went to work . . . She said herself, "I can't manage money. What I see, I have to have, and then by the fifteenth [of the month] . . ."' This suggests that both Frau M. and her acquaintance subscribed to the view that a housewife should be able to manage on her husband's income, and that going out to work was an admission of failure at this task.[192]

Articles on the subject of household economy generally presented the wife as coping with a situation beyond her control – a fixed housekeeping budget – but other articles emphasized the economic power of housewives as consumers. Perhaps the individual could accomplish little, but in theory the millions of West German housewives had an imposing amount of power.

In times of rising food prices the magazines urged housewives to take action. They should refuse to pay the higher prices, either going from shop to shop trying to find the best prices or changing their plans and substituting other, less expensive goods. 'Learn to say no! That is your most powerful weapon and your democratic right in the shopping battle that you must fight for yourself and your loved ones every day. Don't let anyone dictate excessive prices to you!'[193] The combination of metaphors is interesting. One would not normally expect democratic rights to matter much in the heat of battle. Women's right to refuse to buy at prices they considered excessive, a rather ancient form of protest, was presented as a benefit accruing to them from the new regime in West Germany. The consumer stood up to the authority figure of the shopkeeper, striking a blow for self-determination – in contrast to the rationing under the Third Reich or the lines and shortages of the Eastern bloc. This article was entitled 'My Husband Doesn't Earn Enough' and was clearly intended to shift the burden of responsibility for a tight household budget from the husband's employer to the shopkeeper and, in the end, to the wife.

One reader responded enthusiastically to this call for more assertiveness in shopping, saying that the article had shaken her out of her previous indifference. In two weeks of following the magazine's advice, she had not had much material success, but found the contest itself satisfying: 'the feeling of satisfaction from having won still another "victory" in a shop is priceless'. To keep from slackening, she had cut out the article and carried it in her appointment calendar. She expressed the hope that the idea would receive wider publicity. She concluded, 'The individual woman can do little. Only if many people think and act the same way could it happen that one day your visionary "economic miracle" will be achieved.'[194]

Women as Consumers: the Dangers of Extravagance. While some articles and advertisements praised the economical housewife, condemnations of extravagance were not lacking. There were repeated accusations that young women were becoming too demanding, 'too expensive to marry'. As single women earning wages and living with their parents, they were spoiled, spending ridiculous amounts on nylons and hairdos rather than saving to equip their future households.[195]

Housewives were sometimes blamed for driving up the cost of living through extravagance. This did not just mean too many new hats, but too much luxury food. A 1956 *Ratgeber* article took the view that consumers' dissatisfaction was based less on rising prices than on rising expectations which outran their means. Butchers, the article claimed, complained that housewives only wanted the best cuts of meat, while the cheaper cuts could not be sold. Grocers reported that customers wanted vegetables which were out of season. 'It's not the cost of living which is too high, but the cost of satisfying our excessively high demands. We could be much more relaxed, happy and contented again if we would learn to cut back.'[196] A 1955 article in *Stimme der Frau* claimed that about 40 per cent of the increase in expenditures over the period 1950–54 resulted from higher prices and 60 per cent from quantitative and qualitative increases in consumption.[197]

Women were portrayed not only as extravagant but also as easily persuaded. In discussions of the dangers of consumer credit, the housewife victimized by the persistent door-to-door salesman was a common image. In proposing a reform of the law regulating instalment payments, SPD representative Reischl also criticized advertising presentations made in cinemas. A period in which a contract made outside the normal business premises of the business involved could be cancelled without penalty (one of the provisions of the bill as initially proposed) was needed so that people seduced by the presentation would have time to sit down 'as a family, husband and wife together,' and reconsider the decision to purchase.[198]

One article in *Ratgeber* depicted the full-time housewife as 'frugal by nature' but suggested that women who worked for pay were more likely to be extravagant. A reader of *Ihre Freundin* took a similar position in a letter in response to an article on housewives being blamed for excessive spending:

> I myself can't imagine that there are women who are 'just housewives' who always feed their family members chops and cauliflower ... The fact that consumption of these items, chops and cauliflower, is so high can no doubt

be credited to employed women, who have to calculate more closely with their time . . . I'd like to see the head of household who wouldn't prefer skilfully prepared *Jägerkohl* or Irish stew to cauliflower, but, as I say, dishes like that take more time and effort and also a knowledge of cooking that young working women mostly lack.[199]

Some articles questioned the attribution of blame for higher prices and extravagant styles of living primarily to women. One article accepted that criticisms of housewives for buying only the most expensive goods were partly justified, but insisted that men shared the blame. Many women, the author stated, would be perfectly happy to eat more vegetables and less meat for the sake of their figures or because of modern knowledge about nutrition. It was the husbands who protested: 'I'm not a rabbit.'[200]

Some of Michael Wildt's interviews support this view. Speaking of the late 1950s, Frau H. said, 'Sometimes I refused to go along with it, I said, "We don't need to have that all the time." And then my husband said, "Haven't we got the money to fulfil the wishes that we'd like to? So get it."'[201] Here, the husband is presented as depicting his own desires as those of the couple. It is of course also possible that some women, brought up to indulge their families but not themselves, projected their own desires on to their husbands.

Women could derive pleasure and satisfaction, as well as practical benefits, from their success in managing money. They could see their economic role, both in the family and in the larger world, as important, a view which was reinforced in the press. Husbands also valued thrift, even if they were not necessarily accepting of its implications for their diets. Ultimately, though, it was the husband, as principal wage-earner, who had the real financial power in the family, while on the macroeconomic level financial power was even more firmly in the hands of men. House-wives had responsibility rather than power, though much of the discussion in women's magazines tended to disguise this fact.

The Supermarket: Danger and Promise

The 1950s saw a major change in the way groceries and many other household products were sold in Germany: the rise of the self-service shop. Initially, shopkeepers were very sceptical about whether this American innovation would be accepted by German housewives. After all, shopping was not just a matter of exchanging money for goods, it was an occasion for exchanging gossip as well. Furthermore, the traditional shop offered advice on products. Some 1950s advertisements portrayed the white-coated shopkeeper as an authority figure extolling the advantages of the latest laundry detergent or floor-polish. None the less, the self-service shops proved extremely successful. Difficulty in finding sales help provided an additional incentive to switch to this method.

A 1961 report in *Ihre Freundin* indicated that some customers welcomed the lack of personal interaction in self-service shops because they felt more pressured to buy in traditional shops or preferred a certain anonymity and privacy in making purchases which permitted their neighbours to draw conclusions about their financial circumstances. Two of the customers interviewed spoke positively of having the option of looking at something and then putting it back on the shelf. One of the readers who wrote letters in response to the article appreciated not having to tell the shopkeeper out loud, in the presence of waiting neighbours, what she needed, giving the neighbours a look 'into my cooking pot and thus into my purse'. Some shoppers felt under pressure to buy more or more expensive wares than they really wanted. One wrote: 'With products where there are three or four price categories, I can choose a middling or cheap sort without embarrassment, without being subjected to critical looks. I don't have to listen to the question, "Is that all?"'[202]

Two men found that they felt more comfortable shopping in self-service shops. One experienced traditional shops as an oppressively feminine environment. 'Stuck in a – pardon me – crowd of gossipy women shoppers at the baker's, the butcher's, the dairy shop – no, that's not for a man.' Another man, on the other hand, preferred the corner shop because the shopkeeper knew what kind of bread, what brand of margarine his wife preferred, so there was less risk of a mistake. He also didn't like to feel he was being manipulated.

While some shoppers evidently felt under psychological pressure to buy when they shopped in traditional shops, the self-service shops introduced new techniques of manipulation, which were regarded with suspicion. Products had to sell themselves. Eye-catching packaging, long regarded with scepticism by consumers because it increased the price of the product, now paid off. Product placement was geared towards increasing sales by promoting impulse purchases.[203]

In the effort to save money, the new self-service grocery shops were potential enemies of the economical housewife. *Ratgeber* warned in a 1965 article about the dangers of being led by placement and packaging to buy items which were not on the shopping list or which were not the best value for money. 'It is no doubt very tempting to stroll along the overflowing shelves and fill one's basket on wheels with all the fine things piled up all around the shopper. But this is an expensive journey.' The self-service shops were also criticized by *Ratgeber* as a temptation to juvenile delinquency, since they made shoplifting relatively easy.[204]

The self-service shops had come to stay; while they accounted for 4.4 per cent of grocery sales in 1956, the figure rose to 34.8 per cent in 1960 and 62.0 per cent in 1964.[205] If some housewives of the 1950s saw the advent of self-service as a reduction of unpleasant social pressures to buy, they were evidently not actually buying less. The reduction in social interaction may also have contributed to feelings of isolation among housewives in subsequent decades.

The Good Life and Bad Health

References to health dangers were notably frequent in warnings of the perils of a higher standard of living or the pursuit of it. These concerns had some basis in fact. In addition, in an increasingly secular society, fears of danger to the body replaced fears of danger to the soul. Worry about one's health was modern and scientific, while worry about one's salvation wasn't. Finally, there were plenty of conservative members of the medical profession ready to perform studies and make public state-ments pointing to factors such as the employment of women or the use of consumer credit as health risks.[206]

While a cookery book of the 1950s still contained the assertion that there was little danger of overconsumption of meat 'simply because the mass of the population can't afford that financially',[207] this situation was already changing. Part of the problem was simply cosmetic. A *Ratgeber* article in 1954 commented,

> For a long time, the war made worrying about our figures unnecessary. And when we'd finally got to the point where we could get all those good things again, we enjoyed what was offered us. Now, though, some of us are eyeing with concern the lovely curves in places we'd rather not see them.[208]

But of course there were real health risks as well. Overeating played a prominent role in depictions of the *Wirtschaftswunder* in popular culture. A piece comparing conditions in 1950 and 1960 through depictions of 'Familie Jedermann' celebrating New Year's Eve dealt extensively with food. In the 1950 vignette, the people were slim and cleaned their plates. In 1960, they were watching their diets because of health problems.[209]

Financial difficulties were also linked to health risks. A notice on 'dangerous instalment payments' in *Ratgeber*'s news column stated,

'Doctors have concluded that circulatory problems, weakness of the heart and nervous ailments can often be traced to the excessive burden of [financial] obligations.' An article in the same magazine, arguing against buying in instalments and for a more modest standard of living, expressed the view that new purchases were more satisfying if they did not involve a continuing financial obligation. 'More than a few psychologists', the article asserted, blamed stress, nervousness and insecurity on the 'epidemic' of instalment buying.[210]

If concerns about family life predominated in attacks on women's employment, another popular approach was to warn of the health risks resulting from the strain of combining work outside the home with housework. *Ratgeber* conducted a steady campaign on this issue in the 1950s. Its miscellaneous-news column (Das interessiert die Frau, Nachrichten für die Frau) repeatedly spoke of studies showing that working women and especially working wives suffered frequent illness. On one occasion, it repeated a plea by gynaecologists for the elimination of *Doppelverdienertum* (two-wage families) in cases where there were children. It cited statistics on chronic illness among women and warned of the financial costs. *Ratgeber* also linked employment for mothers to higher rates of miscarriage and stillbirth.[211]

Overwork was a potential problem not only for women who worked outside the home but also for men who sought to 'get ahead' through hard work. One author, while admitting that some people called in sick when they weren't, worried more about overwork and exhaustion: '[Many people] take sick leave only when it is already too late.'[212] An article in *Brigitte* came close to comparing the *Wirtschaftswunder* itself to an illness:

Of course it's an astonishing accomplishment, to create normal conditions and a visible prosperity in Germany in less than ten years after the catastrophic collapse. But many of those who created this miracle seem to have done it in a fever, and this fever has not yet left them.[213]

This article warned that the husband's overwork might be the wife's fault. In earlier days, a husband would have refused to overstrain himself in order to satisfy his wife's desire to live beyond his means, but, in the postwar world, 'the exaggerated craving for earnings and property, for social prestige and career success has taken on a decidedly unhealthy character'. *Ratgeber* printed a cautionary tale about a wife who pushed her husband to climb ever higher on the career ladder until finally he had a heart attack.[214]

Technology vs. the Family: the Dangers of Television

One of the changes the *Wirtschaftswunder* brought to the West German household was television, the classic example of modern technology seen as a threat to the family. There was a rapid fall in the price of television sets in the mid-1950s. The price of a small (36 cm diagonal) set fell from DM 1200 in the summer of 1952 to DM 600 early in 1955, a price which *Der Spiegel* noted was below the price proposed in 1939 for a *'Volks-fernsehempfänger'* (RM 650). In 1958, 15 per cent of households had television sets; eight years later, the figure had climbed to 66 per cent.[215]

In the 1950s, not only the violence portrayed on television was seen as threatening to children, but even the simple fact of moving images. Children, it was believed, could not distinguish fact from fiction and could easily be overstimulated and become nervous as a result of exposure to television. Consequently, television viewing was inappropriate for children below school age. As early as 1954, *Ratgeber* warned: 'If we want to preserve a peaceful, happy and secure life for our children in their little world for as long as possible, we will have to reject television viewing, at least for them.'[216]

Reports from the US on the dangers of television for children began even before the advent of regular television broadcasts in Germany. *Der Spiegel* reported in 1950 that 'Fernsehen macht dumm.' American children, the article stated, spent so much time watching TV that they didn't do their homework and consequently got lower test scores. It also noted that 'the numerous "crime shows" with gunfire, robbery and murder were particularly popular with young people'.[217]

A 1961 article began, '"TV disease" is threatening our children.' It cited a survey indicating that 28 per cent of children between two and sixteen watched television. Worse, many of them watched in the evening, when the programming was intended for adults. 'Unrestricted television viewing in the developmental years', the article warned, 'is no less dangerous than alcohol and nicotine.' The dangers were emotional disturbance and loss of concentration. An eight- or nine-year-old child might be permitted to watch children's programmes once or twice a week, but younger children had no business in front of the screen.[218]

Concerns about television were readily developed from existing concerns about film and radio. A 1958 article warned about the dangers of leaving the radio on all day:

Many doctors have already warned against this, because the continual exposure to all sorts of musical or other sounds has a bad effect on the nervous system, the ability to concentrate, and on mental performance. How often children and even babies are unthinkingly exposed to this background noise! And the sound of the radio is especially bad for the small child; scientific studies have unequivocally shown that it produces very bad and unpleasant sensations in the little person – and in order to develop properly, it needs a consistent state of well-being![219]

It is striking to the present-day reader that this great sensitivity to seemingly minor disturbances of children's rest developed so soon after the war. Less than a generation earlier, children had been exposed to much more disturbing stimuli and seemed, by and large, to have survived and developed. But perhaps it was precisely the inability to protect children in past years which intensified the concern now.

The cinema was another example of the stresses to which modern life exposed both children and adults. Life was too fast-moving, too busy. By not allowing children to go to the cinema, the parents could at least exercise control over one aspect. *Ratgeber* warned of 'the endangerment of young people through film'. Children might think real life was like the films. The particular danger was that girls would expect young men to be perfect gentlemen.[220]

With both film and television, a chief danger for children was seen to lie in the flood of sensory impressions which they were not yet prepared to interpret. There were also occasional warnings that television encouraged an excessively passive attitude in adults. 'It is not appropriate for us to always let life be presented to us from outside. We shouldn't always [sit back and] let ourselves be entertained.'[221]

Despite the concerns, television was extremely popular. Other products used this popularity in their advertisements. For instance, one advertisement suggested that an evening of participating in the goings-on of the wide world from the comfort of one's own home properly included snacks baked with Dr Oetker baking-powder.[222] The 'well-known TV chef' Clemens Wilmenrod lent his prestige to a processed-cheese product as well as to magazine recipes.[223] In 1960, *Für Sie* regularly featured recipes introduced by 'TV chefs'.

A 1951 article in *Stimme der Frau*, not a magazine ordinarily given to philosophy, expressed concern about the nation's moral well-being:

If one is completely honest, one notices suddenly that something has happened to all of us. Some wise old men of science, who ponder the development of mankind, find that we – the generation since the Second World War – have lost our inner centre, and that we try to compensate for this loss with a reorientation towards external things, with a craving for material possessions.

After the First World War it was not so different. But it had not assumed such a broad form. It only affected one class: namely the *nouveaux riches*, those who had suddenly come up in the world. Now this craving doesn't seem to be limited to a small class.[224]

One might argue that there were more pressing moral questions for the Germans to consider at that time than materialism; none the less, it was a concern. However much the achievements of the *Wirtschaftswunder* might be appreciated, both materially and as a source of national pride, there remained a degree of ambivalence, of concern about the physical and spiritual price. Concrete fears included excessive consumer debt, inflation, stress and overwork. These concerns were especially acute in the 1950s.

Concerns were related not only to class issues – were the workers getting too ambitious? – but also to gender. Shopping was women's work, and they were open to praise or criticism as the 'economics minister of the family', an important but subordinate role. The money women spent was, in most cases, earned mainly by their husbands; work outside the home for married women was controversial, and those women who did work tended to be clustered in low-paying jobs.

Women's place was still primarily in the home. As we have seen, though, the *Wirtschaftswunder* had changed the material conditions of day-to-day life profoundly. The effects of this change, and of the notion of equal rights, on women's and men's domestic roles will be the subject of the next chapter.

—4—

Men, Women and Machines

Equal Rights, Different Roles

In postwar West Germany, the discussion over women's proper role in society had to be taken up again after the simple answers of the National Socialists and the obviously atypical conditions of the predominantly female society present at the end of the war. The constitution of the new state, one early (and binding) declaration of principles, featured a compromise between feminist calls for equal rights and Christian concerns about the family. Thanks to the efforts of the Social Democrat Elisabeth Selbert and the women's groups who supported her position, the new constitution included the simple formulation 'Men and women have equal rights.' Another article guaranteed state support for the institutions of marriage and the family. These two provisions, both of which were included among the guarantees of basic civil rights at the beginning of the Basic Law, would frequently come into conflict.[1]

Several parts of the Civil Code, which dated from the turn of the century, clearly contradicted the guarantee of equal rights. The authors of the constitution gave the parliament until 31 March 1953 to effect the necessary changes.[2] The deadline was not met. The Social Democrats refused to support the Christian Democrats' move for an extension, so April 1953 brought a legal vacuum, which was ended only with the Equal Rights Law of 1957. In the meantime, the courts managed as best they could.[3]

One of the provisions of the Civil Code which was declared unconstitutional was Paragraph 1354, which gave the husband the right to make final decisions in all areas related to the marriage if the husband and wife could not reach an agreement. An attempt was made to replace the paragraph with a modified version rather than simply dropping it, but this failed in 1956 by a narrow margin. The husband's rights to represent the children and to make final decisions regarding them (Paragraphs 1628 and 1629) were eliminated by a decision of the Federal Constitutional Court in 1959. In contrast, French husbands retained extensive rights, including the right to determine where the family would live and the right to contest a wife's decision to work outside the home, until 1965.[4]

Although some on the right strongly favoured retaining the husband's rights as set down in the old Paragraph 1354, this position did not have universal support even among conservatives. *Ratgeber* sharply criticized the government's support for the husband's prerogative in a short piece in its miscellaneous-news column in December 1952:

> It may be of interest that neither the marriage laws of the Nordic countries nor the relevant laws of the USA and England contain such provisions. The legislators of those countries have not presumed to regulate the private relationships of spouses in this one-sided manner.[5]

If the right of the husband to have final say as head of the household was widely questioned by the 1950s, the different roles and obligations of husband and wife in family life were not. Equal rights did not mean that men and women were the same. Until the marriage law reform of 1977, the law was quite specific in spelling out the duties of each partner. The wife was to run the household. Her right to work outside the home was limited; her duties to marriage and family came first.[6] The husband lost his right to unilaterally terminate a contract of employment made by his wife, however.[7] In a financial emergency, the wife could be required to earn income, but, if the husband's income was sufficient to support the family, the wife was not required to work outside the home. Ordinarily, the wife's contribution to the support of the family came through her administration of the household.[8]

Outside the family, too, equality was not construed to mean sameness. The existence of a guarantee of equal rights in the West German constitution not only failed to lead to unisex toilets and compulsory military service for women, it did not even affect protective legislation for women workers. Wage discrimination on grounds of sex was successfully challenged in the courts, but the solution reached was to rename the job categories in terms of 'heavy' and 'light' work rather than the sex of the worker.

In the first years after the war, women's magazines discussed political issues relatively often, though their attention was generally limited to 'women's issues'. Political re-education was a major goal of the occupation authorities, who issued licences and allocated paper supplies. The coverage given to politics declined once the constraints were removed; the public wanted entertainment instead.[9]

The support for equal rights, defined in a fairly limited sense, on the part of producers of women's magazines seems to have been genuine enough. References to politics did not disappear in the 1950s, but they were frequently phrased in a way which suggested a sense on the part of the authors that the audience wasn't really interested. When in 1953 those provisions of West German law not in accord with the constitutional guarantee of equal rights became null and void, an editorial in *Constanze* commented on the event as follows:

> How have you been feeling for the last eight or ten days? Do you always walk across the street or through your flat with your head held high? Do you see your husband – if you have one – differently from before? No? None of that? You feel that nothing at all has changed since you have had equal rights with your husband and all other men – since midnight on 31 March 1953? Don't be angry with us if we can't agree with you this time. There have been a number of changes, even if you haven't noticed much yet.[10]

The article went on to enumerate some of the rights the husband had lost. The reader, however, was expected to take the position that nothing had changed. The light-hearted tone, which was very typical of *Constanze* at this time, served to emphasize the distance between the 'women's world' of the magazine and the 'men's world' of politics.

The discussion of women's employment is one example of the coexistence of assertions of equality with acceptance of the status quo. Mention of women in 'men's jobs' was generally positive. These women were seen as exceptions, however. An article in *Ihre Freundin* painted an admiring picture of a female radiologist but also took the view that few women had the qualities necessary to be successful in this demanding profession.[11]

A review of an American film about a woman doctor provided an occasion for *Constanze* to discuss the careers of early women doctors in Germany, crediting the 'unparalleled idealism of the first women doctors' for the fact that 'young girls of today study with equal rights alongside young men in the lecture halls and clinics of the universities'. This statement managed both to deny lingering inequality between men and women and to demonstrate it through the use of the terms '*Mädchen*' and '*Männer*' to describe the allegedly equal students.[12]

The assumption that some jobs were women's jobs and some jobs were men's jobs which would not attract more than a few women remained generally unchallenged. Columns of advice for young women choosing professions generally included almost exclusively typically female occupations, sometimes with a discussion of why the particular occupation was especially suitable for young women. One *Ratgeber* article expressed the view that it was nice if a girl chose an occupation 'which allows the womanly qualities to develop; [in other words] occupations which have to do with people, children, plants, animals'.[13] As we have already seen, the assumption that young women would quit work when they married or at least when their children were small remained powerful. This implied that women would not require extensive education; their economic security, and social status, would be based on their husbands' occupations, not their own.

The public discussion of the question of equal rights was reflected only occasionally in advertisements. One advertisement for Bosch mixers showed a judge, finger upraised and mouth open in mid-lecture, with a pile of thick law books. The slogan was 'Equal rights for the housewife'.[14] In the text of the advertisement, this was translated as the right to mechanical help with the housework. An advertisement for the artificial fibre Perlon showed a man and a woman at twin sinks washing clothes. 'Equal rights, equal duties' read the headline.

The Bosch advertisement spoke of equality within the traditional division of gender roles – the woman should have the same technological assistance for her housework as the man had for his paid labour. The Perlon advertisement was more radical, although it is somewhat difficult to imagine it translated from the line drawing of the advertisement to a real West German bathroom.

The advocacy of equal rights, however hedged in with qualifications, shared space in magazines with criticism of 'too much' equality. The woman who was too determined to prove her competence in the male world eliminated her feminine charms. She was likely never to marry (it was apparently unthinkable that a woman might be so unfeminine as to choose to remain single, or to prefer a companion of her own sex). An article in *Constanze* lamented the domestic ineptitude of successful career women:

> The higher a woman ascends on the ladder of her career these days, the further she often removes herself from her natural duties . . . Equal rights and emancipation are unfortunately often misunderstood by modern women . . . As little as it is possible to take from a woman the act of becoming a mother is it possible to transfer the office of housewife to the husband. It is of course no discredit to him to help in the household as often as possible. But very few men are by nature such gifted 'housewives' as to be able to transform a bare flat into a cosy home.[15]

Freude an perlon

Gleiche Rechte . . . Gleiche Pflichten

PERLON macht aus Pflichten ein Vergnügen.

Meine Damen . . . waschen Sie Ihr PERLON oft -

meine Herren . . . waschen Sie Ihr PERLON selbst

Figure 4.1 Advertisement for Perlon (synthetic fiber) (detail), *Stimme der Frau* 5 (23 February) 1955, p. 25.

The assumption here was that women had a 'natural' ability to create cosy homes. The learned skills and the work which went into this task were as discreetly hidden as the messy physicality of the 'act of becoming a mother': To use Ingrid Langer-El Sayed's expression, 'a necessary connection is postulated between the ability to bear children and the ability to vacuum and wash dishes'.[16] Such a logic implied on the one hand that men were inherently incapable of doing housework satisfactorily, and on the other hand that women's success in maintaining orderly, comfortable homes was due to their inherent female nature rather than to their individual skills and work.

Wives' career success was sometimes presented in the 1950s as threatening to their marital happiness. A woman who wrote to *Stimme der Frau* about marital difficulties received the following advice from another reader: 'Your delight over your professional successes is understandable, but if I were in your place I'd conceal it in the presence of your husband and, if the subject does come up, speak of good fortune, not of a proper appreciation of your abilities.'[17]

The conformity to social norms of feminine behaviour required by marriage had to begin even before the marriage took place. Too much independence in young women reduced their chances of marriage. One author stated that only nonconformists would possibly be interested in 'excessively mannish or tomboyish, excessively independent' women, intellectual bluestockings and successful female athletes. Ordinary men considered such women 'unemotional, too unsympathetic, too inflexible'. Such a woman, he theorized, was 'usually the victim of a difficult youth and in general also of equal rights, the ugly reverse side of which is very often a loss of womanly qualities'. Forced to take care of themselves like men, such women lost their femininity. They lacked:

> the most important qualities of a good wife: motherly warmth, joy in caring for others, adaptability . . . No doubt Bärbel [the exemplary case under discussion] could learn quickly, with the help of understanding girlfriends, how well pretty dresses and longer hair would suit her, or even painted fingernails. She would be amazed to discover how highly men esteem a woman who sometimes cries at the cinema and will never understand how a car motor works . . . Bärbel would surely discover how much further a woman gets when she accepts without reservation the role towards which nature and society direct her and plays it and lives it to the best of her ability.[18]

This article discussed a 'deviant' woman and how she might be helped to become more properly feminine. Often, especially in *Constanze* and *Ihre*

Freundin in the 1950s, the assumption was that all women naturally shared certain characteristics, notably a great concern with their own physical appearance (convenient for many of the magazines' advertisers). 'Despite military and labour service, the women in Israel have remained true daughters of Eve,' found one reporter, using a popular expression.[19]

By the end of the 1960s, the second wave of the women's movement was evident in women's magazines. Political issues took on greater importance. *Brigitte* announced a series of pieces on the reality behind the equality proclaimed by law.[20] *Für Sie* carried an article discussing the progress which had been made in changing women's legal position and the legal and social inequality which remained. A particular target of criticism was men's unwillingness to help with the housework, which, however, was blamed not on individuals but on society: 'As long as a helpful family man is ridiculed by society as henpecked, male willingness to help is understandably very limited.'[21]

In 1969, *Constanze* reported critically on a public-opinion survey which had found that most women saw home and family as their primary purpose in life and an overwhelming majority thought mothers should not work outside the home. The position taken in the *Constanze* article was that this was a shocking state of affairs and that women who were 'just housewives' suffered from disappointment and depression.[22] As the survey results indicate, however, *Constanze* was trying to change opinion, not reflecting it. Evidence of ambivalence remained, however: an admiring article on a female politician earlier that same year was not complete without the insistence that the woman in question was 'no virago, no bluestocking, no dried-up old maid, but a very lively woman'.[23]

Men and Housework

The question of equal rights for men and women was (and is) intimately bound up with the distribution of household labour. As we have seen, the idea that women and men had equal rights was not generally construed to mean that they were fundamentally similar types of human beings. The idea that men and women had complementary roles to play in marriage, the husband responsible for earning income and the wife for running the household, was enshrined in West German family law as well as being accepted custom. Theoretically, this meant that the husband and wife had equal roles. If the wife also worked for pay, this equation no longer held. Even if the wife did not work outside the home, however, the division of labour might seem unequal if her housework required more hours and more physical exertion than his paid employment. If the couple's income permitted, some of the housework could be shifted to a paid third party. Another solution, of course, was for the wife not to work outside the home. As indicated in the previous chapter, this was strongly supported.

Some of the women interviewed reported that their husbands had done occasional housework. Frau K.'s husband enjoyed cooking, as a hobby, something which she found surprising. 'He actually really liked to cook – on Sundays, when he was at home, the kitchen was his kitchen. Which was really never the case earlier, because I'd never known that from my father. He only saw the kitchen from the outside.'[24]

In this case, the work was done voluntarily, for pleasure. Herr K. took on more responsibility for housework in the last years of his life, when he was no longer able to work outside the home. Frau Ge. reported that her father did some of the shopping after he retired.[25]

Herr Ma. helped his wife when there was a lot of work to be done, for example when she was bottling: 'In the summer, I was grateful, my husband liked to be a *Hausmann* – He wasn't forced, he enjoyed it – We did the bottling together.' He also pitched in sometimes on Saturdays in order to get the housework finished earlier so they would have more free time to go hiking. Frau Ma. emphasized the voluntary nature of her husband's participation and her appreciation of it. His willingness to help evidently raised rather than lowered her opinion of him, but her statement suggests that she did not believe a woman had a right to 'force' her husband to help.[26]

Several of the women interviewed spoke of the great changes they saw as having occurred between their generation and the present one. Frau Pr. saw young men of today as more willing and able to participate in housework than those of her generation, though she gave no clear reason for this change: 'Well, with this whole generation, that was women's work, cleaning, men couldn't do that, and nowadays they're somehow very different.' Frau K. and Frau Ga. both gave themselves some of the credit, since they'd required their children, boys as well as girls, to help around the house. Frau Ga. reported that her children's friends had teased them about having to do chores, and the boys had complained about it, but that as adults they and their partners were glad that they had the skills.[27]

The views on men doing housework presented in the pages of women's magazines in the 1950s and 1960s varied. A 1958 article on the men's page of *Ratgeber* took the view that the argument that the wife had to work outside the home often did not hold water. Even if it did, the wife had no right to insist on help with the housework:

> The management and to a great extent the work that a household involves are still absolutely the wife's area . . . If a man values a comfortable and well-kept home and his wife helps to support them through her work, it is every man's duty to make the double burden of work and household a little easier for his wife to bear. On the whole, however, it contradicts the nature of men and women if their responsibilities get too mixed up, so it is preferable for the wife only to work full-time in case of urgent necessity.[28]

'Making the double burden a little easier to bear' clearly falls far short of bearing it oneself. The responsibility for managing the household (on a very tight budget, presumably, if the wife worked out of economic necessity) remained with the wife, who could not count on help from her husband.

At the other extreme, a 1960 *Constanze* article presented as an 'ideal couple' one in which both partners worked and a grandmother took care of the small child during the day. The author argued that, in a two-career marriage, both partners had the same duties and rights. 'When it comes to the household, it won't do for the man always to ride first class, so to speak, while the wife is back in the wooden-seat section. The marriage train is bound to derail eventually.' While this was an extreme position, there was some support for the idea that the husband should help at home if the wife worked.[29]

A 1956 article in *Ratgeber* called for more help from husbands and more acceptance of men's doing housework. Here, the call for help was not targeted only at men whose wives worked outside the home. Instead, the article argued that men's paid work required fewer hours than formerly and, often, was not physically strenuous.

> 'For my family, nothing is too much,' alleged model husbands like to say with conviction. But, if one looks more closely at these gentlemen, it turns out to be not seldom the case that after eight hours of office work they're not even capable of fetching potatoes from the cellar or going shopping, much less helping with the cooking or the washing-up.[30]

While women had demonstrated their ability to perform in traditionally male professions, the article went on, men were reluctant to do 'women's work'. The author condemned mothers for encouraging such attitudes on the part of their sons. Other articles also criticized women's role in discouraging men from performing housework.[31]

The author of the *Ratgeber* article regarded men's refusal to help as uncivilized.

To be sure, there are said to be Negro tribes in which the men stretch out on coconut-fibre mats in the shade of tall palm trees while their wives, in the broiling heat, cultivate the fields, take care of the livestock and watch the children. But to reintroduce such customs in civilized regions is going a bit too far.

By associating a one-sided division of household labour with the practices of 'barbarians', the author made it seem inappropriate for civilized Europeans. Another variation on this technique was the application of the term 'pasha' to husbands who expected their wives to wait on them. The demands made in this article were not very far-reaching, extending only to occasional help. Still, the author was determined to see women's household work taken seriously and to see men and children helping with it.

Brigitte published a piece in 1970 entitled 'Should Men Help around the House?' The heading at the top stated, 'Studies have shown that only seven men in a hundred assist their wives in the household. Do equal rights stop at the apron?' The piece consisted of responses by seven couples to questions on the subject. In three cases, in all of which the wife worked outside the home, the husband participated actively in the housework. The responses ranged from 'housework is women's work' to 'Of course [the husband should help]. After all, it's not my household, it's ours.'[32]

There were certain household tasks which were regarded as appropriate for men. One was household repairs which required manual skills and technical knowledge in which men were supposed to be superior to women. Another was heavy work, such as carrying coal upstairs and ashes and rubbish down. Here, men were allowed to apply their superior strength. In the most modern blocks of flats, oil stoves or central-heating systems and rubbish chutes eliminated much of this work. Changes in lifestyles would add one additional responsibility: washing the car. A woman interviewed in a 1970s study reported the following exchange: 'Yes, I already told him . . . you wash dishes and tidy up the same as I do. I work, too. At first, he just stared, "I don't have to do all that, I wash the car." Then I said, "We don't *have* a car yet."'[33]

Taboos against men doing 'women's work' represented a barrier to male participation in most household tasks. Sometimes magazines worked against these taboos, particularly in recommending that boys be educated in household tasks. This was often portrayed as leading to more appreciation for their wives later rather than to practical usefulness, however, except for bachelors. For instance, one author thought thirteen-year-olds of both sexes should be able to make their beds, cook a simple meal, clean up the kitchen, darn socks and sew on buttons.

> If I extend this in principle to boys as well, it is because women have been complaining for generations that most men did not properly appreciate their housework. How can they be expected to, if they never had to do it themselves?[34]

In the schools, home-making was largely a girls' subject; as of 1966, it was mandatory for both sexes in only one state, though it was available to boys in some others.[35]

If the magazines sometimes opposed taboos against men doing 'women's work', they often reinforced them. Men were sometimes portrayed as totally incompetent in domestic affairs. This may have been a welcome counterweight to men's assertion of superior ability in most areas of life. In any event, an assumption of masculine incompetence in housework could reassure women that they were needed. A husband who could not cook was dependent on his wife, unless he could afford to eat out all the time.

The supposition of incompetence also meant that men could not be called on to do much housework. In an article on preparations an expectant mother should make, *Ratgeber* suggested that a husband might not remember to air the bedroom or notice that the bread and butter were running low. 'Surely you've already revealed to him where the shoe polish for his shoes is, and the socks and underwear.'[36] In other words, an adult male ought to be able to dress himself and polish his shoes without instructions from his wife, in an emergency, but probably not much more than that. Another article gave advice to wives who were going on trips and leaving their husbands to cope:

> The grass widower who ties on an apron and reaches for the wooden spoon rather than going to the nearest restaurant shows courage. The clever wife makes preparations in order to make the unfamiliar kitchen work easier for him.[37]

These preparations included leaving behind simple recipes and menus, doing the shopping in advance and explaining in writing where the various ingredients were kept. The wife was also advised to leave some prepared dishes in the refrigerator. Similar portrayals of men as incompetent in housework were present in French women's magazines during the same period, though there seems to have been more emphasis there on women's ability to outsmart their husbands.[38]

Men doing housework could be figures of fun. Two cartoons which appeared in *Constanze* in 1959 presented dishwashing husbands as substitutes for servants. The woman in the first said, 'I feel soooo sorry for my husband – but there's simply no [household] help to be had!' In the second, the words of the rather aggressive nationalistic song the husband was singing were placed in ironic contrast to his performance of demeaning labour: 'The God who made the iron grow / He never wanted [men to be] slaves.'[39] In both cartoons, the men were depicted with aprons and the women with cigarettes, emphasizing the 'world turned upside down' image. A third cartoon on the same page showed another apron-clad, dishwashing man explaining to a more masculinely dressed visitor, 'Yesterday I married my housekeeper.' The heading for the three cartoons was 'Herr im Haus'.[40]

A letter from 'Anni K., Frankfurt' published in *Ihre Freundin* in 1958 complained about her husband's help around the house on the grounds that, except for cooking, housework was not appropriate for a man and made him unappealing to her. Furthermore, she felt unneeded. Interestingly, most of the women whose letters responding to hers were published in a subsequent issue took the position that she should be grateful, though one writer agreed that a man looked ridiculous running around with a shopping bag and thought she should discourage him from that particular task. On the other hand, one man responded, 'I would like to congratulate Frau K. for maintaining her natural sense of what constitute decidedly feminine areas of work and for her very reasonable position on the question of the spouse's help in the household.'[41]

Women as well as men subscribed to ideas about proper gender roles which could cause them to see male help in the household as 'unmanly'. In addition, male involvement in housework threatened female autonomy in an area which was important to many women. For the vast majority of women, the sense of 'being one's own boss' could only be achieved in the home, not in the outside world. This sense could more easily be maintained if the husband stayed out of the kitchen.

Overall, then, the depiction of men and housework in magazines presented a mixed message. There was a tension between the idea that men and women were inherently different types of human beings with different abilities and the idea that men and women should be equal and labour distributed fairly. If only women could be good housekeepers, then it was not right to ask men to help with the housework and in any event they'd make a mess of it. On the other hand, if the wife worked outside the home or the husband's job was less demanding of time and energy than her housework was, the division of labour seemed unfair.

This is the same conflict between equality and difference which was played out in the legal arena. In the household, too, difference tended to come out the winner.

Images of Foreign Men and Housework

One reflection in women's magazines of German attitudes about proper gender roles was the depiction of gender roles in other countries. As we have seen, Africa could be used as a bad example. Discussion of countries supposedly more 'progressive' than Germany showed the ambivalence about this type of 'progress'.

America appeared to some Germans as a land where women had achieved a remarkable degree of power. This attitude was well established by the 1950s. Many travellers from Germany in the 1920s had commented on the role of American women; their attitudes on the subject varied according to where the authors stood on the 'woman question' in Germany. The feminist Alice Salomon envied the freedom of American women, while more conservative observers saw America as a place where men were enslaved by women as well as machines. Hermann Scheffauer presented American husbands' help with the housework as a parody of European courtly love. Babbitt did not sing serenades (to a lover Scheffauer depicted as 'tap-dancing like a Negro') or write sonnets. 'Rather, he pushes the baby carriage, sets the table, carries the dishes into the kitchen, puts on an apron, washes up, goes shopping and in winter takes care of the heater.'[42] The image of the apron-wearing, dishwashing American husband was a popular stereotype in the 1950s.

An item in the miscellaneous-news column of *Stimme der Frau* in 1955 reported on the existence of 'his and hers' aprons in the USA as a 'symbol of women's equal rights' and further noted that American women had indicated in a recent Gallup poll that they regarded dishwashing as a responsibility to be shared by marriage partners. 'It is no wonder', the piece concluded, 'that major American newspapers fear that there could one day be a revolution by men, who are now burdened way beyond their strength.'[43]

Concerns that American women were 'too liberated' and not a fit model for German women to emulate continued to be voiced in West German women's magazines throughout the period under review. In a series of articles in *Constanze*, the conservative writer Hans Habe compared German and American women.[44] Habe saw American women as still competing with men after they'd achieved equal rights and claimed that American men died young because they were unhappy. According to

Habe, more and more American men were letting their wives support their families, especially in the rural South. Finally, though, there were signs that the relation between the sexes were becoming 'normalized'. A poll conducted by a women's magazine revealed that 74 per cent of American women wanted a man they could look up to – something which in Habe's opinion no American woman would have confessed twenty years earlier. Normality included, for Habe:

> the division of roles in private life. Where the man ceases to be the head of the family and has to content himself with the role of babysitter, a state of psychological distress develops such as we could observe in the past decades in America. Where the wife takes over the husband's responsibilities, either a male rebellion simmers or the husband – worse still – accepts his humiliating role and ceases to be the man that his wife, in the end, wants him to be.[45]

American women, in Habe's view, confused equal rights with sameness, refusing to acknowledge the existence of distinctly male professions and qualities. Habe also saw American women as 'comfort-loving', blaming this characteristic for, among other things, the higher rate of Caesareans in the US. He also portrayed American women as sexually frigid and incapable of growing old gracefully. His opinion was not totally negative, though – he saw American women as more cultured than American men.[46]

Other voices expressed envy of American women and the 'respect and admiration'[47] with which their men treated them. A defender of the dishwashing American man reported:

> In America, I've seen male dinner guests take off their jackets after dinner, roll up their sleeves and wash the dishes. There, they have the proper sense that if you can't keep a maid you just have to help out yourself. Our wives aren't our slaves, they're our companions in life.[48]

The author suggested to German husbands that they should help out with the dishes and polish their own shoes. In addition, they should buy their wives household appliances – and flowers. Still, the ideal solution would be for the husband to lighten his wife's burden by employing another woman to assist her.

In an article in *Ratgeber*, one of a series on the lives of housewives in other countries, the Englishman also received praise for his consideration of his wife. According to the article, 'Mr Smith' brought a cup of tea to his wife's bedside in the morning, washed the dishes and cleaned the family's shoes 'until the sons are big enough to help him'. The help with the housework, like the morning tea, was an 'expression of respect' for the housewife.[49]

Ihre Freundin, campaigning for more household appliances in 1950, attributed the greater progress which the US had made on that front not so much to greater wealth as to the greater willingness of husbands to recognize their wives' needs.[50] German husbands, the article implied, should be less selfish and more considerate of their wives' legitimate demands.

The comparison went both ways. While some German authors used American husbands as role models for German husbands, many American authors, especially in the late 1940s, saw European women as models for what American women should be like. Marriages between American servicemen and European women were taken as a sign that American women had become too unfeminine, too materialistic and generally too demanding. An article entitled 'Do European Women Make Better Wives?' portrayed the American husband's life as miserable. An army personnel officer was quoted, listing the advantages to a man from marriage:

> But what does he get in return, beyond the 'privilege' of intimacy? Check it off: He gets to make his own breakfast . . . He gets to live in an almost mechanically run household – for which he has to buy the gadgets . . . And even with all the gadgets, he still has to pitch in on any chores that don't get done during the day. Then he has to top this off by providing an escort-and-entertainment service to compensate the little woman for her 'imprisonment' in the household he's breaking his back to support . . . Over here the women give their men something that most American women don't: a sense of being the boss, a sense of security.[51]

Another author took the argument a step further, arguing that it was precisely because of the new appliances that American husbands had been lured into doing housework: 'The American male is a sucker for anything that whirs or hums or lights up, and women know this.'[52] There was something of a backlash in America at this time, not so much against feminism as against the power of women, whether achieved through non-traditional means or not. This meant that German authors critical of the supposed excesses of female power in America could draw on a good deal of American literature in support of their argument.

Ihre Freundin reported in 1961 on a course which three American women were giving in Berlin for German brides of American soldiers to prepare them for life in the US. *Ihre Freundin* took the position that the major function of the course was to teach properly bad manners. The

American GIs, the article stated, were concerned that their female compatriots wanted to 'enlighten' their German sisters and eliminate their 'healthy respect for men'. 'Then the German woman would lose her charm (for American men). "Then we could just as well have married American women to start with," said the GIs.'[53]

By the late 1960s, it was possible to find examples of foreign men doing more than occasional dishwashing. The 17 April 1967 issue of *Constanze* featured an article on marriage in Sweden, which was written by a man and reflected both a rather hesitant admiration and an obvious insecurity.[54] It depicted both a couple in which the husband and wife alternated days of working and staying at home and one in which the wife worked and the husband stayed at home full-time. This lifestyle was so shockingly radical the author could find no word for it, describing the husband as the 'male housewife (in Sweden they already say *Hemmaman*)'. To translate this term into German as *Hausmann* evidently seemed to him impossible.[55]

The author portrayed the position of the German husband as unfair: 'We all know how it is here. The German husband has really nothing against his wife earning money. None the less, after five he allows himself to be waited on like a pasha.' He stated that this was not the way to bring about equal rights for women in employment and attributed the equality of Swedish women to their husbands' willingness to share the housework and child care. But this was, he implied, a high price to pay. He stated that the Swedish husbands were not henpecked (*Pantoffelhelden*) but didn't seem to believe this entirely. Not only were the women demanding about housework, they were also demanding in bed – having premarital experience with other men, they were in a position to compare.

One exchange he depicted served both to reinforce stereotypes about American marriages and to question whether things were really better in Sweden. He quoted the wife:

> 'We don't rule over our husbands and families like the American women do. I can [compare] because we lived in New York for two years. We're just good partners in marriage. That's all.'
>
> Sven, who had now finally got his son into his nappy, heard the last two sentences. He wanted, hesitantly, to contradict them.
>
> Whereupon Margaretha [said] energetically, 'That's my opinion and I stand by it.' Sven remained silent and smiled.

One of the photos illustrating the article showed the extremely radical image of a man powdering his baby's behind and kissing his wife as she left for work – dance practice. While she was pursuing a glamorous career, her husband was left to cope with the most disagreeable aspects of parenthood.

Foreign women were occasionally interviewed about their views of German women. In one 1970 article, a Swedish women attributed the continuing use of old-fashioned kitchens in Germany to 'romanticism' and the continual cleaning to lack of self-esteem. An Indian woman found German women too bossy: 'The German woman, because she's so diligent and competent, thinks she's a little better than men.' Both she and the Japanese woman found that German women neglected their children. By putting such criticisms in the mouths of foreign women, it was possible for magazine authors to simultaneously express them and distance themselves from them. 'Are we really like that?' asked the headline of this particular article, stressing the possibility that the foreign women's impressions might not be accurate. If negative portrayals of German women in the foreign press were reported, it was generally with indignation. For example, an article in *Ihre Freundin* in 1955 took issue with American newspaper articles (not cited specifically) which portrayed German women as oppressed. The article pointed to German women's wearing make-up despite men's disapproval of it as evidence of their independence.[56]

In articles on the division of household labour in foreign lands, German authors played with different options for gender roles. The act of choosing foreign examples placed a distance, literally, between the practices discussed and the German audience. Taken as a whole, these articles did not represent a ringing endorsement of a radically egalitarian division of household labour. Such ideas seem to have been greeted in some quarters with a fair amount of male sexual anxiety. There were also objections to the notion that German women were necessarily oppressed if they did all the housework or preferred to look up to their husbands. Still, the idea of a token male participation in housework out of courtesy to the wife met with some positive responses. By expressing male help with housework in terms of a positive male image, the gentleman, rather than in terms of the negative image of the henpecked husband, authors sought to make it more palatable to men and women.

Men and Housework in Advertisements for Household Products

On the whole, the images of men in advertisements were even less challenging to the status quo than the discussion of men and housework in articles. Men rarely appeared at all in advertisements for household products. Ordinarily, if such an advertisement showed a person, it was a young woman. Many of the male figures used were non-humans, such as the Erdal (shoe polish) frog. When human males did appear, they usually weren't working.

One type of image which did crop up occasionally in the 1950s was the overworked or inept man trying to do housework, with the message that, since he wouldn't be able to cope without proper equipment, there was no reason why his wife should struggle with old-fashioned methods. The argument that men would be positively eager to purchase labour-saving appliances if they were the ones who had to do the housework was evidently popular. One advertisement showed a man standing at a washtub, with the text, 'If Father had to do the washing, he'd buy a Miele electric washing-machine today.'[57] Similarly, a 1955 advertisement proclaimed, 'If men had to clean, in ten minutes they'd call for help from FAKIR, the electric waxer with unbeaten versatility.'

In a 1955 Braun advertisement, a husband who was doing the house-work while his wife was away decided that they needed a mixer.[58] In part, these advertisements made use of the stock comic depiction of the man as inept housekeeper. The men were portrayed as cartoon figures. The Braun advertisement, in which the man was not seen, included a recounting of the husband's kitchen adventures. The advertisements also communicated the message that women should not be willing to work harder than men would, however.

Men in white chef's hats could occasionally be found in advertisements for products such as hand mixers or pots. Husbands who cooked as a hobby also made occasional appearances in advertisements (as they did in the text of magazines, presenting favourite recipes). One advertisement for an electric grill held out the possibility that one's husband would be so enthusiastic about grilling one wouldn't be able to get him out of the kitchen.[59]

While these depictions were ostensibly positive images, not parodies, they showed some ambivalence. The men in question were often not terribly attractive. To be sure, in 1950s magazine advertisements even the women did not always look like fashion models. Among men, the handsome ones tended to be those who were drawn rather than photo-graphed. One of these, in an advertisement for detergent, was washing laundry in a hotel sink (thus not challenging the division of *household* labour). But other men depicted doing housework, such as the pudgy man with dark-rimmed glasses presented as a hobby cook in one advertise-ment for saucepans, are hard to imagine as attractive role models.[60]

The text of one furniture advertisement took issue with the viewer's expected merriment at the idea of the man of the house in an apron. It

Figure 4.2 Advertisement for Fakir waxer, *Ihre Freundin* 7 (15 March) 1955, p. 50.

praised the husband's consideration. The same consideration was presumably supposed to motivate the male reader to buy kitchen furniture. Still, the actual portrayal of the dishwashing husband in the advertisement was not very flattering. The inclusion, for reasons which are not altogether clear, of an outsize dog in the illustration did not contribute to the attractiveness of the image. It was clear from the text of the advertisement that the husband was merely helping out in what remained primarily his wife's territory. The advertisement went on to speak of the housewife's joy at the sight of such a fine kitchen.

Ach, wie komisch: der Hausherr mit der Schürze!

No, so komisch ist das doch gar nicht, wenn der Hausherr mal ein bißchen in der Küche hilft und sich dazu eine Schürze vorbindet, um den Anzug zu schonen. Die männliche Würde geht ja dabei keineswegs verloren, denn häusliche Hilfsbereitschaft ist ja immer auch ein Zeichen

Unterhalten Sie sich doch einmal ganz zwanglos mit Ihrem Musterring-Möbelhaus über Ihre Heim- und Möbelwünsche – Sie werden staunen, welche Möglichkeiten sich Ihnen dabei eröffnen!

Stadt gibt es ein Musterring-Möbelhaus! Der neue Musterring-Katalog, jetzt noch umfangreicher (56 Seiten!), noch reichhaltiger illustriert mit vielen farbigen Raumbildern und Wohnbeispielen, berät Sie in allem, was Sie vor dem Möbelkauf wissen möchten und wissen müssen. Sie erhalten

Figure 4.3 Advertisement for Musterring furniture (detail), *Ihre Freundin* 8 (8 April) 1958, p. 45.

Male as well as female children were sometimes portrayed using appliances to suggest how easy they were to use – child's play. Some of the items portrayed in this fashion would have been quite dangerous for a child to use in reality. The text in one advertisement for a hand-held chopper and mixer made clear that, though the photo showed a boy holding the device, its use was the province of women: Peter was said to prefer the foods his mummy prepared using the gadget (with the revealing name the Housewife's Magic Wand) and, since he had such a good appetite, 'our little man is getting big'. Although the boy was depicted holding the mixer, his real role was that of consumer.[61]

This role of beneficiary rather than performer of housework was also favoured for adult males in advertisements. One advertisement for a household cleaner showed the young husband looking on admiringly as his wife washed a kitchen wall.[62] In another advertisement, for dishwashing liquid, the husband was seated in his easy chair, looking up from his newspaper to say how pleased he was that his wife had more time for the children and for him now that she used Lux.

Figure 4.4 Advertisement for Lux dishwashing liquid (detail), *Constanze 1* April 1959, p. 117.

Husbands, much more often than other women, were portrayed in the role of recipient/critic of housework. In an advertisement for Miele washing-machines, a husband carefully inspected the pile of sheets his wife held. He was evidently satisfied by what he saw, as shown by the smile half-seen over the top of the pile. The wife, whose painted finger-nails, neatly styled hair and lack of an apron subtly suggested the advantages of using a washing-machine, beamed. On the one hand, the portrayal of these figures suggested that housework was a labour of love, something she did for him and which, done well, would assure her of his

Figure 4.5 Advertisement for Miele washing machine (detail), *Ihre Freundin* 8/1960, p. 117.

continued admiration. On the other hand, he was entitled to inspect her work and judge it. He was her supervisor. A series of advertisements for Wipp laundry detergent used a very similar theme, showing couples and clean laundry with the slogan, 'For you, I wash perfectly.' The phrase could either refer to the relationship of the wife to the husband or the laundry detergent to the wife.[63]

Men appeared as authority figures in advertisements not only as husbands but also as 'experts' of various types. Frequently, this status was symbolized by a white coat, whether the man was being portrayed as a scientist or a salesman. One laundry detergent advertisement provides an interesting juxtaposition of male and female experts. In the top photograph, a brunette friend told the blonde woman of the merits of the laundry detergent. The friend was positioned slightly higher than the prospective consumer and her head was tilted slightly less, but she still showed very non-aggressive body language and a broad smile. The instruction took place in a private setting and the female 'expert' had provided her friend with a cup of coffee or tea. In contrast, the male 'expert' in the second picture, presumably a shopkeeper, held up his index finger in a classic 'lecturing' gesture and had an unsmiling face. His considerably larger size enhanced his authority. He bent over the woman in the manner of an adult talking to a child. Here, unlike in the first photo,

Figure 4.6 Advertisement for Schwanweiss laundry detergent, *Constanze* 8 (6 April) 1955, p. 101.

the blonde woman looked attentively at her instructor. The lecture presumably took place in a public setting, the shop (she was wearing a coat), though the setting was not shown, the background being a plain and somewhat ominous dark colour. The third photo was a textbook case of what Erving Goffman termed 'the feminine touch', in which women's hands were used as a sort of decorative frame for the product, touching it very lightly rather than grasping it or manipulating it.[64]

A pair of advertisements for Zanker washing-machines also made use of male and female experts. The female expert was an experienced housewife in a white apron advising a younger woman. In the text, she based her authority on having done extensive comparison shopping before she decided to buy the Zanker. Her expertise came from the company as represented by the appliance dealers rather than from her experience as a housewife. Another advertisement from the same series showed one of these male experts instructing a fellow man. The point of view was that of the husband being advised: 'We men are also interested in how our wives solve the laundry problem nowadays.' As a consequence, they sought out professional advice (and, unsurprisingly, wound up buying a Zanker). Ultimately, it was the men in white coats who had 'solved the laundry problem' for the women.[65]

A 1958 advertisement for floor polish portrayed a man, somewhat improbably, as interested in and enthusiastic about floor polish, but it was clear that he was investigating the claims made by 'housewives' about the polish rather than actually cleaning the floor. This was emphasized by the clothing that the adults in the illustration were wearing: she had on an apron, while he wore a shirt and tie and a cardigan, the clothing of someone who worked outside the home and relaxed in it.

In another scene in the same advertisement, two children were portrayed in sex-typical floor-endangering play – the boy 'repairing' a toy truck with a hammer, the girl, who was watching him in a possibly envious manner, washing in a toy washtub.[66] A photo series in *Ratgeber* enlarged on the theme of playing washday. The photos, accompanied by verse, showed a little girl, perhaps three years old, with a kerchief on her head. She was fully equipped with a little wooden washtub on a stand or table, a washboard, a wringer and a laundry basket. The text praised her concentration and diligence. Such images were variations on the very popular theme that children imitating adult behaviour were 'cute'. For little girls, evidently, playing 'mummy' did not necessarily just involve playing with dolls. These two examples do not indicate how popular such games were in reality, but they do demonstrate that such toys existed and were unremarkable.

Demands Not Made

One line of argument found especially in the 1960s was that the wife had a theoretical right to her husband's help around the house but because of her good nature would not insist on it. Instead, by using the advertised products, she could perform 'her' work satisfactorily without his assistance.

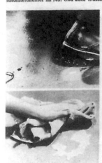

Figure 4.7 Advertisement for Seiblank floor wax, *Ihre Freundin* 5 (25 February) 1958, p. 35.

A variant of this was the transformation of a demand for the husband's help into a demand that he purchase a particular appliance. The appliance would then fulfil his obligation to help his wife.

The substitution of the commercial product (in this case, a low-tech one) for the husband was particularly explicit in an advertisement for soaped steel-wool pads. 'Specialist for grill-cleaning', read the first line of the text. The text initially related this to the husband. Visually, however, the primary reference was to the outsize package of steel-wool pads on which the husband was seated. The wife was not going to ask her husband to clean the grill, even if he was the 'specialist', in other words, even if this was a task he had performed satisfactorily in the past and which was within the category of household tasks which could appropriately be performed by a man (grilling being a 'male' activity). 'It's Sunday and, not only that, it's time for his sports programme.' The steel-wool pad, the advertisement stated explicitly, was the wife's business.[67]

The advertisement was aimed at a female audience – not only did it appear in a women's magazine, but it advertised an everyday, low-cost product which would ordinarily have been selected by women. It is impossible to tell whether the advertisement was really effective. Evidently, however, neither the advertising agency nor the firm expected that the image of a wife indulging her husband's desire to relax and enjoy a favourite television show on his day off, while she performed a rather unpleasant cleaning task, quite possibly made necessary by his hobby, would prejudice women against the product.

The scenario in an advertisement for dishwashing liquid was that the father had returned home early and offered to help his wife and daughter (the young son did not appear to be actively participating) with the washing-up. The kitchen contained enormous piles of clean dishes reminiscent of illustrations intended to emphasize how much work housewives did. Here, however, the intention was not to dramatize the work the woman did, but to emphasize how easily she could do it with Pril. Pril, not the husband, helped with the dishes. In an instant, she would be done with the dishes and happy family life could commence.[68]

An advertisement for fluorescent lights presented a hierarchy of possible wishes a wife might have for her husband's assistance. 'If your husband can't cook and doesn't like drying the dishes, he should at least see to it that you have the same good light in your kitchen that he has in the office.' It would be nice if the husband would help around the house, but it was not necessary, even if the grounds for refusal were simply personal preference. His responsibility was limited to making sure that his wife had acceptable working conditions in what was explicitly 'her' kitchen.[69]

Figure 4.8 Advertisement for Pril dishwashing detergent, *Constanze* 1 April 1959, p. 27.

Through buying an appliance, a man could help his wife with the housework while remaining within his role as provider. According to one advertisement, the model husband bought a Lavamat washing-machine.[70] One 1969 advertisement suggested that a dishwasher, still a very rare luxury in German households at that time, would allow a man to show consideration for his wife without getting his hands wet. 'There are men who wash the dishes themselves. There are men who expect their wives to do it. And there are gentlemen who simply point to the FAVORIT DELUXE dishwasher from AEG and its advantages.'[71] They pointed to it; they did not load it. The dishwasher replaced work which might otherwise be done by men or children.

There were other, lesser ways in which the good husband could ease his wife's housework without doing it himself. One underwear advertisement stated that a man wore Jockey underwear for his wife's sake: both because he looked good in it and because it was easy to wash and required no ironing. Another advertisement suggested that men should buy long-lasting socks so that their wives wouldn't need to spend so much time darning.[72]

Overall, then, while calls for men to participate in household tasks and depictions of them doing so were not absent from women's magazines, they were often weakened by qualifications and tended to make only limited demands. Positive depictions of men doing housework were more common in the text of magazine articles than in the advertisements, but even there male participation in housework was generally depicted as 'help', placing the husband in the role of the gentleman showing his affection and appreciation for his wife. This implied that it would be occasional and voluntary.

Other depictions of men doing housework were ambivalent or hostile. Particularly in the 1950s, there were suggestions that men who did housework made themselves laughable and would in any event not do a good job. Depicting men in 'female' roles as figures of fun, in a rather ancient tradition of humour, could serve to increase women's sense of their own skills and of being needed, but would also tend to discourage men from doing housework and women from asking them to. Magazine articles about male participation in housework often reflected the concern that men who did housework might be seen as 'unmanly', in other words sexually unattractive. This concern may have been more acute among men than among women. Some articles simply condemned the performance of housework by men as inappropriate, while others showed a great deal of defensiveness on the question of whether a man who helped around the house was a *Pantoffelheld*. Advertisements tended to reinforce the view that men who did housework were sexually unattractive.

In the 1960s, the idea that it was not unreasonable for women to ask for men's help with the housework, at any rate if they also worked outside the home, seems to have gained ground. Some advertisements attempted to channel women's desire for help with the housework into a desire for products which would allegedly ease their burden without imposing burdens (except financial ones) on their husbands. A change in how housework was done would prove much easier to bring about than a change in whom it was done by.

Gender, Money and Household Technology

A potential problem for sellers of household appliances was that, while the appliances were perceived as benefiting mainly women, the money to pay for them was earned mostly by men. Sibylle Meyer and Eva Schulze have noted the different speed with which new technological developments were adapted in the household in the areas of home entertainment and housework.[73] They note that the radio and the television set were found in a majority of German households a few decades after their invention, while innovations such as washing-machines and refrigerators long remained restricted to industry. Even when usable household models were developed, they spread slowly compared with radios and television sets.

Meyer and Schulze attribute this difference primarily to the fact that appliances were seen as benefiting housewives only, while the radio or television or record-player was seen as benefiting the whole family. This was compounded by women's socialization to put the family's needs ahead of their own. Their argument is supported by their interviews with Berlin housewives.

Other factors played some role as well – the 'thin end of the wedge' in entertainment technology, the primitive radio, was relatively inexpensive to build and drew little, if any, current in operation.[74] Household appliances, especially those involving electric heat, had high operating costs as well as high prices. Television came on the scene at a time when the purchasing power of average families was beginning a terrific rise – under other circumstances it might have remained a rarity for decades, as the telephone did. Thus economic factors tended to favour the rapid expansion of entertainment technology. It is also arguable that a status symbol in the living-room is more effective than one in the kitchen, since it will probably be seen by more guests.

This does not rule out gender as a factor. Meyer and Schulze's argument echoes many contemporary voices. Some advertisements addressed this issue by explicitly pointing out benefits to the whole family accruing from the purchase of the device (and from the wife's housework). A 1970 article in *Brigitte* on five au pairs' perceptions of life in Germany included somewhat contradictory comments on this subject. In the Swedish woman's view, 'In the family, one person makes the decisions, and that's the man. He decides: first a car and a TV, then a washing-machine or a dishwasher.' An Irishwoman saw appliances as a high priority, but one which perhaps required sacrifices for the wife rather than the husband: 'They [German women] would rather do without a trip or new clothes and instead get a washing-machine, a dishwasher, a freezer and things like that.'[75]

A 1970 article on dishwashers admitted that they were not among the cheapest household appliances. Still, they cost much less than colour television sets. 'Whether money for a dishwasher is set aside in the family budget depends first of all on how the housewife's work is valued by her family and whether or not there is room in the kitchen for the machine.'[76]

Women's magazines, and of course advertisements, provided arguments in favour of the purchase of appliances. Some of these were strongly gender-based, appealing to a guilty conscience on the husband's part or a feeling of being discriminated against on the wife's part. One argument, for example, was that technology had thus far aided only men in their work while women still worked at home much as their grandmothers had. Certainly, as indicated in Chapter 2, the technology of the home had tended to lag behind that of the factory. On the other hand, office jobs generally predominated in magazine depictions of men's work and the machines most widely used in office work tended to be used by women rather than men. But in arguing in favour of household technology it was convenient to ignore matters of class and occupation and divide people simply into male and female.

> Technology has developed machines and devices for the housewife's work, too. They could make life much easier – if one had them. The main objection: I can't afford that. But isn't it the case that the husband's wishes, say for a larger radio, are always fulfilled, while the wife's request for a water-heater is rejected out of hand? Any man who was denied the tools for his daily work would go on strike immediately. He would simply refuse to work with antediluvian devices when he knew that there were modern tools available in every shop. But for the housewife that's supposed to be a luxury![77]

Five years later, the same magazine was still arguing that '[in West Germany], the mechanization of work has so far benefited only men'. Before the men voiced further wishes, the article demanded, a modern electric cooker, a food processor and especially a washing-machine were needed in the kitchen. The article cited figures to the effect that the German housewife had a work week of 118 hours, compared with 63 for the American and 98 for the French. Meanwhile, the men were talking about a 40-hour week.[78]

Did household technology perpetuate the sexual division of labour by making it possible for women to manage both work outside the home and all the household work? Charles A. Thrall has suggested this.[79] Other scholars support this view for the German case.[80] This is an interesting argument, but overlooks other possibilities for reducing the amount of household labour done by housewives: the reduction of standards of housekeeping or the use of commercial services (laundries, restaurants, maids), a possibility which is linked more to the availability of a low-wage labour force than to technology. In addition, it neglects the factor of differing male and female attitudes towards housework: if both husband and wife regard housekeeping as primarily her responsibility, and if she sees the condition of the household as a reflection of her personal worth in a way he does not, the husband's inclination and ability to offer active and passive resistance to participation in housework are considerable regardless of whether the wife works outside the home or not.

As we have seen, the magazines and their advertisements helped in many ways to reinforce such attitudes. Even if they were committed to equality of the sexes in principle, women's magazines reinforced stereotypes about appropriate sex roles. The equality they advocated was a narrowly defined, formal equality between people whose differences were fundamental and innate.

Appliances – a Solution to the 'Servant Problem'?

While the division of labour which assigned housework exclusively to women was not unchallenged, it remained powerful. Men were much more likely to be recipients of housework than participants in it. Housework was generally done by women for their families, without paid assistance. In one 1951 survey, 8.5 per cent of housewives had the support of a full-time maid, while another 10 per cent had some paid assistance. These were much larger numbers than the percentage of women who had help from their husbands (less than 1 per cent), but over 70 per cent of women had no help at all.[81]

As a paying job, housework had been declining in popularity since the late nineteenth century, as other 'women's jobs' opened up in industry and in the service sector. Families were increasingly unable to compete for workers with other employers who offered better wages and shorter hours. In 1895, 18 per cent of all employed women and 30 per cent of single employed women were in personal service. This had declined dramatically by the mid-1920s. In 1950, 9 per cent of employed women were in service. The absolute number of women in this category rose slightly in the early 1950s, reaching a postwar peak in 1954/55 (at over 100,000 below 1938 levels) and then declined. By 1961, this group made up less than 3.5 per cent of all employed women and 5.5 per cent of employed single women.[82]

The struggle with the 'servant problem' was one of the traditional concerns of the organized housewives' movement. Calls for professionalization of housework often occurred in this context, with middle-class housewives setting themselves up as mistresses of the trade who could teach 'apprentices' from working-class families. This promised to kill two birds with one stone, improving the general well-being of the lower orders and providing free help for the middle-class housewife. In addition, it promoted the housewives' own role as socially valuable and requiring skills which had to be learned, rather than being a basically instinctive attribute of females as a sex.[83]

In the 1950s, there were still attempts to reverse the decline in household help, but optimism that this could be accomplished seems to have been limited. One attempt to make housework more attractive as a paying job involved regularizing (and shortening) working hours. The German Housewives' League negotiated a contract in 1955 with the union representing workers in the restaurant business, in which some maids were also organized, but this could be nothing but a gesture since the vast majority of both employers and employees were unorganized. Not the least of the obstacles to such efforts was the reluctance of housewives to accept shorter working hours for their maids. An article in *Stimme der Frau* held out some hope: 'If Fräulein Else is happy, she surely won't calculate every minute. If she knows that she is taken seriously as a person and that her work is appreciated, she surely won't look at the clock – or at the contract.'[84] Still, a tone of resignation was frequently to be found in the pages of women's magazines on the subject. Another article in *Stimme der Frau* gave decorating suggestions for small rooms – like the now-vacant maid's room.[85]

In the 1950s, matters were worsened by international competition. Both Switzerland and Sweden had markedly higher standards of living at that time than did Germany, which could make housework more pleasant as well. One article reported on a woman who had found a job in a Swedish household: 'Even the least-loved work, washing dishes, is fun here, because the Swedish households are very modern, equipped with the latest technical achievements.'[86] The modern technology in question, judging by the photograph, was running hot water. The article also went on to say that the young woman was treated well by her employers. Sweden was described as 'the land of milk and honey, not only for those who have a lot of money but for all who are willing to work and who accomplish something in their profession'. Young women who went to work in England or France or the USA (which, with air travel, was no longer quite as far away as it had been) could learn useful languages as well as domestic skills.

The attractiveness of foreign countries decreased as conditions in West Germany improved. At the same time, however, opportunities for factory and office work in West Germany increased. In May 1960, the *Badische Zeitung* reported on the shortage of domestic help in Freiburg.

> Even a room with a private bath and other comforts can hardly lure young (and older) girls into going to work in a household these days. The young ladies, who have already found out what life can offer them, can only be recruited by households which guarantee that they won't be on the job more than nine hours a day and will have Saturdays and Sundays completely free as in industry or office work.[87]

The article reported that there were at least 500 jobs available and many families had simply given up looking.

Advertisements for household appliances had long suggested that the machines were substitutes for servants. This tactic continued to be used occasionally in the 1950s and 1960s, but sometimes in ways which suggested that the days of full-time maids were past and only appliances remained. For example, an advertisement which referred to a mixer as 'the household help who never gets tired' showed a maid in rather old-fashioned dress: the mixer was the modern equivalent.

A 1969 advertisement for a food processor personified the device with a cartoon of a curly-haired young maid saying, 'I'm a "pearl" looking for work. Lots of work.' The firm's various small appliances were described as the 'household pearls of the modern age'. The advertisement's creators believed they needed to add in small print at the bottom the explanation that 'pearl' was a popular expression for a particularly dependable servant.[88] Magazine articles also associated appliances with servants. An article on new household products in *Für Sie* in 1960 was entitled 'Household Help: Kitchen Technology' and stated:

> The exodus of workers from the household has long since answered the question of whether or not the kitchen should be technologically transformed and equipped with machines – answered it in favour of the time- and labour-saving device.[89]

Eine Küchenhilfe,
die nie müde wird

Eine Küchenhilfe, die nie müde wird, die viele der so zeit-
raubenden und anstrengenden Küchenarbeiten im Nu er-
ledigt – wäre das nicht etwas für Sie, verehrte Hausfrau?

Figure 4.9 Advertisement for Bosch mixer, *Constanze* 3 April 1957 (detail), p. 115.

The author of one *Ratgeber* article on spring-cleaning resorted to mythological imagery, referring to modern cleaning products as 'a whole troop of *Heinzelmännchen*' (helpful mythical characters) to assist the modern housewife.[90] The Siemens company paper *Der Anschluß* claimed that one could buy a complete set of household electrical devices, ranging from a washer to a hair-drier, for the price of a year's pay for a maid.[91] Even more common than explicit comparisons were implied comparisons: appliances were depicted as 'doing' housework for housewives.

Appliances weren't literally substitutes for servants. Some wealthy families had both – indeed, appliances which reduced the amount of hard physical labour required were an asset in the competition among employers for maids. By the end of the 1960s, mechanical 'servants', which unlike real ones could be mass-produced, had spread to a much larger portion of the population than could have been provided with human maids. Still, the maid had left a place in the popular imagination of the household which could be filled by household appliances. This correspondence tended to disguise certain aspects of machine-assisted housework – maids were, for instance, self-cleaning.

Pay for Housewives? The Problematic Nature of Housework

Many of the characteristics of housework which made it unattractive as a paid occupation, such as long and irregular hours and manual labour, also applied to women's work for their own families. In addition, housework done by housewives did not provide pay and benefits, at least not directly. This was also true of work in family businesses or on family farms, but their number had declined with industrialization. By the 1950s, paid employment was a long-established norm for men, which also meant that it was normal to define the value of work by the wage or salary received for it. Housework was hard to quantify; it was not paid, nor did it generally result in the production of goods for sale. Economists did not include it in the gross domestic product. Housewives were listed in the employment statistics as not economically active. Bourgeois housewives themselves had contributed to the invisibility of housework as work when they conformed to an ideology that required the home to be seen as a place of rest and relaxation. As long as servants were available, they had in fact been able to avoid the heaviest work.[92]

In the 1950s and 1960s, given the reduction in the number of full-time domestic servants, it was less feasible than it had been to shift domestic work from women of one class to women of another. Sharing housework equally between men and women was theoretically an option, though, as we have seen, the overall depiction of men doing housework in women's magazines of the 1950s and 1960s did little to encourage that. Until the marriage law reform of 1977, West German law specifically spelt out men's and women's responsibilities in marriage, officially endorsing the notion that housework was women's work.

The unequal distribution of household labour between the sexes has long been recognized as a barrier to women's equality. In the nineteenth century, the striking changes brought about in daily life by industrialization led some to believe that the problem would solve itself as more and more work was taken out of the home and women entered paid employment. Others advocated the socialization of housework through various kinds of communal living arrangements. In Germany, Lily Braun had been an early advocate of the socialization of housework.[93] Lenin saw it as a necessary prerequisite for women's equality.[94] The idea had never really caught on in its socialist form, although in urban areas commercial laundries and other services took some housework out of the home in a capitalist context.

In the 1950s and 1960s, however, such notions were not widely promoted. The war years had provided large numbers of people with involuntary experiments in communal living, which was eagerly rejected for one's 'own four walls', while provisions for day care, after-school child care or full-day schools smacked of East German efforts to mobilize women for the labour force. Young people on the political left in the late 1960s and subsequently would have a different perspective, however; day care would be a key demand of the 1970s women's movement, while the youth movement launched new experiments in communal living.[95]

The notion of solving the problem of unpaid housework by paying for it was around in the 1950s and 1960s – it was considered and rejected in a 1950 article in *Ihre Freundin*[96] – but rarely mentioned. *Ratgeber* approvingly noted a Swedish initiative to extend paid sick leave to housewives, however. It was not simply a matter of money, but of principle: 'Her [the Swedish housewife's] work in the household was thus officially recognized as professional work.'[97] How far this recognition extended into Swedish society is open to question, but at any rate West German housewives did not enjoy such benefits, nor did they acquire pension claims in their own right. Wages for housework would become a divisive issue in the 1970s women's movement. Income tax benefits for single-wage households did exist, but benefited the husband as taxpayer rather than the wife. The Christian Democrats proposed a DM 300 monthly allowance for housewives in the early 1970s, which made it that much easier for opponents of pay for housework within the women's movement to brand the idea as reactionary.[98]

Women's magazines of the 1950s and 1960s, which were aimed in part at housewives, paid less attention to radically changing the economic or social conditions under which housework was performed than to increasing its social status. 'When I applied for a new identification card recently and under "Occupation" wrote simply "Housewife", I did not fail to notice the slightly disdainful smile of the [female] official,' wrote Irmgard Becht in a 1960 article in *Ihre Freundin*. Becht placed the blame for the low status of housewifery on women themselves and urged housewives to think about the positive aspects of their occupation and stop complaining so much.[99] Housewives' organizations campaigned for higher status for housewives. There was ideological support from the government as well; for instance, in 1956, the Family Ministry advocated the substitution of the expression '*Ganz-Hausfrau*' for the more usual but somewhat derogatory '*Nur-Hausfrau*'.[100] This did not catch on.

Advocates of recognition for housewives used several tactics. Some chose to emphasize the amount of work done by housewives. While this resonated with the value attached to industry in German culture and could be a useful corrective to male perceptions that housework was trivial, the image of the housewife as drudge was not particularly attractive, especially to middle-class women. Consequently, the tendency to conceal housework, to emphasize the role of lady of the house rather than that of maid of all work, persisted as well. Emphasizing skill rather than effort was also an option. In advertisements and articles, household appliances and other modern household products were held up as a solution to the housewife's dilemma, making it possible for her to have sparkling dishes and blinding white laundry without wearing herself out, but it was the product rather than the housewife's skill which got the credit.

Polishing the Housewife's Image

The Industrious Housewife

Praise of the industrious housewife was nothing new. One classic example is in Schiller's 'Song of the Bell', which Frau Ge. had to memorize as a schoolgirl. While the man must go out into the hostile world, the 'modest housewife' rules the home. She 'ceaselessly moves her / Industrious hands' and 'rests never'.[101] A woman's work was never done. This fitted in with a more general work ethic, which was still strong in the 1950s. There was, additionally, the traditional association of sloppy housekeeping with sexual immorality (evident in the term *Schlampe*, slut). The National Socialist regime had regarded bad housekeeping as a symptom of 'asociality', a somewhat ill-defined but undesirable condition. The good housewife worked hard and worked well, applying her skills and experience for the good of her family. Consequently, she was entitled to society's respect.

Amount of Work. One evidently popular method of soliciting respect for housewives was the exercise of multiplying, for instance, the number of dishes washed in a day or the distance a housewife walked in a day by the number of days in a month, a year and so forth. This represented, sometimes in a quite literal sense, an effort to make visible the work which was normally invisible. Instead of the reality, in which the same plates were washed and then used and washed again, over and over, here the washed plates stayed clean and formed a permanent monument to the housewife's industry.

In the course of 25 years, claimed a two-page spread in *Ratgeber*, a housewife with a family of four would cut half a million slices of bread, clean the equivalent of a city the size of Kassel, wash enough plates to make a pile 1800 m high, clean as many windows as there were on the Empire State Building.[102] The article held out hope that mechanical innovations could help housewives save a little time, although it was not terribly optimistic. Instead, it concluded with a plea to those who benefited from the housewife's work to help make her life a little easier.

An advertisement for dishwashing detergent used a similar illustration to dramatize the amount of washing-up a housewife did in the course of a month. The selling point here was that, with so much work to do, the housewife could never manage with (cheaper) soap or soda, but needed the specialized product. In the illustration, the husband seemed to be impressed by the imposing pile of dishes and pots. A note at the bottom of the full-page advertisement suggested cutting it out and laying it on the breakfast table for the benefit of one's own husband.[103]

Training. To keep busy all the time was not the sole point, of course. If a woman never got done with her housework because she was so inept at it, that did not reflect well on her. Skill and knowledge, as well as sheer physical labour, mattered. The combination was expected to result in an orderly home and a neatly dressed, well-fed family.

An emphasis on the need for proper training was one way to gain professional status for housewifery. Women also set standards for themselves (and, to some extent, for their neighbours), standards which allowed them to judge whether or not their housekeeping was adequate. Advertisements for household products promoted higher standards of housekeeping and praised the good things the housewife, properly equipped, would be able to do for her family. Inevitably, however, they gave most of the credit to the products rather than to the housewife herself.

All but one of the women interviewed for this study had some formal training in housekeeping skills. This ranged from the basic course for school-leavers attended by Frau P. to Frau Sch.'s studies at a women's institute (*Frauenfachschule*). Here, the normal course of education for

Hausfrauen leisten Mammutarbeit

Während in immer mehr Berufszweigen die Fünf-Tage-Woche und der Acht-Stunden-Tag zur festen Gewohnheit werden, leistet ein Berufszweig nach wie vor Schwerarbeit, ohne große Aussicht auf eine Besserung, ohne Murren, in aller Stille: die Hausfrau! Längst aufgestellte Erhebungen haben ergeben, daß eine Hausfrau mit vierköpfiger Familie und einer Dreizimmerwohnung wöchentlich etwa 70 Stunden arbeitet, also 10 Stunden pro Tag, den Sonntag inbegriffen. Dreieinhalb Stunden verbringt nach diesen Untersuchungen die Hausfrau durchschnittlich in der Küche, 2 Stunden wendet sie zur Reinigung auf, $1^{3}/_4$ Stunden näht und flickt sie, 1 Stunde widmet sie ihren Kindern, eine $^3/_4$ Stunde wird gewaschen und geplättet, während die restliche Zeit mit dem Einkaufen und den vielen tausend „Kleinigkeiten" vorbeigeht.

Ebenso imposant sind die auf das Jahr umgerechneten Arbeiten dieser „Durch-

▲
Eine halbe Million Brotscheiben schneidet eine Hausfrau in 25 Jahren für eine vierköpfige Familie. Sie reichen, aufeinandergelegt, bis zur Spitze des 4800 Meter hohen Montblanc. Die Arbeit des Brotschneidens nimmt den Hausfrauen niemand ab, aber sie kann ihnen heute wenigstens durch Maschinen erleichtert werden.

Wie sehr müssen sich Hausfrauen plagen, ▶ wenn sie die einfachsten Hausarbeiten verrichten. Viele Schweißperlen kostet das Wischen, Fegen und Bohnern der Fußböden, das Klopfen der Polstermöbel und Teppiche. Die Reinigung einer dreiräumigen Wohnung ein Vierteljahrhundert lang entspricht der Säuberung einer Stadt von der Größe Kassels.

886

Figure 4.10 *Ratgeber* September 1961, p. 886.

girls who had completed the intermediate level of school preparation (*Mittlere Reife*) was two years of classwork alternating with two years of practical work. The degree allowed several career options, including teacher of home economics.[104] Women's magazines reported occasionally on courses for brides at private institutions.[105] There were also special courses to permit practising housewives to earn the status of masters.[106]

There was some concern about whether young women were being adequately prepared for their future as housewives. One article warned of the possible consequences:

> There may be no statistics about the unhappiness that results from an unsystematic handling of the housekeeping money, from unsatisfactory knowledge of cooking and inadequate experience in housekeeping – but any divorce lawyer will confirm that there would surely be far fewer separations if it weren't for the fact that more and more brides walk into the register office without any preparation for their chosen profession of housewife.[107]

There were periodic suggestions in the magazines that, whether men indicated their appreciation or not, an orderly home, good meals and staying within the allotted budget were conducive to marital happiness.

Standards of Housekeeping. Formal training in housework was one source of standards. Frau Sch. was still pleasantly aware that she was breaking the rules whenever she hung up her laundry without having it all carefully sorted and each piece hung just so. Housewives themselves also helped to set and strove to live up to personal and community standards, thus proclaiming that housework was worth doing right. Home economists and authors sought to influence such standards, as did advertising for household products. Actual enforcement, however, was in the hands of neighbours, mothers and mothers-in-law, husbands and, especially, housewives themselves, who were the closest inspectors of their own work and measured it against the standards they had learned and adapted to their own and their families' needs. Meeting such standards could give women a sense of accomplishment.[108]

Neighbours traditionally enforced community standards. The dutiful, energetic and skilful performance of housework reflected well on a woman's character and her family's respectability. In some areas, at least, there was enough visiting among neighbours to ensure that the condition of kitchen floors and stoves was adequately inspected.[109] Windows and their curtains and laundry hanging out to dry were on public display. Not only was laundry to be spotlessly clean, it was to be hung up in an orderly fashion.[110]

While being looked down on as a bad housekeeper was no fun, looking down on others could be. A 1954 article in *Ratgeber* discussed the cleaning of bedding in the form of a conversation in which a wise mother got to show off her encyclopaedic knowledge of the proper care of down and horsehair to her enthusiastic but ignorant daughter. The daughter asked the mother, who was looking out the window, why she was shaking her head.

> 'See for yourself what Frau Kurz across from us has done with her duvets. So careless!'
>
> 'Why careless? She's laid them on the window-sill to sun, I see. Don't we do that too?'
>
> 'Dear child, I see how terribly necessary it is for you to spend this half year before your marriage learning from me in the household and paying attention – because your skills as a secretary won't be enough for the two of you. Up until now, you've only been interested in things that had to do with your profession, but I hope that for Walter's sake you'll take just as much pleasure in your household. No, of course we don't lay our duvets in the full sun, that would make the feathers break down.'[111]

When they came to brushing and vacuuming the mattresses, Hilde's mother said, 'It would be better for you to do it in the garden, but you're still inexperienced and don't need to give the nosy neighbours anything to laugh about.' Clearly, Hilde's mother was just as nosy as the neighbours were. She judged Frau Kurz, Frau Kurz and the other women judged her. Hilde needed to learn to do her cleaning skilfully so that her future neighbours would find nothing to laugh at.

The point of this little piece, beyond imparting practical information about cleaning and caring for beds and bedding, was to emphasize the importance of the type of knowledge possessed by the real author and the fictional mother. The daughter might enjoy her profession and earn money, but that would not be enough when she was married. Now she was learning to appreciate her mother's skills. Possibly this was wish fulfilment on the author's part – both in this article and in the articles expressing alarm at young women's lack of housekeeping knowledge, one gets the sense that the daughters' respect for the mothers' skills was not taken for granted.

Household Products and Higher Standards.   Advertisements for household products sometimes referred to, and encouraged, the need to impress others with one's skills as a housewife. Laundry detergents in the 1960s competed for customers by promising blindingly white laundry which would impress the neighbours.

Figure 4.11 Advertisement for Sunil laundry detergent, *Constanze* 3 April 1967, p. 96.

Some advertisements clearly sought to set high standards for housework in order to increase consumption of the advertised products. Advertisements for cleaning products sometimes suggested that, since they made the cleaning so easy, it could be done more often. Proclaiming that 'a well-kept home without a sparkling clean, odourless toilet is simply unthinkable nowadays', one advertisement for toilet cleaner advised using the product daily. An advertisement for window polish suggested that the windows could be cleaned easily and quickly – 'even between house-cleaning days'.[112]

One 1958 advertisement showed a happy husband in a fresh vest and suggested that, with the half-automatic washing-machine being advertised, it was possible for him to have a clean one every day. A 1957 advertisement for another washing-machine also proclaimed the benefits of frequent changes of underwear: 'One feels so clean, so completely well-groomed. Simply wonderful! And wonderfully simple with the Miele express washing-machine!'[113] A 1970 series of underwear ads took a more aggressive approach, depicting men wearing pig masks to dramatize the results of a poll which had shown that only 10 per cent of men changed their underwear daily.[114] An advertisement for bedlinen encouraged changing the bed more often, stating that the linen in question would stand up to frequent washing.[115]

Advertisements for kitchen appliances promised better meals and better health. 'Special treats' were presented as expressions of a wife's love for her husband, a mother's love for her children. These could be prepared more easily with products ranging from mixers to mixes.

Offer him something.
   Even if the way to a man's heart isn't always through his stomach – he's always in favour of tasty meals. The housewife has a lot to do if she wants to keep on serving him delicious surprises.
   And that's why it's so important to have not only a BOSCH refrigerator . . . but also a BOSCH food processor. It's an ideal help in many tiring and time-consuming kitchen tasks . . .
   And, if everything's so simple, the menu can be more varied and more interesting.[116]

The food processor came with a recipe book to provide 'lots of ideas for using the machine to its full potential'. The consumer was buying not only help with some of the more tiring and boring parts of food prepara-tion, but also knowledge. Without a food processor, the advertisement implied, the wife would be compelled to serve her husband the same old thing day after day. With it, she could cater to his tastes and maintain her hold over him. The machine and its associated cookery book, rather than the wife's skill as a cook, were what mattered.

Children also appeared as beneficiaries of appliances, although less frequently than husbands. One advertisement for a cooker featured a photograph of two children, perhaps three and one, the smaller one smeared with a light-coloured food substance. The text spoke of the children's increased delight in Mummy's cooking and implied that Mummy was more willing to make special treats for the children now that she could cook 'automatically'.[117]

The wife's duty to please her family by providing them with tasty meals and snacks predominated in the depiction of cooking in advertisements. Another duty was the protection of the family's health through the provision of nutritious food. As noted in Chapter 3, the improvement of the standard of living with regard to diet had potential negative side-effects. Manufacturers offered many solutions, presenting appliances and prepared foods as a means to achieving a more 'natural' and healthy diet.

One advertisement for an electric cooker promised that foods cooked on it would retain their vitamins as well as their full flavour.[118] Appeals based on the health benefits to the family were particularly popular in advertisements for food processors, blenders and similar devices. A fiendishly grinning tot holding a glass of juice proclaimed:

My mummy does it right!
    Everybody says I'm a fine, healthy boy. No wonder: Mummy makes me delicious raw fruit and vegetable juices every day with the Trifix. They're great for me. Since we've had the Trifix, all of us feel good, and Mummy has it a lot easier.[119]

Another advertisement for the same product showed a pile of fruit and vegetables and next to it, crossed out, a bottle of medicine. It urged consumers to drink fruit and vegetable juices every day in order to maintain 'health – the most valuable possession'.[120] In other words, health, ordinarily regarded as non-purchasable, could in fact be bought by buying the processor.

Years of propaganda from nutritionists had already got across the idea that fresh fruits and vegetables were healthy; the advertisements associated the appliances with this healthy image. Somewhat paradoxically, they implied a need to prepare foods whose health value was based on their not being prepared in the usual sense, i.e. cooked. Of course, it was still possible to eat fresh fruit instead of making juice out of it, or to grate carrots or other vegetables for a salad with a simple, easy-to-clean hand-grater.

Fresh foods, a refrigerator advertisement asserted, were healthy and wholesome. This much most nutrition experts would probably have agreed with. The advertisement went on to promise: 'As the owner of a Bosch refrigerator, you always have plenty of tasty, fresh foods and drinks on hand.' The advertisement treated this as an inevitable consequence of

Meine Mutti macht es richtig!

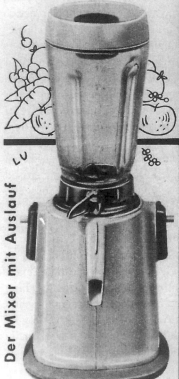

Der Mixer mit Auslauf

Jeder sagt, ich sei ein prächtiger, gesunder Junge. Kein Wunder: Mutti bereitet mir jeden Tag mit der Trifix köstliche Obst- und Gemüse-Rohsäfte. Die bekommen mir wunderbar. Überhaupt: seit wir die Trifix haben, fühlt sich bei uns jeder wohl, und Mutti hat's im Haushalt viel leichter.

PREIS: Kernstück und Mixer DM 175.—

Weitere Aufsteckteile: Saftzentrifuge,
3 Rohkostraspeln, Zitruspresse

Bauknecht Trifix

mixt · zerkleinert · entsaftet

Gutschein Nr. 345 für den interessanten Trifix-Prospekt. Ausschneiden, auf Postkarte kleben, als Drucksache senden an G BAUKNECHT GMBH STUTTGART-S

Figure 4.12 Advertisement for Bauknecht blender, *Ratgeber* October 1956, p. 641.

refrigerator ownership. The time-consuming and sometimes strenuous work of shopping for fresh food and carrying it home and the organizational skills required to prevent it from getting pushed to the back of the shelf and forgotten were invisible in the advertisement. Fresh food and beverages magically emerged from the refrigerator.[121]

Washing-machines, cleaning products and vacuum cleaners were also advertised as promoting family health through better hygiene. For example, a series of Constructa advertisements proclaimed that the firm's new washing-machines were capable of washing at temperatures of 100°C, not merely 95°C like the competition.[122] While the Constructa campaign promoted a new way of carrying out an old-fashioned practice (boiling laundry), an advertisement for a combination vacuum cleaner and floor polisher suggested that old methods were positively dangerous. The advertisement showed a drawing of a woman sweeping the floor near a baby in its crib. 'Clouds of bacteria are stirred up when the broom and mop storm through the rooms. Cleaning with the vacuuming Fakir electric floor waxer could prevent this danger.' While the necessity of cleanliness in a baby's environment was reaffirmed, the traditional methods of achieving it were depicted as counterproductive.[123]

Even when appliance advertisements praised the benefits of housework for the family, they tended to claim the credit for the product advertised at least as much as for the housewife. 'Praise for the industrious housewife, praise for her Pre-fresh wash', proclaimed one detergent advertisement.[124] In addition, changes in household products rendered some existing knowledge useless. There was no need to know how to tell whether an oven had reached the correct temperature to bake a cake if one had an electric or gas oven with a thermostat. Old methods of cleaning might not be appropriate for new types of flooring. Permanent-press clothing temporarily threatened to make the difficult art of correctly starching and ironing a man's cotton shirt obsolete. An ever-increasing variety of commercial cleaning products, each with instructions on its label, made it less necessary to know how to use established cleaning agents such as ammonia and alcohol.[125]

The Invisibility of Household Labour in Advertisements for Household Products. Advertisements for appliances and other household products rarely showed manual labour being performed. If they did, it was as a bad example of the old-fashioned way of doing things. A few washing-machine advertisements showed someone putting in or taking out laundry, but more commonly the happy owner was shown engaging in leisure activities or simply gesturing toward the machine. Mixers were almost

Figure 4.13 Advertisement for Miele washing machine (detail), *Ihre Freundin* 12 (4 June) 1957, p. 46.

never shown in use – they looked better clean. Some advertisements went to considerable lengths to conceal housework in order to suggest that the product in question would make it effortless. For instance, in one advertisement for dishwashing liquid, the dishwashing was relegated to one of the small sketches at the bottom of the advertisement, while the big picture showed a housewife in a clean apron sitting in a lawn chair, wearing shoes that one would not care to stand at a sink in and apparently floating in the air along with the clean dishes. Another advertisement, for margarine, depicted Mum as a magician, effortlessly conjuring up elegantly garnished dishes.[126]

In her study of advertisements for household equipment in *Ladies Home Journal*, Bonnie Fox found that promises of liberation from housework did not play a major role in advertising, peaking at 21 per cent of appeals in 1909/10.[127] In West German advertisements of the 1950s and 1960s, savings in time and effort were frequently among the selling points listed, especially around 1955–57.

Love and Leisure

Making housework invisible was nothing new. The ideal of the leisured lady with her soft, white hands pressed nineteenth-century bourgeois housewives to conceal housework which was necessary but beneath their station. The notion that the home should be a place for the husband to rest from the cares of the hostile world meant that the hustle and bustle of housekeeping should be confined to the times when he was off at work.[128] For women of the twentieth century, emphasis on women's beauty and charm, on their loving nature as wives and as mothers produced a feminine ideal opposed to, and more attractive than, the image of woman as domestic drudge, unpaid maid-of-all-work, especially for middle-class women. Perceptions of the twentieth-century world as particularly fast-moving and stressful only added to the desire for the home to be a place of peace and quiet.

The twentieth century added another ideal – the modern 'superwoman' effortlessly juggling the demands of an outside job with those of the household. One author contrasted the acceptable behaviour for a woman working outside the home with that for a man:

> or have *you* ever encountered a woman who, after the office or the shop closes, throws herself on the couch with her feet up and calls to her returning spouse, 'Ghastly day at work again today. I'm dog-tired. Need my rest. Call me when dinner's ready and keep the kids off my back. I'm too worn out!' No, dear sisters, none of us would be so heartless as to destroy the image of the modern woman – never tired, always happy, dependable, easily juggling household and work – in the imagination of the good man into whose earthly life one should, according to the poet's instructions, weave roses.[129]

Although, as we have seen, women's magazines often argued for more recognition for housework, this was not to be achieved through making it conspicuous in everyday household life. Housework could be allowed

Figure 4.14 Advertisement for Lux diahwashing liquid, *Constanze* 1 April 1959, p. 117.

to disturb a husband's relaxation only under special circumstances, such as washday or spring-cleaning. Even then, the wife should make every effort to be attractive and cheerful. An article in *Ratgeber* suggested wearing a pretty apron and tying one's kerchief in a 'coquettish' manner, with perhaps a curl peeping out, and wearing lipstick.[130]

A 1952 article in *Ratgeber* warned that it was possible for a housewife to be too diligent. While defensively stating that this was not an argument in favour of sloppiness or bad housekeeping, the article warned that doing too much endangered household comfort. The housewife should remain calm, be 'the heart of the house, which always beats with a steady rhythm, even if something unexpected happens'.[131]

The notion that the housewife should always be cheerful and relaxed was reflected in innumerable advertisements for patent medicines. There were tonics and tablets of all kinds. There were various pain relievers to help women maintain their good moods despite headaches and the 'critical days' of the month. One advertisement suggested that a glass of coffee liqueur (35 per cent alcohol) before the husband returned would make the evening twice as pleasant.[132]

Some advertisements for appliances and other household products played on the idea that the wife's calm and good cheer were necessary to balance the stresses and strains which his active life out in the hostile world put on the husband. As one advertisement put it, 'The good mood of the well-rested housewife is always a joy for "him". At least one person in the family should not be overworked – the housewife.'[133]

Other advertisements suggested that, by making it easier for women to clean up after their families, the products advertised would help them be more tolerant mothers and wives. Mummy would be less angry with her children when they got their clothes dirty if she had a washing-machine.[134] She could allow more types of indoor activities with modern floor-care products to protect floors and make cleaning up easier. One advertisement for floor polish showed a young mother looking on with a smile as her small daughter skipped in the kitchen.[135] It was not just children who needed to be cleaned up after, of course: 'Doesn't a man have a right to get dirty once in a while? A considerate housewife won't let that get her down. Because for really dirty and stained things, there's Henko.'[136] Here the statements about sex roles were clear – a man had the right to get his clothes dirty, but the obligation to get them clean again belonged to his wife. Fortunately for her, Henkel had produced a prewash which would soak out 'even the toughest dirt' effortlessly.

Sex Appeal. One place housework was supposed to be invisible was on the body of the housewife. One argument made in favour of buying appliances was that the wife's exhaustion could damage a marriage. This was an especially relevant consideration in the early 1950s when the high divorce rate and the so-called 'surplus of women' resulting from the war made married women nervous. A magazine article warned:

> the International League of Home Economics recently attested that the German housewives, through their diligence, increasingly endanger the happiness of their marriages. '*Too much work*', the article states, '*is the reason why many*

women in the Federal Republic lose their health and with it their attractiveness for their husbands too early.'[137]

The article, which was aimed primarily at promoting the spread of household appliances, called the 'reform of housework in Germany' an issue on which 'the happiness of countless families and the survival of many marriages depends'.

Many advertisements, especially those for washing-machines, played on this theme. One attributed a man's love for his wife to the fact that she was 'always well-groomed, well-rested and in a good mood' and this in turn to the husband's having bought her a washing-machine 'in time'.[138] Another made a washing-machine sound almost like a cosmetic product:

to be a beautiful woman . . .

Beauty brings you happiness and success. But in order to be beautiful, you must be well-rested. That's only possible if you leave time-consuming, strenuous household tasks to modern electric appliances. AEG washing-machines immediately relieve you of one of the heaviest chores – washing.[139]

In another advertisement, the husband's provision for his wife extended to the purchase of an entire kitchen. The advertisement showed him congratulating himself for this brilliant idea. He was embracing his wife, who had a decidedly flirtatious expression on her face and held a stirring spoon so that its shadow emphasized her cleavage.

These advertisements attempted to win male buyers for household products by promising them sexier wives. The two goals of being a diligent housewife and being an attractive woman were not entirely compatible. This tension is also evident in some advertisements aimed primarily at women. Advertisements for cosmetic products, especially hand cream, sometimes emphasized the products' ability to combat the uncosmetic effects of housework. An advertisement for hairspray illustrated its ability to preserve the hairdo on washday.

Such advertisements, and many articles as well, promoted the view that beauty was not only of concern to single women trying to land husbands but remained important in marriage as well. Being a perfect housewife was not enough. One woman who wrote to a magazine colum-nist – her husband was cheating on her – received the following advice:

perhaps you should consider whether you haven't forgotten yourself a little, with the overly cared-for home and the excessive efficiency. A 'model' housewife is a fine thing, but not always a husband's ultimate dream. Many prefer a little less perfection and a charming, lovable, good-looking wife.[140]

Nur echte „**Musterring**"-Möbel tragen dieses Zeichen

Im Bundesgebiet bieten Ihnen über 120 Verkaufsstellen die Vorteile des „**Musterring**"-Programms!

Ein Blick durch die Tür, ins nächste Zimmer:

So einladend und gemütlich läßt sich mit echten „**Musterring**"-An- und Aufbaumöbeln eine Eßnische im Wohnzimmer

Köpfchen, Köpfchen...!

Meine liebe kleine Frau ist immer so hübsch und kreuzfidel. Daß ich ihr eine **Musterring**-Küche geschenkt habe, war der beste Einfall meines Lebens. Sie sagt: Du glaubst ja gar nicht, wie leicht und einfach mir jetzt die Arbeit von der Hand geht — man ermüdet überhaupt nicht mehr. Einfach wunderbar!

Ja, einfach wunderbar. Das ist die treffendste Bezeichnung für eine moderne **Musterring**-Küche. — Hunderttausenden schon sind **Musterring**-Möbel ein echter Begriff für

● glückliches Wohnbehagen —
● zuverlässige Qualität —
● erstaunlich niedrige Preise.

So einfach ist es, an echte **Musterring**-Möbel zu kommen: Sie brauchen nur ein Kärtchen an die untenstehende Anschrift zu schreiben. Schon nach wenigen Tagen erhalten Sie kostenlos und für Sie völlig unverbindlich den großen, reich und farbig illustrierten **Musterring**-Katalog mit Preisliste. Ungestört und von niemandem gedrängt können Sie dann planen, prüfen und wählen — in Ruhe und Muße. Ist das nicht ein gutes Angebot? Also heute noch schreiben an

Musterring-Kontaktstelle

OELDE/Westfalen , Postfach 49 / I F 3

Name. ....

Anschrift:

Ich interessiere mich besonders für:

Gutschein

Figure 4.15 Advertisement for Musterring furniture, *Ihre Freundin* 18 (28 August) 1956, p. 65.

Figure 4.16 Advertisement for Taft hair spray, *Constanze* 2 October 1957, p. 105.

While the idea that a woman ought to be able to stop worrying about her appearance after marriage and concentrate on her housekeeping did not disappear from society, magazines which focused on beauty and fashion were hardly going to advocate it.

More Time for the Family.   Reducing the burden of housework could not only make the wife more attractive but also give her more time to spend with her family. Here, too, the housewife's duties conflicted – housework was done for the family members, but it also distracted her from them. Many advertisements for household appliances operated on the assumption that spending more time with the children, or with the husband, was the most appealing use of the additional free time they promised. One advertisement showed a mother reading to her son and daughter:

New Happiness

How often must this woman have longed to be completely a friend and mother to her children? Hurry and overwork in her household always stood in the way. But now everything is different. She is the overjoyed owner of a Constructa, free of her heaviest duty, the washing. The new-won time and inner strength now benefit what is dearest to her in the world: her family.[141]

An advertisement for another brand of washing-machines featured a mother playing with her son. 'Time for Peterle even on washdays!' the advertisement proclaimed.[142] A mixer could also promise more time for the family.

Of course cooking and baking is lovely, but, if one can free oneself from the arduous part of this lovely activity, one should, as a good mother. Because much time is saved which one can more usefully devote to one's husband and children. Therefore, a Krups 3-Mix belongs in the kitchen of every progressive woman.[143]

Many women no doubt did desire more time with their children. The economist Wolfgang Fischer conducted a study, published in 1972, in which 576 women were asked what they would do with additional free time resulting from the use of appliances or services: 45.87 per cent of them listed 'more extensive education of the children' in first place and 16.32 per cent listed it in second place.[144]

These advertisements also reinforced the idea that a mother's duty to her children went well beyond ensuring that they had clean clothes and a warm dinner. While the mother's simple physical presence, 'being there for the children', was seen as important, demands for more active involvement with her children were growing. The more cars there were, the less possible it was for young children to play outside without supervision. Ideas about child-rearing changed towards more parental concern with the individual child's personality and less emphasis on order, obedience and doing chores. This also tended to increase the time required of mothers.[145]

More children attended advanced schools, and even in the lower grades there seems to have been increased emphasis on parental supervision of homework.[146] In West Germany, the transfer of child-care and educational functions to the state was less extensive than in many other countries. The school day typically ended in the early afternoon, at which time the children returned home for their midday meal. The expectation that somebody should be there and have prepared a hot meal when the children came home from school caused conflicts for mothers of school-aged children who wanted to work even part-time outside the home.[147] Social expectations of mothers' duties corresponded with the state's desire to limit expenditure on education and with teachers' desire for more class preparation and grading time.

The Value of Leisure. The argument that household appliances would give the housewife more time for herself was less frequent than the argument that they would give her more time for her family, but not unknown. Leisure time was a valued commodity in the 1950s and 1960s. Unions pushed successfully for shorter working weeks and longer vacations. The contrast between the workers' five-day week and the housewives' seven-day week did not go unnoticed.[148] One washing-machine advertisement spoke of 'every housewife's wish' to 'for once, not to have to toil and drudge, to have time for oneself'. With the washing-machine, this wish was 'easy to fulfil'. A competitor's advertisement from the same year showed the proud washing-machine owner writing a letter to a friend. Another manufacturer offered 'more leisure time for "her" – time to create something lasting [which clean laundry is certainly not]. For your husband, for your children and – not last of all – for yourself.' But the advertisement did list that last, as did the happy housewife in the Constructa advertisement in the same magazine who was now 'free for my family and for myself'.[149]

Articles spoke of women's need for relaxation, for time for themselves. In one article, a woman who had learned during a long illness that not all of the housework she did was really necessary warned a friend:

> Do you really think your family appreciates your ambition not to be able to find any dust in the most hidden nooks and crannies, to be able to eat off the floors, so to speak? Aren't you driving yourself into the role of the 'overworked housewife'? Nobody is demanding it of you![150]

Magazine images presented a contrast between the ideals of the dutiful housewife and the relaxed, attractive wife and mother. Housework was presented as essential to the smooth running of the household and the happiness of its members, but also as opposed to these aims. Housewives were open to criticism if they were too diligent – *Putzteufel*, cleaning demons. Calls for a relaxation of housekeeping standards, like the one above, were rare, however. Rather, household products were presented as the solution to the dilemma.

Labour Saving and Standards: the Example of Cooking. The conflict between the desire to reduce labour and the need to maintain standards was particularly evident in the area of cooking. In the 1950s and especially the 1960s, many products were available to shorten cooking time by moving some or all of the activities involved in food preparation from the home to the factory. This could, however, come into conflict with established norms of economy, taste and what constituted a proper family meal.

Some types of convenience foods were well established by this time, particularly the packaged soup mixes dating back to the days of Julius Maggi and Carl Heinrich Knorr in the late nineteenth century. Maggi intended his bouillon and soup mixes for women factory workers who had little time to cook. Pudding mixes and dried noodles were also nineteenth-century inventions, and dried-potato products made their appearance around the time of the First World War.[151] *Constanze* listed in 1955:

> Ready-to-cook soups, made according to delicious recipes, vegetables and potatoes which are already cleaned and ready to use (though so far only here and there), ready-to-use sauces, potato dumpling mix, tinned goods (including complete dishes), cake mix (just add liquid), ready-to-bake puff pastry and strudel pastry, ready-made sponge cakes and other practical items as well.[152]

Over time, the variety of these products increased. Frozen foods came to play more of a role, though this development was still in its early stages in 1970.[153]

Advertising for prepared foods sometimes emphasized the wife's desire to please her husband. This was perhaps intended to counter the perception that a wife who used ready-made foods or mixes was not showing her love for her husband as she should have done. One pudding mix promised simply, '"HE" is even fonder of "her" if she serves him Aromax Chocolate Pudding with dinner.'[154] Later, 'HE' apparently became more sophisticated. A 1970 advertisement for tinned bouillabaisse showed a happy, white-haired couple. The slogan was, 'With Jensen's in the house, the honeymoon lasts a little longer.' A wife who loved her husband, the text continued, would cook meals which would appeal to him. If she loved him a great deal, she would buy the (very appetizingly described) soup in question.[155]

While the need for 'fast food' was established, there were reservations about the use of processed foods to save time. In the late 1950s, *Ratgeber* ran a series called 'Time-Saving Menus' with recipes for housewives who were pressed for time. The introductions to these recipes indicated that they were intended for washdays, for spring-cleaning, for women who worked outside the home or for single people.[156] The introduction to one set of recipes explicitly stated, 'The idea of "time-saving menus" is not to use mainly tinned goods or dishes which have been prepared ahead of time.'[157]

While *Ratgeber*'s objections to such practices seem to have stemmed primarily from a sense of what constituted a proper meal, there were other concerns about tinned goods as well. In 1955, *Stimme der Frau* reported getting many letters from women unable to do their own bottling because of cramped living conditions or the lack of a garden and expressing concerns about the alternative: 'Are tinned vegetables of inferior quality? Do they really contain no vitamins and nutrients?' The article, which was illustrated with photographs of a male nutritionist and female cannery workers, reassured readers that commercially prepared tinned goods were perfectly nutritious, in fact more so than home-bottled produce, and less likely to go bad. Hans Jürgen Teuteberg reported in a 1979 article that mistrust of industrially processed foods, especially tinned goods, persisted.[158]

High prices were also a problem. Since the housewife's time was not assigned a monetary value, transferring food-preparation work out of the home did not make economic sense. In a 1970 study, only 24.2 per cent of the 619 women surveyed indicated that there was no reason not to use ready-made main dishes in the home. Of those who had objections, 50.97 per cent listed the high prices in first place. Many of the women in this study also found that prepared foods didn't taste as good as home-made. The limited selection available and the lack of opportunity for individual creativity were rated as less serious problems.[159]

While there were reservations, there were also clear advantages to be gained by the use of short cuts in meal preparation. *Constanze* was rather more open than *Ratgeber* to the use of prepared foods. One menu from 'Constanze's Time-Saving Menus' featured tinned ravioli and a herring soup made with tinned herring in horseradish sauce. The recipes in the series were for two persons, which suggests that they were seen as acceptable for young two-career couples without children but perhaps not for families.[160]

In 1970, *Für Sie* sponsored a cooking contest which emphasized the use of convenience foods to save time and proposed to crown the 'Free-Time Cooking Queen of 1970'. The article spoke of the invisible 'portion of free time' inside 'every bag, every packet, every tin, every jar', whether it was a matter of sauce or soup mixes, tinned or frozen meals, even spice mixes or (presumably, instant) coffee.[161]

There was a clear upward trend in the consumption of tinned fruits and vegetables, though fresh produce continued to predominate, especially in fruit. In 1950, under 10 per cent of the vegetables and just over 4 per cent of the fruit consumed by the four-person households with moderate incomes who kept records of their consumption for the government statistical office came out of tins and jars (the figure for fruit includes jam). By 1960, this had risen moderately, to 13.3 per cent and 5.1 per cent respectively. In 1970, 28.5 per cent of the vegetables were tinned and another 3 per cent frozen, while 7.2 per cent of the fruit was either tinned or dried and another 2.2 per cent consumed in the form of jams and jellies.[162]

In addition to the quantitative increase in the consumption of convenience foods, there were qualitative changes. In the 1960s, for instance, tinned soups gained on powdered soup mixes, though without seriously challenging the predominance of the latter. At the same time, while sales of ordinary bouillon cubes and powder remained stable, there was an increase in sales of powdered broth mixes with bits of vegetables in them. Both of these developments indicate that housewives were buying relatively more higher-quality prepared foods, despite the higher prices.[163]

Convenience foods could always be dressed up a little, to better meet the family's tastes and to give the housewife the sense of having done something. *Constanze*, which asserted that 'hardly any housewife has time nowadays to make soup according to the good old recipes', had suggestions on how to improve the packaged mixes.[164] This technique was not limited in its application to soups:

> Many housewives don't have the time to stand for hours at the kitchen stove. In these cases, tinned goods, and especially complete tinned meals, are very welcome. The danger of monotony in a tin-can menu can be easily avoided. With little effort, very original dishes can be conjured up.

The recipes include jazzing up tinned chicken with rice with saffron, cayenne, madeira and lemon juice, or rinsing the tomato sauce from tinned ravioli, making tomato soup with it and frying the ravioli with egg.[165] While the article spoke of 'little effort' and used the very popular term 'conjure' (*zaubern*), suggesting no effort at all, it actually advocated arguably unnecessary work.

As in kitchen technology, America, the 'legendary land of the tin can',[166] led the way. Interestingly, *Ihre Freundin* claimed with pride in 1955 that the inventor of a series of cake and other baked-goods mixes popular in the US was a native German.[167] But there were often traces of disdain as well as envy in accounts of the American way of cooking. 'They have it easy!' pronounced *Ratgeber* in 1955. 'In American grocery stores there are five hundred types of prepared food on hand which can be brought to the table after briefly warming them.' The negative side was that they cost about a third more than other foods.[168] In 1963, an executive in the frozen-foods business expected to meet his goal of quadrupling West German consumption of frozen foods by the following year, because 'West German wives have recently been becoming more and more "American", that is to say more comfort-loving and, like their husbands, concerned with shortening their working hours.'[169]

Ratgeber reported in 1959 that 'many housewives' in the US took less than half an hour to prepare family meals, 'because industry, by providing tinned goods, deep-frozen foods and pre-cooked meals, has taken most of the kitchen work away from her. Many big companies sell their employees ready-made meals to take out. At home, they only need to be thawed and warmed.' The heading of this short item, in the miscellaneous-news column, was 'Is the art of home cooking superfluous?'[170] The magazine, with its extensive recipe section, had a vested interest in home cooking *not* being superfluous, and this was no doubt true for most of its readers as well. Women could more easily achieve a measure of recognition as good cooks than in most other areas of housework.

How fast was too fast? *Der Spiegel* reported on the decline of family life in America:

> Twenty-three million US citizens spoon a TV dinner into themselves every evening in front of the set. This is a pre-chewed dish on a plastic plate which can be mastered without knife and fork. The side dishes – potatoes, vegetable, dessert – are always heaped in the same places on the plate, so that the viewer can find them and devour them even in the dark, without having to avert his gaze from the screen.[171]

The allegation that TV dinners could be eaten with a spoon alone seems intended to create an association between American eating habits and those of very small children. Civilized adults eat with a knife and fork. Clearly, there were limits to the extent to which household labour could be reduced without violating cultural standards.

Labour Saving in Practice. The desire to maintain certain standards of housekeeping marked one limit to saving time and effort in housework. Another was of a practical nature – only some types of work could actually be assisted by appliances, and the care of the machines themselves created new work. A refrigerator would keep food cold, but it couldn't shop. The refrigerator also had to be cleaned and defrosted. Electrical devices could aid in some cooking tasks, for instance beating egg whites, but by no means in all, and they couldn't plan meals. No machine could make a bed.

If time were saved from one household task, for instance the washing, it might be applied to other housework rather than being set aside as 'free' time. A Constructa advertisement provided a textbook illustration of Friedan's thesis that 'housewifery expands to fill the time available'.[172] One of the small photographs in the advertisement showed the housewife fitting a home-made dress for her daughter. The caption spoke of the pleasure involved in sewing the children's clothes rather than buying everything ready-made. Another picture showed the housewife cooking. The caption indicated that she finally had enough time to try out new recipes.[173]

These suggestions about how additional time might be spent were presumably less threatening than the suggestion that a housewife might go out to work. But they also pointed to potentially genuine pleasures. Frau P. enjoyed experimenting with new recipes, while Frau Ma. liked to make gifts for her nieces and nephews. Her enjoyment was heightened by their appreciation of her skills. Housewives did not necessarily put a high priority on reducing the total amount of time they spent on housework. If time saved from an unpleasant task were applied to a pleasant one, this could be seen as a gain by the person involved, though not by the statistician counting working hours.

In view of these and other factors, a number of scholars have questioned the assumption that changes in household technology have steadily reduced the time and effort required for housework. Looking primarily at nineteenth-century America, Ruth Schwartz Cowan came to the conclusion that, while some types of heavy labour were made easier, the work which was eliminated from the house was often men's or children's work, such as butchering livestock or fetching water. Standards in housekeeping rose enough to more than make up for the potential savings in time produced by technology. Joann Vanek examined time-budget studies done in the United States from the 1920s to the 1960s and came to the conclusion that there was no reduction in the time spent in housework by full-time housewives, despite the increased use of household appliances.[174]

Similar results have been found for Germany. Irmhild Kettschau, examining results of several studies done in the 1970s on time spent on housework, concluded that women's standards were the deciding factor determining how much time they devoted to housekeeping; not only did appliances not reduce the time spent, even work outside the home had little effect. Better equipment might actually be associated with an increase in the time worked.[175] Recent work by Sibylle Meyer and Eva Schulze suggests that the observation made by Karin Hausen for the nineteenth century, that the rise in standards preceded the wider availability of technological help, also applies for the postwar period.[176]

Even if no time was saved, some types of products certainly could significantly reduce the amount of physical effort required for housework. The washing-machine was perhaps the clearest case of reduction of labour — for those women who had previously done the household laundry themselves. Washing the old-fashioned way involved lifting heavy buckets and pots of water as well as sodden clothing. The heat and steam were unpleasant and the water chapped one's hands. It was recognized as hard work — on washday, a wife could prepare simpler meals and look tired in the evening.[177]

The savings in hard work brought about by the washing-machine were such that one article advocated getting together with other families to purchase one for the communal laundry room. With the ability to do her laundry by machine, in a clean, well-ventilated room, the housewife would be able to, 'come evening, take on her duties as a housewife, or an occasional evening out, fresh and in good spirits, without being painfully reminded of the past day and without fearing the next washday's toil'.[178]

Dr S., who had her washing done commercially before she got a washing-machine, none the less regarded it as a significant labour-saving device, compared with the washing techniques she remembered from her childhood in the 1920s.

> I still feel that the washing-machine is the most effective appliance. Because to do the laundry oneself nowadays the way I still [saw it done] as a child . . .
> Down in the cellar there was a great big built-in thing with running water and with a wringing machine, with two rollers, at the far end. And there was a built-in boiler which was heated from underneath with wood and maybe some

coal, because we lived in a coal-mining area. And when that was hot and had boiled for so long, then [the laundry] was heaved over into this basin to be rinsed and then run through [the wringer] and then hung up. So when I think of all those procedures, and nowadays I just turn on the washing-machine, click-clack, then I must say, it's enchanting. This easing of the work.

The refrigerator, which she had years before she had a washing-machine, was less of an improvement over the old way of doing things.

earlier, if you had a big house and a basement . . . then there was all the running up and down stairs, down to the basement and back up, but that worked out, too. People didn't keep so much on hand, you went shopping every day. Nowadays everyone wants to just have one major shopping expedition in the week, at most. So I didn't find that such a relief.[179]

For women who sent most of the family washing to a commercial laundry, the washing-machine was at best a minor labour-saver. The amount of work saved depended on how much of the washing that was still being done at home was not considered too delicate to be entrusted to a household washing-machine. If the ironing had also been done by the laundry, moving the procedure to the home entailed an increase in the amount of housework. For women who did their washing in a communal laundry room or a commercial laundromat, the labour saved depended on the distance travelled. Women with experience of older methods were very aware of the labour saved by using a washing-machine versus washing by hand; younger women growing up with washing-machines would take this for granted.

Dr S. did not find the refrigerator as significant a labour saver, though she was aware of the effort saved (the trips down and up the cellar stairs). Frau M., who lived in the suburbs, without convenient shopping, found it more useful. The time saved by making fewer trips to the shops was more substantial for her. She worked part-time and she and her husband liked to go hiking at the weekends, further reducing shopping opportunities. In addition, she pointed to the inadequacies of cellar space in modern buildings – too little and too warm, suitable for tinned goods or potatoes but not for food that needed to be kept cold.[180] Naturally, the possession of a refrigerator does not inevitably result in a reduction in the number of shopping trips. It is partly a matter of personal preference and partly of transportation – women who did their shopping on foot were generally limited to what they could carry.[181] As far as shopping was concerned, the automobile was at least as important a labour-saving device as the refrigerator, though also more expensive.

The food processor has a rather bad reputation as a labour-saving device, due to the time required to set it up and clean it. Frau Pr. never got one, seeing it as too much work.[182] Even this appliance had some benefits, however. Frau Sch. recalls that, after her father, who worked for Bauknecht, gave her one of the new food processors produced by the firm, she would use it to make an extra *Christstollen* at Christmas for her mother, who did not have a food processor. Mixing the heavy dough by hand was strenuous; the machine made it easy. Later, living alone, Frau Sch. found the machine unnecessary and gave it away to a family with children.[183]

Modern housing design and modern furniture also had the potential to reduce the effort spent on housework. To the established linoleum were added more and more new, easy-care floor coverings.[184] Modern furniture styles featured less dust-catching ornamentation. Many pieces of furniture were lighter in weight and hence easier to move when cleaning. Synthetic curtains were much easier to wash than cotton lace curtains. The small size of many postwar flats also lessened the work involved in cleaning.

New flats were likely to have a toilet and a bath or shower, though sometimes in the same room, which was a source of complaints. Over time, older buildings which were not so well equipped were upgraded. As of 1960, just over half of all flats featured both bath and toilet and more than two-thirds had at least a toilet. Housing featuring neither of these modern conveniences predominated only in communities with fewer than 2,000 inhabitants. In cities of over 200,000 less than 10 per cent of the housing stock was so poorly equipped.[185]

If a flat was modern enough to have central heating or use oil rather than coal or wood stoves, a considerable amount of mess was eliminated. This transition did not proceed very rapidly at first, but by 1968 the proportion of dwellings equipped with central heating approached one-third.[186] The use of central heat or non-solid-fuel stoves led to a considerable reduction in work in the wintertime. One magazine estimated that a modern coal stove in a medium-sized room would burn 20 hundredweight of anthracite or 30 hundredweight of brown coal in the course of a winter.[187] The coal had to be carried in and the ashes carried out. An article in *Ihre Freundin* in 1955 proclaimed the advantages of oil stoves:

> There's no more hauling coal. The tiring wood-splitting, the dirty work of starting the fire, with the bothersome smoke in the room, the work of stoking the fire, etc., all of that is obsolete. The morning chore of cleaning out the ashes, with the annoying dust, is eliminated.[188]

Even if a husband or son could be persuaded that carrying up coal and carrying down ashes were 'men's work', at least if there was a man at home at the time it needed to be done, cleaning up the coal dust or wood chips and ashes which were bound to go astray remained the responsibility of the housewife.

Modern Housework

Characteristics of 'Modern' Housework. As we have seen, in the 1920s there was a move to 'modernize' housework by applying the lessons of industrial engineering to work processes in the home and by increasing the efficiency of kitchen design. The notion of the modern housewife competed with the notion that the truly modern woman was the young, single, employed woman. The image of modern housework presented in the 1950s and 1960s focused not so much on organization and efficiency as on technology and style. The modern housewife was young and carefree, liberated from the burdens of 'old-fashioned' housework through modern products.

Explicit praise of the modernity of household products was more common in advertising of the 1950s than in the 1960s. This approach was especially popular at the end of the 1950s, though many 1951 advertisements in *Constanze* also praised products as modern. Direct references to the high-tech nature of products followed a similar pattern, though they were much less frequent than general references to modernity.

Although the overall popularity of this approach was lower in the 1960s, this decade featured some of the most striking examples as people in 'spacesuits' began to appear in advertisements for household products. An advertisement for floor polish featured a woman in tight white coveralls with a curious cutaway plastic fish-bowl on her head. She was evidently intended to personify the product. Further signs of its modernity were the rocket shape of the bottle and the use of a lower-case initial letter in the product's name.[189]

The particular 'modern' characteristic to which the rocket symbolism pointed was speed, a message made explicit in the text of the advertisement. An advertisement for Progress vacuum cleaners also emphasized speed as a characteristic of modern housework, using an image of an aeroplane. The text as well as the illustration attempted to associate the speed of the jet plane with the vacuum cleaner. The advertisement praised the machine's appearance as well as its efficiency.[190]

Another characteristic of modern housework was the absence of manual labour – with the new products, housework could be performed

Wissenschaft ist unbestechlich

.' :h'ige Erkenntnisse der CONSTRUCTA-Forschung haben zu einer besonders
.. :s:regerechten und kostengerechten Weise des vollautomatischen Waschens geführt,
zum neuen **CONSTRUCTA-Waschverfahren:**

Figure 4.17 Advertisement for Constructa washing machine (detail), *Ratgeber* June 1959, p. 590. A similar advertisement appeared in *Constanze* 29 April 1959, p. 59.

'effortlessly'. In the floor cleaner advertisement, this idea was communicated through an old-fashioned image: the rocket pilot was also cast in the role of a maid. A woman in a 1965 advertisement lamented that she had been 'an unmodern woman', cleaning her windows with water, before her discovery of Sidolin. The 'modern' cleaning method was described as 'much easier and faster'.[191]

An advertisement for Constructa washing-machines depicted labour saving as the result of technological progress, stating:

> Technology and research have changed the face of the world.
> Heavy, arduous labour is taken out of human hands. 'Thinking' machines perform the same work better and faster.
> A new way of life – everyone can participate in it.
> For the housewife with her whole family, that means:
> Washday – the no. 1 source of household unrest – is no more.
> The washing is done *fully automatically!*[192]

Here, mechanization in the home was implicitly tied to mechanization in the factory. If work was taken out of human hands, that was a good thing – the question of whether those hands would find other employment was not raised. 'Everyone' could participate in the new way of life – but in reality not nearly 'everyone' could do so by buying a Constructa, which was a very expensive machine.

The advertisement went on to say that the housewife 'trusts in Constructa research with all its experience and modern (*neuzeitlichen*) discoveries'. Another Constructa advertisement from 1959 featured a white-coated scientist peering intently at a test-tube above the headline 'Science is incorruptible'. The 1958 AEG Lavamat was a 'miraculous achievement of technology'.[193] In the field of washing-machines, there had in fact been significant technological progress since the war. But advertising for other household appliances also emphasized technology. These advertisements were obviously designed in the hope that the audience would have a generally positive view of science (notwithstanding the fact that its corruptibility had been amply demonstrated) and this cachet would also attach to household products.

One area in which the 'modern' cleaning method was heavily advertised was floors. Traditional floor wax polish competed with newer products which did not require the heavy work of buffing. One advertisement proclaimed that, in Sweden, polishing the floor in the traditional manner was old-fashioned (*unmodern*).

Sweden is in many respects the most progressive country in Europe . . . and progress shows itself in housework, too. For floor care, 90 per cent use no-buff floor finishes – like Glänzer. That means: for 9 out of 10 housewives, using wax polish is old-fashioned – they've long since gone over to modern floor care, which saves much time and effort.[194]

Meanwhile, manufacturers of the 'old-fashioned' wax polishes emphasized their superior cleaning properties, implying that floors treated with the newer polishes were not clean.[195]

New, labour-saving methods of cleaning were open to charges that they could not possibly be as effective as old-fashioned methods. Market researchers attempting to explain the discrepancy between survey results and sales figures concluded that housewives underreported their use of labour-saving synthetic detergents out of fear of being thought lazy.[196] The emphasis on the positively valued characteristic 'modernity' was probably in part to counter such consumer reservations; in the advertisements saving time and effort was associated not with laziness but with being up to date.

Modern Style and the Invisibility of Housework. Well before the 1950s, the modern aesthetic had come to dominate appliance design. The days of highly ornamented and unusually shaped sewing-machines were past, the day of the freezer designed to look like a country chest had not yet come.[197] White enamel predominated, with here and there a flash of chrome. The author of a manual on interior design noted that the tendency of the small, single-function kitchen to look like 'a sort of laboratory for the housewife' was intensified by the appearance of modern appliances.[198] One critic conceded that in the area of refrigerators, mixers and gas stoves there were 'almost more decent and tolerable forms than bad ones' (in contrast to the situation with regard to lamps and radios).[199] What appeared to be a slightly modified electric iron stood in the centre of the control panel of the spaceship *Orion* in the 1960s TV series *Raumpatrouille* (*Space Patrol*), looking right at home with the rest of the fake high-tech apparatus.

Modern style, along with modern technology, could be advocated as a reason to replace the only home appliance likely to date from an earlier fashion era: the manual sewing-machine. *Ratgeber* proposed a less drastic remedy, giving instructions for decently hiding such 'old-timers' with their 'ungainly cases and the ugly metal base with the driving wheel'.[200]

In his study of industrial design, *Objects of Desire*, Adrian Forty interprets design of household appliances as a reflection of the myth that housework was not work. He cites in particular the small appliances produced by Braun, which earned an international reputation for modern design in the late 1950s.

> The styling of Braun products suited the deceits and contradictions of housework well, for their appearance raised no comparisons with machine tools or office equipment and preserved the illusion that housework was an elevated and noble activity.[201]

The question of whether Braun appliances resembled office equipment is at least debatable. As for the image of housework transmitted by the designs, it was more one of non-existence than nobility. One notable characteristic of the Braun mixer was that the beaters were concealed within the high mixing bowl. The motor was, of course, completely hidden. The actual work performed by the machine was made as invisible as possible. The fact that the design, while discreet, was quite elegant by modern design standards added to the impression of a decorative rather than useful object. Braun products' cool simplicity in line and colour (or lack thereof) made them excellent status symbols, since they would be admired by people trained to appreciate classical modern design, i.e. educated white-collar people, and probably found very plain by those who had not.

Larger appliances tended to disappear almost completely. Refrigerators fit under countertops or hung from walls along with ordinary cupboards. The tendency in washing-machines was also toward smaller models which would fit under the counter. Sometimes even the window in the door disappeared, as in top-loading machines and one AEG model with an extra door. The advertisement spoke of how the machine hid the disturbance of the moving laundry.[202] A washing-machine in the spin cycle might shake the entire flat, but its external form was static.

Aesthetic considerations were mentioned only occasionally in advertisements, though many included photos or drawings of the product. One washing-machine was advertised as an 'enchanting beauty in the kitchen', designed by a 'well-known Swedish designer (*Formkünstler*)'.[203] A 1951 food processor was praised as 'modern, beautifully formed and efficient', in that order.[204]

The modern kitchen with the latest appliances could itself function as a symbol of 'modernity', and did so in one of a series of advertisements for Temagin, 'the modern pain reliever for modern people'. Other advertisements from the series used more conventional symbols of modernity such as aeroplanes. The mixer and juicer shown on the counter are Braun models, although they are turned around so that the firm's logo is not visible.[205]

Technology and Women.   The use of a modern kitchen and fashionably dressed housewives to represent 'modern people' implied that there was nothing inherently 'unmodern' about housewives. In fact, however, many advertisements testify to a certain uneasiness on the part of the advertisers about the association between women and the traditionally male area of technology. Some advertisements directed technical information specifically at men. Others linked the products advertised with non-technical, traditional images.

One 1956 refrigerator advertisement pictured a happy couple admiring a refrigerator. 'Both are united in their confidence in the Bosch refrigerator.' But their admiration was for different aspects of the appliance. The man was interested in the technology. As breadwinner, he was also concerned with economy. The woman was interested first in the appearance and secondarily in the practical usefulness of the machine. Another advertisement assumed that in watching a demonstration of a washing-machine, '"He" evaluates the technology, "She" the practical value.'[206]

Many advertisements which stressed the high-tech characteristics of appliances were clearly aimed at men. German advertising agencies and executives may well have shared the view that 'women can be sold much

Figure 4.18 Advertisement for Temagin pain reliever, *Ihre Freundin* 7/1960, p. 82.

– 167 –

more easily on appearance than on mechanical superiority'.[207] One advertisement associated refrigerators and cookers with cars: 'You have the newest models of car in your head. And your wife is stuck with old-timers in the kitchen. You should look into two top-of-the-line models that are of interest to your wife.'[208] The assumption was that the wife was not interested in cars (or the husband, ordinarily, in household appliances). The text emphasized the technical features of the appliances, saying that they were also interesting for a man. 'Your wife can programme this electric cooker effortlessly – like a future household robot.'

Some manufacturers chose advertising strategies which either avoided direct reference to technology or tried to assimilate it to more old-fashioned ideas. One 1958 advertisement announced that it would refrain from weighing the reader down with technical details, advising her to try out the product for herself. 'Then no words are necessary.' Another advertisement by the same firm reassured women that using the washing-machine was just a matter of setting two controls: 'You simply can't do it wrong!' The advertisement went on to state that the appliance was 'made with love'. [209]

The Linde refrigerator was 'the refrigerator of the modern housewife'. Instead of using a modern image, however, the refrigerator in its role as the housewife's pride and joy was compared to the hand-woven linen of the medieval housewife. The refrigerator united 'economy and beauty in perfect harmony'. These were characteristics which the medieval housewife would also have appreciated. The Linde refrigerator was to be associated with a general air of progress, but also with traditional values.[210]

A Constructa advertisement using a picture of a violin in the background described the product as a masterpiece for the modern age.

> Talent and ability were the virtues of the old violin makers. Their creations were masterpieces.
>
> In our modern, technical age there are still achievements of an unusual level. The Constructa – valued in many European lands as the pinnacle of German automatic washing-machine construction – combines classical beauty of form with the achievements of fully developed technology. In the life of the progressive housewife, it plays 'first violin'.[211]

While the advertiser evidently expected the housewife to enjoy being called 'progressive', the comparison was with a preindustrial product, a hand-made violin. The advertisement both emphasized the technological perfection of the Constructa and wrapped it in more traditional images. Even the technology was 'fully developed', not new and untested but established and dependable.

Figure 4.19 Advertisement for Frigor refrigerator, *Ihre Freundin* 9 (26 April) 1955, p. 44.

A more extreme example is a 1955 refrigerator advertisement which took the unusual approach of comparing the product to a flower. It surrounded and protected heat-sensitive foods and beverages the way a flower's petals protected its delicate stamens. Through this odd analogy, the machine was associated with a natural, beautiful object.

Such advertisements suggest a fear on the manufacturers' part that women would see modern technology as threatening. Rather than emphasizing the technological modernity of the appliances, the advertisements put them in a premodern, even natural context. There was ambivalence about the relationship between women and technology, even within the 'female' realm of the household.[212] Attempts to construct an image of the 'modern housewife' coexisted with attempts to put technological change in a traditional framework.

When advertisements for household products used words like 'modern' and 'progressive', they were meant in a positive sense. The image of 'modern' people in the advertisements was consistent, if vague. It emphasized open-mindedness, cheerfulness and youth. In terms of household work, 'modernity' meant that the work could be performed quickly, with little physical effort. This reflected an increase in emphasis on leisure, which was also shown in concerns about the health effects of overwork, interest in vacations and the push for the five-day working week.

This view of modern life conflicted with other ideals. Modern furniture, however practical it might be, could seem cold and *ungemütlich*. Images of machinery and technology did not quite fit in with traditional views of home, hearth and women. The use of labour-saving products conflicted with ideas of how housework should be done properly and with the value attached to labour.

There were efforts to increase the status of housework in the 1950s, as there had been earlier in the century. These efforts were motivated in part by dissatisfaction with the discrepancy between women's supposed equality and the continuing social inequality between the sexes. In part, they were motivated by fears that more and more women would choose to continue working outside the home even after they married and had children.

Due to the nature of housework, however, these efforts were constantly contradicted by other, negative messages. Housework took time away from the family, it was drudgery, it rendered women unattractive and old before their time. In addition, in advertisements, credit for the achievements of housewives was given to machines and chemicals.

These new household products made a real difference in the level of physical effort required to perform some household tasks, notably the washing and floor care. They did not necessarily result in an overall reduction in the time spent on housework, but then this was not necessarily an objective of all women. They did contribute to the perception that housework was not a full-time job (except during the period when there were small children who required a great deal of attention). They reinforced tendencies to lessen the perceived value of housework.

Developments made the traditional housewife image, the housewife whose skill and thrift made possible a higher standard of living for her family, difficult to sustain. The higher standard of living was attributed to earnings, and planned obsolescence meant that the work of preserving the family's property was no longer needed – items would be replaced as old-fashioned before they wore out anyway. The new image of the modern housewife was hardly satisfying, either – it suggested a freedom from work which conflicted with women's actual experience of housework. It promoted ever-higher standards, but promised little reward for achieving them, because in the modern world that was all taken for granted. In the end, it did seem that 'modern housewife' was a contradiction in terms. The 1950s and 1960s saw the heyday of the stay-at-home housewife in West Germany. The next generation of women would be increasingly reluctant to accept the housewife role.

–5–

Conclusions

The economic changes which occurred in West Germany, and elsewhere in Western Europe, in the 1950s and 1960s are easily overshadowed by the more dramatic events of the 1940s. None the less, the creation of the 'first world' of today, with an extremely high general standard of living compared with most of the world or most of European history, is a development of great historical significance. It has encouraged the migration of people from other parts of the world to Europe in search of a better life, but also resentment of the newcomers by the natives, who see them as threatening their own economic position. It helped to promote discontent among Europeans east of the Elbe and erode the legitimacy of their governments. It has the potential to erode the legitimacy of Western governments as well, should 'market forces' result in a significant lowering of standards of living.

In West Germany, the transition of the 1950s and 1960s was particularly dramatic against the background of rubble left by the Second World War. While the rise in the standard of living was uneven and took years to reach most families, it had profound effects on domestic life. More and more families lived in new, modern flats or houses. The new prosperity made it possible to have a more varied diet while spending less of the family's income on food. There was more money left over with which to sample both the products of domestic industries and the offerings of the wider world.

One of the changes which resulted was the increasingly broad distribution of household appliances. In the interwar period, they were rare; even many wealthy families did without, transferring housework to maids rather than machines. In the mid-1950s, a refrigerator was a status symbol and an automatic washing-machine a prohibitively expensive luxury. When Frau P. married in 1963, however, a small refrigerator was one of the 'necessities' the young couple bought, though their means were modest.

The use of household appliances did not generally result in a lessening of the time spent on housework, but it did change work processes. Washing could be done at home, as needed, without the steam and heavy lifting involved in doing it the old-fashioned way. Shopping for perishable items like milk did not necessarily have to be done every day. If one chose, a food processor could do the chopping and mixing, although cleaning the food processor had to be done by hand.

Advertisements often implied that appliances and other household products would make housework effortless and instant. The aesthetics of the objects themselves reinforced this myth of housework as non-existent. Moving parts were concealed beneath quiet, static forms. Magazine articles emphasized the amount of work performed by housewives in order to argue in favour of the purchase of appliances, but the implication was that once the appliances were in place the housewives would no longer need to work hard.

It was, for the most part, housewives who were doing the work; fewer and fewer families could find full-time paid help and men rarely did housework. The transformation of day-to-day domestic life which occurred during the course of the 1950s and 1960s took place within the framework of gender roles which had become established by the 1920s: men were primarily responsible for earning income and women were primarily responsible for housekeeping. This division of roles was endorsed by law as well as custom.

Advertisements for appliances and other household products generally presented these new items within the familiar framework of established gender roles. Even in the cases where men were shown performing housework, the manner of the portrayal often made clear that these were not examples to be imitated. More usually, men were portrayed as recipients and critics of housework. Some articles in women's magazines called for more male help around the house, but rarely for equal responsibility, while other articles endorsed the existing division of labour or portrayed men as so incompetent in domestic tasks that they *couldn't* be really helpful.

While economic prosperity and the preservation of the housewife marriage were both widely held political goals, they were not entirely compatible. The changes of the *Wirtschaftswunder* tended to make women's housework seem less valuable. Its economic importance was lessened as families had more disposable income, less need to count every mark and pfennig and accumulate the small savings accrued through darning socks or using cheap cuts of meat. Appliances helped to make housework invisible, hiding it away behind their smooth enamel. Advertisements created a fiction of the leisured housewife, always pretty and well rested because her mechanical and chemical servants did all the work.

Conclusions

Advertisements for appliances and cleaning products gave credit for successful performance of household tasks to the products rather than their users. They presented the purchase of the advertised product, rather than the housewife's skill and knowledge, as responsible for the delicious cake or the clean, wrinkle-free shirt. Use of some products, such as prepared foods or no-iron shirts, really did reduce the amount of knowledge required. Younger women who grew up doing the washing by setting a dial would find it harder than their mothers had to develop a sense of professional pride in their housekeeping.[1]

Advertisements sought to create a new image of the modern, attractive, leisured housewife, but this faced the serious obstacle that modern products did not in themselves reduce the time spent on housework, just the physical labour. In addition, some advertisements expressed a tension between the notion of modernity and views of women as natural and unchanging. Some emphasized technology while explicitly directing their appeals to a male audience. Others worked against the notion of household appliances as technical objects, using preindustrial or natural imagery which their creators evidently expected to be more appealing to women.

Despite efforts to update the housewife's image, the employed woman still seemed more modern. Work outside the home for married women without children was becoming more common by the 1960s; the housework involved in maintaining a small, postwar flat for two adults was not necessarily a full-time job, and the extra income helped the couple to participate in the rising standard of living. There were those who felt that altogether too much emphasis was being given to material prosperity, and both employed women and insufficiently thrifty housewives were targets of their criticism.

There was still strong opposition to mothers working outside the home, which found expression in a lack of social provisions such as day-care centres and full-day schools. Magazine articles, especially in the 1950s, worried about mothers' neglect of their responsibility to 'be there' for their children, and about the overwork which resulted from attempting to combine work and family responsibilities. In the 1970s, an increasing number of couples opted to remain childless or have only a single child, and the number of people who did not marry or did not stay married was also increasing. Among the causes of this development were the rising standard of living, which made children more expensive because they required more accessories, and the postwar building boom, which had out of necessity produced mainly small flats.[2]

In the 1970s, more and more wives opted for work outside the home, which offered them social contacts and some money of their own. Many preferred to work part-time, since their increased work outside the home was not matched by their husbands' increased work inside the home, and this became increasingly possible as the number of part-time jobs increased. The expansion of office work also contributed to an increasing number of jobs for women. Increasingly, young women expected to combine work and family, although this still proved difficult in practice.[3]

In the 1950s and 1960s, there was very little in the way of an organized women's movement. This changed in the 1970s. The new feminists recognized the unequal division of household labour as an important subject, but did not agree on its solution. Consequently, there was no possibility of building a widely supported, focused movement like that for the legalization of abortion. The women's movement developed into an active subculture, but tended to remain isolated from the majority of the female population, who were more likely to express discontent by filing for divorce than by participating in demonstrations. Still, issues such as abortion, violence against women and unequal educational and employment opportunities received more attention, and women came to play more of a role as participants in rather than simply subjects of public discussion.[4]

Looking back across the protest movements and economic crises of the past quarter of a century, the 1950s and 1960s (up to about 1967) appear rather quiet. None the less, they were a period of significant change in very basic aspects of life. In terms of women's roles, these years appear conservative, but in fact the *Wirtschaftswunder* itself was generating challenges to traditional values.

Appendix

Biographical Sketches of Interviewees

For further information about the interviews, see Chapter 1. The interviews with members of the housewives' organization were conducted on 25 October and 6 December 1993. Frau Sch. responded to a handbill. I have known Frau Ge. and Dr S. for several years. Frau P. and Frau M. are the mothers of acquaintances.

Explanation of Terms

Mittlere Reife – intermediate educational qualification between the required elementary education (to age fourteen) and the *Abitur*.
Abitur – set of examinations, usually at age nineteen, qualifying for university study.
Frauenfachschule (Women's Institute) – school with three- or four-year course in home economics.

Biographical Sketches

Frau Ga. *Interview 6 December 1993.* From Freiburg, oldest of four children. Finished school in 1940 with the *Mittlere Reife*. Labour service in family with six children. Apprenticeship as office worker with local publishing firm, completed in 1944. Subsequently sent to work on the fortifications of the *Westwall*. The family home was destroyed in the big Freiburg air raid (27 November 1944) and the house to which the family subsequently moved was confiscated by the French when they occupied the area, whereupon the family was temporarily split up. First child born 1947. Married 1949; husband worked for the railways. Frau Ga. had an office job with a state agency, which she left in 1950 at her husband's urging. They had a total of seven children. Frau Ga. had summer help from au pairs, mostly Swedish. She returned to occasional office work after her husband took early retirement.

Appendix

Frau Ge. *Interview 27 December 1993.* Born 1922 in small town near Rottweil. Father a painter; parents also had a small farm, which they gave up in their old age. Elementary education. After leaving school, went to live with and work for relatives in Stuttgart for two years to learn the finer points of housekeeping. Married 1944; husband a painter, discharged from military service on medical grounds. He died in 1947. They had two children, born 1945 and 1947; Frau Ge. later had a third child (born 1961). During and after her marriage, Frau Ge. continued to live in her parents' house (with her husband, while he was alive). She helped with farm work, both for her parents while they had a farm and later for neighbours, and worked occasionally in local factories and restaurants.

Frau K. *Interview 6 December 1993.* Originally from Upper Silesia (now in Poland), Frau K. went to the Ruhr area in 1945. She married in 1949 and left work when her first child was born. The family lived at first with her parents in a two-room flat with a glassed-in balcony. They moved to a flat of their own in 1953, shortly after the birth of the second child. Her mother bought her a primitive washing-machine in 1953 or 1954, which she had for about ten years before buying a modern one. She acquired a refrigerator in 1958 or 1959. When she was first married, the first priority was to get furniture, not appliances. Frau K. stayed home full time for fifteen years, until her husband became disabled from cancer, whereupon she went back to work because they found it difficult to get by on his pension. He died in 1969.

Frau M. *Interview 21 July 1992.* Born in a village near Lahr, not far from Freiburg. She was one of four children. Her father was a tile-layer. Her mother was frequently ill, and her older sister took over much of the household work until she married. Frau M. had an elementary education, did one year of labour service in households and went to work as an unskilled labourer in a cigarette factory. The family needed her income, so there was no possibility of an apprenticeship. She had to stop working at the factory after she developed eye problems from the dust. She married in 1949. Her husband worked for the post office, eventually achieving civil-servant status. They lived with his parents for the first year, then got a flat of their own. They initially sublet part of it for additional income. They had two children, one with health problems. Frau M. started working in a grocery shop in 1960 or 1961. She did not have an apprenticeship, just a six-week training period.

Frau Ma. *Interview 6 December 1993.*　Born 1928 near Dresden. Mother a teacher. *Abitur* 1946 but unable to pursue university studies, apprenticeship as a hand-weaver. She crossed the border illegally and worked in Hanover as a weaver. She married in 1954. Her husband was a car mechanic. He moved to Freiburg and she joined him in 1956 when he was able to find a flat for them. She was unable to find work as a weaver in Freiburg. In addition, they hoped to have children. This did not happen and they needed more money to pay for further professional training for her husband, so after five years as a full-time housewife she went to work part time in a bank. After they moved to Freiburg, they lived initially in two rooms rented from a widow, moving to a flat after the widow died and her heirs sold the house. They purchased a refrigerator in 1957, an automatic washing-machine in 1960 or 1961.

Frau P. *Interview 14 July 1992.*　Born 1935 in Breisach, on the Rhine not far from Freiburg. The family moved to the nearby town of Ihringen at the end of the war. After leaving school, she lived for two or three years with an aunt in Switzerland, helping in her business (cosmetology) and household. Subsequently, she worked in a hotel in Freiburg. She married in 1963. Her husband was a skilled factory worker. The firm for which he worked owned some blocks of flats, and they were able to rent a flat in one of these. They were able to purchase a refrigerator and an electric cooker at the time they married, a vacuum cleaner (in instalments) in 1964 and a washing-machine in 1967, until which time she had the washing done commercially. Two children, born 1963 and 1966. While the children were small, Frau P. did home work sewing aprons for extra income. The family moved to Freiburg in 1968, after Herr P. changed jobs. Frau P. worked part time while the children were in school. In the mid-1970s, they built a house in a small town near Freiburg on land inherited from Frau P.'s father. She established her own cosmetics business at this time, in the house.

Frau Pr. *Interview 6 December 1993.*　Left East Prussia (now partly in Poland, partly in Russia) in 1945 with her family. They moved initially to Schleswig-Holstein but her father was unable to find work there and the family moved to a small town near Freiburg when she was 17. She spent one year at a *Frauenfachschule* after leaving school. She married in 1962. Her husband was an electrician. They had a refrigerator from the time they were married. They lived with her parents for three years, during which their first child was born. They subsequently moved to a two-room flat. She worked in a kindergarten part time until her second and third children (twins) were born; her mother took care of the daughter (who was four when the twins were born). She bought a washing-machine when the twins were born. She later wanted to go back to work but her husband was against it.

Frau R. *Interview 25 October 1993.* Born Hindenburg, Upper Silesia. The family was wealthy; Frau R.'s father owned a large department store. They had servants; her mother did not cook. Frau R. was educated in a girls' boarding-school. She married in 1935 and lived first in a small town in the Odenwald (her husband was from Mannheim). Her husband was a chemist and they had a laboratory specializing in adhesives. They moved to Freiburg in 1938 after her husband bought a wine laboratory there, but continued in the adhesive business as well. When her husband was drafted, she sold the wine laboratory and continued the other business until the war made that impossible. Her husband was killed in 1941, four months after the birth of their son. She and her son lived near Lake Constance for one year after their home was destroyed in the 1944 air raid. After the war, she was able to re-establish the business, which she ran for twenty years. She remarried in 1947. She bought a washing-machine in 1967 but had a refrigerator earlier. When she was a child, her parents had an icebox.

Frau S. *Interview 25 October 1993.* From Berlin, husband a technician. Two children, a son and a daughter, born in Berlin. The firm for which Herr S. worked, which specialized in communications and remote-control technology, was relocated during the war to a village near Singen in far southern Germany, near Lake Constance, and was closed when the French occupied the area at the end of the war. Herr S. subsequently went to work for the postal service (which was, until recently, also responsible for telephone and telegraph services). The family moved to Freiburg in 1952, to a flat provided by the postal service. At the time of the interview, Frau S. and her husband still lived in this flat, which was extensively renovated in the early 1970s (central heating, new wiring, double-glazed windows).

Dr S. *Interview 14 July 1992.* Born 1918 in Westphalia. Father an executive with a coalmine. The family lived in a company house. *Abitur*, studied medicine in Münster and then in Marburg, finished her studies in 1942 and worked in hospitals first in Marburg, then in Mecklenburg, finally in Schwäbisch Hall, where she met her husband. They were married in 1950 and lived for one year in Switzerland, then moved to Heidelberg, where her husband worked in a hospital. She worked part time with another doctor, full time when the other went on vacation or maternity leave. They rented a room from a widow initially but were later able to move into a flat with her parents' help. Shortly thereafter, they moved to the Freiburg area, where they shared a flat with another family initially, then moved to an acquaintance's holiday home in the mountains, then to a flat of their own. They had two children, born 1954 and 1956. In 1960, with financial assistance from both sets of parents, they built a house in a community near Freiburg, where her husband had found work. They bought their first washing-machine at this time; they'd had a refrigerator since about 1953. They acquired a dishwasher in the late 1960s. Dr S. worked somewhat irregularly, as a substitute for other doctors who were on holiday. She decided not to set up her own practice due to the expense, but also liked the variety of temporary work and wanted to have time for her children. She has generally had household help at least one day a week. She was divorced in 1970/71.

Frau Sch. *Interview 17 October 1993.* Born 1926 in Freiburg. Her father was an engineer, originally from Quedlinburg; her mother was from Berlin. Her father was unemployed for five years during the Depression. She left school with the *Mittlere Reife* and attended a *Frauenfachschule* but did not graduate due to the destruction of the school in the 1944 air raid. The family owned a house, in which they had a three-room flat, from which they rented two rooms to a French officer and his family. She married in 1949 and moved to small town near Freiburg because her husband could not get a residence permit in Freiburg. They lived in a rented room for the first year and then in a flat. Her husband was an electrician with his own business. They had a son born January 1950. They built a house in 1959/60 and acquired a washing-machine at that time, which also served as a demonstration model. Frau Sch. helped in her husband's business, doing the bookkeeping and running errands. They divorced in 1971. She then moved to Freiburg and did office work until she retired.

Frau T. *Interview 25 October 1993.* Born Lodz, 1935, father ethnic German from Ukraine, mother Pole, both schoolteachers. Left Lodz January 1945 with her mother and sister. They ended up in Niedersachsen, where her mother found a job teaching Polish children in a displaced persons camp. She lost this job when her husband returned. He found employment as a village schoolteacher near Hildesheim in 1947. The family lived in two rooms rented from a local farmer for five years, then moved into a flat in the schoolhouse, at first shared with others. The flat had no bathroom until 1962, though there was a cold-water tap in the kitchen. It was heated with coal stoves until oil stoves were installed in 1964. Frau T. left school with the *Mittlere Reife* and studied for one year at a *Frauenfachschule*. She wanted to use the *Frauenfachschule* training to become a home economics teacher, getting around her father's opposition to her becoming a teacher, but she was not sufficiently skilled at needlework. She left the *Frauenfachschule* and took an office job. After working for very low pay at two different firms, she got a better job with an industrial firm, where she worked for eight years while continuing to live with her parents. She married in 1965 and left her job because her husband had plans to move to another part of the country, though as it turned out this did not happen immediately. They were able to move into their own flat in 1966 and bought a refrigerator at that time. The flat had built-in cupboards and a stove. She had the bulk of the laundry done commercially (in the first year of her marriage, her mother continued to do it for her) and did the rest by hand. She did not get a washing-machine until about 1979. They had two children, born 1967 and 1971. The family moved to Freiburg in 1972.

Notes

Chapter 1 Introduction

1. Werner Abelshauser, *Wirtschaftsgeschichte der Bundesrepublik Deutschland, 1945–1980* (Frankfurt am Main: Suhrkamp, 1983), pp. 93, 101; Knut Borchardt, 'Zäsuren in der wirtschaftlichen Entwicklung', in Martin Broszat, ed., *Zäsuren nach 1945: Essays zur Periodisierung der deutschen Nachkriegsgeschichte* (Munich: R. Oldenbourg, 1990), p. 31.
2. Statistisches Bundesamt, Wiesbaden, *Fachserie M: Preise, Löhne, Wirtschaftsrechnungen, Reihe 18: Einkommens- und Verbrauchsstichproben: Ausstattung privater Haushalte mit ausgewählten langlebigen Gebrauchsgütern 1962/63* (Stuttgart: W. Kohlhammer, 1964), pp. 16–17, 48. The usual estimate of the useful life of major appliances is ten years.
3. Statistisches Bundesamt, Wiesbaden, *Fachserie M, Reihe 18, 1969* (Stuttgart: W. Kohlhammer, 1970), pp. 35, 42, 74–6, 148–9.
4. Sibylle Meyer and Eva Schulze, 'Technisiertes Familienleben: Ergebnisse einer Längsschnittuntersuchung 1950–1990', in Meyer and Schulze, eds, *Technisiertes Familienleben: Blick zurück und nach vorn* (Berlin: Edition Sigma, 1993).
5. Elizabeth Heineman argues that the female experience of defeat in 1942–48 played a key role in the formation of the postwar identity of all of West Germany. Elizabeth Heineman, 'The Hour of the Woman: Memories of Germany's "Crisis Years" and West German National Identity', *American Historical Review* 101 (April 1996): 354–95. For a critical discussion of the literature on women in the immediate postwar period, see Annette Kuhn, 'Power and Powerlessness: Women after 1945, or the Continuity of the Ideology of Femininity', *German History* 7 (April 1989): 35–46.
6. The term '*vollständige Familie*' was commonly used by sociologists and others after the war to differentiate these families from the large number of families in which the father was absent due to death, divorce or desertion. See Elizabeth Heineman, 'Complete Families, Half Families, No Families at All: Female-Headed Households and the

Reconstruction of the Family in the Early Federal Republic', *Central European History* 29 (winter 1996): 19–60.

7. Sibylle Meyer and Eva Schulze, *Wie wir das alles geschafft haben: Alleinstehende Frauen berichten über ihr Leben nach 1945*, 3rd edn (Munich: C. H. Beck, 1985). Meyer and Schulze emphasize that most of the single women did not live alone, but with parents, sisters, children, other relatives or friends, and that some chose not to marry because they did not want to disrupt these households.

8. There were 35.7 divorces per 10,000 existing marriages in 1960, 50.9 in 1970; in both absolute and relative terms, these figures were lower than in 1950, when the postwar 'divorce boom' was still in progress. Statistisches Bundesamt, Wiesbaden, *Bevölkerung und Wirtschaft 1872–1972* (Stuttgart: W. Kohlhammer, 1972), p. 114.

9. Inconveniently, the local supermarkets mostly took down their bulletin boards in the interest of more advertising space around the time I was conducting this study. An attempt to find interview partners through a local retirement home failed – the management felt there were already enough historians snuffling around. The 'snowball method' of asking one interview partner for introductions to others was also ineffective – I suspect this may be in part because, given that the interviews dealt with domestic life, personal matters tended to come up.

10. *Stimme der Frau* (Voice of Woman) changed its name to *Für Sie* (For You) in December 1956. *Freundin* (Girlfriend) dropped the 'ihre' (your) in 1961. *Constanze* ceased publication after 1969 and *Brigitte* was for a few years thereafter officially *Brigitte mit Constanze*.

11. On the history of magazine publishing in the postwar years, see Sylvia Lott, *Die Frauenzeitschriften von Hans Huffzky und John Jahr: Zur Geschichte der deutschen Frauenzeitschrift zwischen 1933 und 1970* (Berlin: Wissenschaftsverlag Volker Spiess, 1985), pp. 312–39. Information on *Ratgeber* from a telephone conversation with its editor-in-chief, Herr Hackelsberger, May 1994. On male readers, Jörg Hagena, 'Die berufstätige Frau in illustrierten Zeitschriften' (diss., Erlangen-Nuremberg, 1974), p. 124. *Brigitte*, for which Hagena also gives figures, had a smaller number of male readers (25.4% in 1954), but the trend was the same (p. 123).

12. Lott, *Frauenzeitschriften*, pp. 560–2.

13. *Auflagenmeldungen erstattet der Informationsgemeinschaft zur Feststellung der Verbreitung von Werbeträgern e.V.* (Bad Godesberg: Zeitungs-Verlag und Zeitschriften-Verlag GmbH, n.d. [1961]); Ingrid Langer-El Sayed, *Frau und Illustrierte im Kapitalismus* (Cologne: Pahl-Rugenstein, 1971).

14. Hagena, pp. 123–4, 128.
15. Both magazines tended toward a younger readership over time. *Brigitte* in the early 1950s, before its change of style, had been read more by older women. Hagena, pp. 123–4.
16. Lott, *Frauenzeitschriften*, pp. 559, 592. Some private households also subscribed to such services, though their number was decreasing over time. John Sandford, *The Mass Media of the German-Speaking Countries* (London: Oswald Wolff, 1976), p. 52. *Constanze* switched to weekly publication in September 1961 because the issues were getting too thick to fit in the covers used by the services.
17. Lott, *Frauenzeitschriften*, pp. 400, 586, 597.
18. Samples consisted of the January, April, July and October issues.
19. Lott, *Frauenzeitschriften,* pp. 312–39.
20. *Ratgeber* generally devoted over 20%, sometimes over 25%, of its editorial content to food and around 5%, sometimes more, to housework (not including sewing and knitting, which were another 5–10%).
21. 'Was will der Ratgeber für Haus und Familie?' *Ratgeber* January 1954, p. 3. The purpose of the magazine is defined as providing advice for all situations in life but especially for matters of housekeeping.
22. *Ihre Freundin* 1 (10 January) 1951, p. 2. An advertisement in *Constanze* from the spring of that year also testifies to the shortage: 'Even without a wrapper, it remains the old Sunlight Soap' (*Constanze,* 28 March 1951, p. 33).
23. Fewa ad, *Constanze*, 28 March 1951, p. 6.
24. *Ihre Freundin* 4/1950, p. 21. For a discussion of the postwar ads proclaiming that the products advertised were available again, see Michael Kriegeskorte, *Werbung in Deutschland 1945–1965: Die Nachkriegszeit im Spiegel ihrer Anzeigen* (Cologne: DuMont, 1992), ch. 1.
25. *Constanze* 7/1950, p. 26.
26. *Constanze* 7/1950, p. 5. See also the defence of a feature on cocktail and evening dresses in *Ihre Freundin* 8 (12 April) 1955, p. 6, which presents fashion photos as a means of educating taste as well as an opportunity for aesthetic enjoyment.
27. *Ihre Freundin* 8/1950, pp. 16–17; 'Kostet Eleganz Geld?' *Ratgeber* September 1954, pp. 426–7.
28. Advertisements for Taft hairspray, *Für Sie* 22 (19 October) 1965, p. 73, and Elbeo stockings, *Ratgeber* November 1961, p. 1201.
29. *Constanze* 42 (9 October) 1967.

30. Gruner & Jahr. Until April 1957, *Brigitte* had been published by Ullstein. See Sylvia Lott-Almstadt, Brigitte *1886–1986: Die ersten hundert Jahre: Chronik einer Frauenzeitschrift* (Hamburg: Gruner & Jahr, 1986).

31. There is some evidence that the two techniques produce similar results: Preben Sepstrup, 'Methodological Developments in Content Analysis', in Karl Eric Rosengren, ed., *Advances in Content Analysis* (Beverly Hills: Sage, 1980), cited in Ellen McCracken, *Decoding Women's Magazines: From* Mademoiselle *to* Ms. (Houndmills, Basingstoke, Hampshire: Macmillan, 1993), p. 312, n. 33.

32. This meant that, in practice, the first year used was 1951 (for *Brigitte*, 1956) and the last year of *Constanze* examined was the last year of its publication, 1969.

33. Sara Mills, introduction to *Gendering the Reader* (New York: Harvester Wheatsheaf, 1994), pp. 5–7.

34. Roland Barthes, 'Rhetoric of the Image', in *Image Music Text*, tr. Stephen Heath (New York: Hill & Wang, 1977), pp. 32–51. Barthes also discusses advertisements, though much more briefly, in some of the essays in *Mythologies*, tr. Annette Lavers (New York: Hill & Wang, 1972), notably 'Soap-Powders and Detergents', pp. 36–40.

35. Judith Williamson, *Decoding Advertisements: Ideology and Meaning in Advertising* (London: Marion Boyars, 1978).

36. Stuart Hall, 'Encoding, decoding', in Simon During, ed., *The Cultural Studies Reader* (London: Routledge, 1993); for a concise introduction, see John Eldridge, Jenny Kitzinger and Kevin Williams, *The Mass Media and Power in Modern Britain* (Oxford: Oxford University Press, 1997), pp. 130–1.

37. Michel de Certeau, 'Reading as Poaching', in *The Practice of Everyday Life*, pp. 165–76, translated by Steven F. Rendall (Berkeley and Los Angeles: University of California Press, 1984).

38. Angela McRobbie, '*Jackie*: An Ideology of Adolescent Femininity', in Bernard Waites, Tony Bennett and Graham Martin, eds, *Popular Culture: Past and Present* (London: Croom Helm, 1982).

39. Janice Winship, 'The Impossibility of *Best*', in Dominic Strinati and Stephen Wagg, eds, *Come On Down? Popular Media Culture in Postwar Britain* (London: Routledge, 1992), p. 91. The reference is to Elizabeth Frazer, 'Teenage Girls Reading *Jackie*', *Media, Culture and Society* 9 (October 1987).

40. Lott, *Frauenzeitschriften*, pp. 586–7.

41. For a discussion of this issue in relation to advertising, see Ronald Berman, *Advertising and Social Change* (Beverly Hills: SAGE, 1981).

Chapter 2 Modernity, Gender and the Home, 1920–1950

1. Detlev J.K. Peukert, *The Weimar Republic: The Crisis of Classical Modernity*, tr. Richard Deveson (London: Allen Lane, 1991), pp. 81–2.
2. Statistisches Bundesamt, *Bevölkerung und Wirtschaft*, p. 145.
3. Angelika Willms, 'Grundzüge der Entwicklung der Frauenarbeit von 1880 bis 1980', in Walter Müller, Angelika Willms and Johann Handl, *Strukturwandel der Frauenarbeit 1880–1980* (Frankfurt am Main: Campus, 1983), pp. 48–51.
4. Ibid., pp. 142, 145.
5. For a discussion of women's economic situation in Weimar Germany, see Renate Bridenthal and Claudia Koonz, 'Beyond *Kinder, Küche, Kirche*: Weimar Women in Politics and Work', in Renate Bridenthal, Atina Grossmann and Marion Kaplan, eds, *When Biology Became Destiny: Women in Weimar and Nazi Germany* (New York: Monthly Review Press, 1984), pp. 33–65.
6. Dagmar Reese, *Straff, aber nicht stramm – herb, aber nicht derb: Zur Vergesellschaftung von Mädchen durch den Bund Deutscher Mädel im sozialkulturellen Vergleich zweier Milieus* (Weinheim: Beltz, 1989), p. 119.
7. Ute Frevert, *Women in German History: From Bourgeois Emancipation to Sexual Liberation*, tr. Stuart McKinnon-Evans (Oxford: Berg, 1989), pp. 180–1.
8. Jill Stephenson, *Women in Nazi Society* (London: Croom Helm, 1975), p. 131.
9. James C. Albisetti, *Schooling German Girls and Women: Secondary and Higher Education in the Nineteenth Century* (Princeton: Princeton University Press, 1988), pp. 291, 300.
10. Frevert, pp. 176–9.
11. Statistisches Reichsamt, *Statistisches Jahrbuch für das Deutsche Reich* (Berlin: Reimar Hobbing, 1930), p. 32. This and Statistisches Bundesamt Wiesbaden, *Statistisches Jahrbuch für die Bundesrepublik Deutschland* (Stuttgart: W. Kohlhammer until 1988, thereafter Metzler-Poeschel) cited henceforth as StJ. See also Peukert, *Weimar Republic,* pp. 7–9.
12. Reinhard Spree, *Health and Social Class in Imperial Germany* (Oxford: Berg, 1988), table 14, p. 204, cited in Frevert, p. 186; Atina Grossmann, 'Abortion and Economic Crisis: The 1931 Campaign Against Paragraph 218', in Bridenthal *et al.*, eds, *When Biology Became Destiny*, pp. 66–86.

13. Frevert, pp. 121–2, 138–9, 169–71, and Eva Kolinsky, *Women in Contemporary Germany: Life, Work and Politics*, rev. edn (Providence: Berg, 1993), p. 222; Britta Lövgren, *Hemarbete som politik: Diskussioner om hemarbete, Sverige 1930–40-talen, och tillkomsten av Hemmens Forskningsinstitut* (Stockholm: Almqvist & Wiksell, 1993), p. 60.

14. Frevert, pp. 172–5. See also Annemarie Tröger, 'Die Dolchstoßlegende der Linken: Haben Frauen Hitler an die Macht gebracht?', in Gruppe Berliner Dozentinnen, *Frauen und Wissenschaft: Beiträge zur Berliner Sommeruniversität für Frauen, Juli 1976* (Berlin: Courage, 1977), pp. 324–55.

15. Renate Bridenthal, '"Professional" Housewives: Stepsisters of the Women's Movement', in Bridenthal *et al.*, eds, *When Biology Became Destiny*, pp. 153–73; Nancy Reagin, *A German Women's Movement: Class and Gender in Hanover, 1880–1933* (Chapel Hill: University of North Carolina Press, 1995).

16. StJ 1927, pp. 12–13, and 1936, p. 178.

17. For a discussion of the development of household technology and the implications of utilities for housework see Caroline Davidson, *A Woman's Work is Never Done: A History of Housework in the British Isles 1650–1950* (London: Chatto & Windus, 1982), Ruth Schwartz Cowan, *More Work for Mother: The Ironies of Household Technology from the Open Hearth to the Microwave* (New York: Basic Books, 1983), Sigfried Giedion, *Mechanization Takes Command* (New York: Oxford University Press, 1948) and Christina Hardyment, *From Mangle to Microwave: The Mechanization of Household Work* (Cambridge: Polity Press, 1988). On Germany, I have made use of a preliminary report from the study 'Technology and Family' conducted by Sibylle Meyer and Eva Schulze at the Technische Universität Berlin (Berlin, n.d.). On specific technologies see Barbara Orland, *Wäsche waschen: Technik- und Sozialgeschichte der häuslichen Wäschepflege* (Reinbek bei Hamburg: Rowohlt, 1991), Gudrun Silberzahn-Jandt, *Wasch-Maschine: Zum Wandel von Frauenarbeit im Haushalt* (Marburg: Jonas, 1991), and Ullrich Hellmann, *Künstliche Kälte: Die Geschichte der Kühlung im Haushalt* (Gießen: Anabas, 1990).

18. For a discussion of the Hamburg system, as well as London, Paris, Frankfurt am Main and Berlin, see John von Simson, *Kanalisation und Städtehygiene im 19. Jahrhundert* (Düsseldorf: VDI, 1983).

19. Manufactured gas (from coal) predominated. Natural gas, mainly

imported from newly discovered fields in Belgium, began to be used in significant quantities in West Germany in the 1960s.

20. Ludwig Koch, 'Das Haushaltsgeräte-Absatzpolitik in Elektrizitäts-versorgungs-Unternehmen' (diss., Munich, 1957), p. 180.

21. Davidson, pp. 127–8.

22. Earl Lifshey, *The Housewares Story: A History of the American Housewares Industry* (Chicago: National Housewares Manufacturers Association, 1973), pp. 265–6.

23. Meyer and Schulze, 'Technology and Family', pp. 12–18.

24. Orland, *Wäsche waschen,* p. 200.

25. Michael Wildt, 'Technik, Kompetenz, Modernität: Amerika als zwiespältiges Vorbild für die Arbeit in der Küche, 1920–1960', in Alf Lüdtke, Inge Marßolek and Adelheid von Saldern, eds, *Amerikanisierung: Traum und Alptraum im Deutschland des 20. Jahrhunderts* (Stuttgart: Franz Steiner, 1996), p. 84.

26. Refrigerators which were not just plugged into a normal outlet but directly wired to a special heavy-duty circuit.

27. Hellmann, *Künstliche Kälte,* pp. 109–17. A '*Volksstaubsauger*' (vacuum cleaner) was apparently also in the works. See Wolfram Fischer, ed., *Die Geschichte der Stromversorgung* (Frankfurt am Main: Verlags- und Wirtschaftsgesellschaft der Elektrizitätswerke m.b.H., 1992), p. 140.

28. On Britain, Davidson, pp. 34–8; on France, Françoise Werner, 'Du ménage à l'art ménager: l'évolution du travail ménager et son écho dans la presse féminine française de 1919 à 1939', *Le Mouvement social* 126 (January–March 1984): 80–1, and see also Robert L. Frost, 'Machine Liberation: Inventing Housewives and Home Appliances in Interwar France', *French Historical Studies* 18 (spring 1993): 109–30; on Sweden, Jan-Erik Hagberg, *Tekniken i kvinnornas händer: Hushållsarbete och hushållsteknik under tjugo- och trettiotalen* (Malmö: Liber, 1986), p. 50. For a discussion of the Norwegian situation, albeit a somewhat sketchy one, see Anna Jorunn Avdem and Kari Melby, *Oppe først og sist i seng: Husarbeid i Norge fra 1850 til i dag* (Oslo: Universitetsforlaget, 1985).

29. Barbara Orland, 'Emanzipation durch Rationalisierung', in Dagmar Reese, Eve Rosenhaft, Carola Sachse and Tilla Siegel, eds, *Rationale Beziehungen? Geschlechterverhältnisse im Rationalisierungsprozeß* (Frankfurt am Main: Suhrkamp, 1993), p. 235.

30. See Mary Nolan, '"Housework Made Easy": The Taylorized Housewife in Weimar Germany's Rationalized Economy', *Feminist Studies* 16 (fall 1990): 549–77. On Bernège, see Martine Martin, 'La

Rationalisation du travail ménager en France dans l'entre-deux-guerres', *Culture technique* 3 (1980): 156–65. Bernège was still influential in France in the 1950s; see Claire Duchen, *Women's Rights and Women's Lives in France, 1944–1968* (London: Routledge, 1994), pp. 69–70.

31. Michael Andritzky, 'Gemeinsam statt einsam: Otl Aicher und die Küchenphilosophie von bulthaup' and 'Eine Küche für den neuen Lebensstil', in Andritzky, ed., *Oikos: Von der Feuerstelle zur Mikrowelle: Haushalt und Wohnen im Wandel* (Gießen: Anabas, 1992), pp. 136–43.

32. Joachim Krause, 'Die Frankfurter Küche', in Andritzky, ed., *Oikos*, pp. 96–112; Lore Kramer, 'Rationalisierung des Haushaltes und Frauenfrage', in Rosemarie Höpfner and Volker Fischer, eds, *Ernst May und das Neue Frankfurt* (Berlin: Wilhelm Ernst & Sohn, 1986), p. 80, cited in Ben Lieberman, 'Testing Peukert's Paradigm: The "Crisis of Classical Modernity" in the "New Frankfurt", 1925–1930', *German Studies Review* 27 (May 1994): 292.

33. Michael Freidank, 'Langfristige Entwicklungstendenzen auf den Märkten ausgewählter Haushaltsmaschinen' (diss., St Gallen, 1966), pp. 124, 129.

34. Martha L. Olney, *Buy Now, Pay Later: Advertising, Credit, and Consumer Durables in the 1920s* (Chapel Hill: University of North Carolina Press, 1991), p. 114.

35. See Olney and also Stuart Ewen, *Captains of Consciousness: Advertising and the Social Roots of the Consumer Culture* (New York: McGraw-Hill, 1976).

36. Theresa Mayer Hammond, *American Paradise: German Travel Literature from Duden to Kisch* (Heidelberg: Carl Winter, 1980), especially pp. 71–87. See also Judith A. Merkle, *Management and Ideology: The Legacy of the International Scientific Management Movement* (Berkeley and Los Angeles: University of California Press, 1980), pp. 172–207, and Mary Nolan, *Visions of Modernity: American Business and the Modernization of Germany* (New York: Oxford University Press, 1994).

37. Rüdiger Hachtmann, '"Die Begründer der amerikanischen Technik sind fast lauter schwäbisch-allemannische Menschen": Nazi-Deutschland, der Blick auf die USA und die "Amerikanisierung" der industriellen Produktionsstrukturen im "Dritten Reich"', in Alf Lüdtke *et al.*, eds, *Amerikanisierung*, pp. 41–4.

38. Erich Welter, 'Rationalisieren wie noch nie', *Frankfurter Zeitung* 9 November 1941, quoted in Hans Dieter Schäfer, 'Amerikanismus

im Dritten Reich', in Michael Prinz and Rainer Zitelmann, eds, *Nationalsozialismus und Modernisierung* (Darmstadt: Wissenschaftliche Buchgesellschaft, 1991), p. 213. See also Detlev Peukert, *Inside Nazi Germany: Conformity, Opposition, and Racism in Everyday Life* (New Haven: Yale University Press, 1987).

39. Jeffrey Herf, *Reactionary Modernism: Technology, Culture, and Politics in Weimar and the Third Reich* (Cambridge: Cambridge University Press, 1984); Michael Prinz and Rainer Zitelmann, eds, *Nationalsozialismus und Modernisierung* (Darmstadt: Wissenschaftliche Buchgesellschaft, 1991).

40. On the Nazi girls' organizations, see Reese, *Straff, aber nicht stramm.*

41. See for example Eva Jantzen and Merith Niehuss, eds, *Das Klassenbuch: Geschichte einer Frauengeneration* (Reinbek bei Hamburg: Rowohlt, 1997), pp. 92–5, 128–30, 136–7. This was a book passed around among members of a 1932 graduating class to keep each other informed about their lives.

42. Claudia Huerkamp, 'Jüdische Akademikerinnen in Deutschland, 1900–1938', *Geschichte und Gesellschaft* 19 (July/Sept. 1993): 318–21, 327.

43. Bettina Bab, 'Frauen helfen siegen', in Annette Kuhn, ed., *Frauenleben im NS-Alltag* (Pfaffenweiler: Centaurus, 1994), pp. 83–4.

44. Stephenson, pp. 103–11; Walter Müller, 'Frauenerwerbstätigkeit im Lebenslauf', in Müller, Willms and Handl, pp. 75–7.

45. Duchen, pp. 101–2; Irmgard Weyrather, *Muttertag und Mutterkreuz: Der Kult um die 'deutsche Mutter' im Nationalsozialismus* (Frankfurt am Main: Fischer Taschenbuch Verlag, 1993); Stephenson, pp. 69–70. The restrictions on birth control continued in most of West Germany until 1961.

46. Gordon A. Craig, *Germany 1866–1945* (New York: Oxford University Press, 1978), pp. 732–3 and 744–5, and Karl Dietrich Erdmann, *Der Zweite Weltkrieg, Gebhardt Handbuch der deutschen Geschichte*, 9th edn, vol. 21 (Munich: Deutscher Taschenbuch Verlag, 1980), pp. 123–4. On the First World War, see Gerd Hardach, *The First World War, 1914–1918* (Berkeley and Los Angeles: University of California Press, 1977) and Jennifer Loehlin, 'Consumers and the State: British and German Food Policy during the First World War' (master's thesis, University of Texas at Austin, 1987).

47. Christoph Kleßmann, 'Untergänge – Übergänge: Gesellschaftsgeschichtliche Brüche und Kontinuitätslinien vor und nach 1945', in Kleßmann, ed., *Nicht nur Hitlers Krieg: Der Zweite Weltkrieg und die Deutschen* (Düsseldorf: Droste, 1989), p. 87.

48. Frau Ga., interview by author, 6 December 1993; Frau R. and Frau S., interviews by author, 25 October 1993.
49. On persons expelled from the eastern territories, see Gerhard Reichling, 'Flucht und Vertreibung der Deutschen: Statistische Grundlagen und terminologische Probleme', in Rainer Schulze, Doris von der Brelie-Lewien and Helga Grebing, eds, *Flüchtlinge und Vertriebene in der westdeutschen Nachkriegsgeschichte: Bilanzierung der Forschung und Perspektiven für die künftige Forschungsarbeit* (Hildesheim: August Lax, 1987), p. 46. Over two million ethnic Germans died either during this expulsion from the Eastern territories or during forced resettlement within the Soviet Union in the 1940s. Frau T., interview with the author, 25 October 1993.
50. Martin K. Sorge, *The Other Price of Hitler's War: German Military and Civilian Losses Resulting from World War II* (New York: Greenwood Press, 1986), particularly pp. 67–71; interviews with Frau R. and Frau Ge.; StJ 1952, p. 25.
51. Frau S., interview.
52. Sociological studies conducted after the war called attention to these problems and in some cases tended to exaggerate their extent. See Gerhard Baumert and Edith Hünninger, *Deutsche Familien nach dem Kriege* (Darmstadt: Eduard Roether, 1954), Hilde Thurnwald, *Gegenwartsprobleme Berliner Familien* (Berlin: Weidmann, 1948), Gerhard Wurzbacher, *Leitbilder gegenwärtigen deutschen Familienlebens* (Stuttgart: Ferdinand Enke, 1952).
53. On children in postwar Germany, see Ulf Preuss-Lausitz *et al.*, *Kriegskinder, Konsumkinder, Krisenkinder: Zur Sozialisationsgeschichte seit dem zweiten Weltkrieg* (Weinheim: Beltz, 1983).
54. Very few German women in the 1950s and 1960s married in their teens, in contrast to the situation in the United States.

Chapter 3 The *Wirtschaftswunder* in the Home

1. Abelshauser, *Wirtschaftsgeschichte der Bundesrepublik Deutschland*, pp. 93, 101.
2. Ibid., pp. 20–4, and Reichling, p. 46. Most prisoners held by the Western allies were repatriated in the first years after the war, but some held by the Soviets returned as late as the mid-1950s. On foreign

workers, Statistisches Bundesamt, *Bevölkerung und Wirtschaft*, p. 148.

3. Gerd Hardach, 'Die Wirtschaft der fünfziger Jahre: Restauration und Wirtschaftswunder', in Dieter Bänsch, ed., *Die fünfziger Jahre: Beiträge zu Politik und Kultur* (Tübingen: Gunter Narr, 1985), p. 58.

4. Hans Günter Hockerts, 'Metamorphosen des Wohlfahrtsstaats', in Broszat, ed., *Zäsuren nach 1945*, pp. 35–40; Abelshauser, *Wirtschaftsgeschichte der Bundesrepublik Deutschland*, p. 143.

5. On the situation of unmarried women and widows, see Meyer and Schulze, *Wie wir das alles geschafft haben* and '"Alleine war's schwieriger und einfacher zugleich"': Veränderung gesellschaftlicher Bewertung und individueller Erfahrung alleinstehender Frauen in Berlin 1943–1955', in Anna-Elisabeth Freier and Annette Kuhn, eds, *Frauen in der Geschichte V: 'Das Schicksal Deutschlands liegt in der Hand seiner Frauen': Frauen in der deutschen Nachkriegsgeschichte* (Düsseldorf: Schwann, 1984); also Elizabeth Heineman, '"Standing Alone": Single Women from Nazi Germany to the Federal Republic' (diss., University of North Carolina, 1993) and Katharina Tumpek-Kjellmark, 'From Hitler's Widows to Adenauer's Brides: Towards a Construction of Gender and Memory in Postwar West Germany' (diss., Cornell, 1994). In 1986, women gained pension rights equal to one year of employment for each child they had. Kolinsky, pp. 68–9.

6. Frau T., interview by author, 25 October 1993.

7. Frau P., interview by author, 14 July 1992.

8. Calculated from StJ 1958 p. 467, 1961 p. 524, 1967 p. 499 and 1972 p. 491, and 1932 p. 321.

9. This is not to discount the importance of the (televised!) World Cup victory of 1954.

10. Thomas Kühne: '". . . aus diesem Krieg werden nicht nur harte Männer heimkehren": Kriegskameradschaft und Männlichkeit im 20. Jahrhundert', in Thomas Kühne, ed., *Männergeschichte – Geschlechtergeschichte: Männlichkeit im Wandel der Moderne* (Frankfurt am Main: Campus, 1996), pp. 188–9.

11. Saba ad, reproduced in Nikolaus Jungwirth and Gerhard Kromschröder, *Die Pubertät der Republik: Die 50er Jahre der Deutschen* (Reinbek bei Hamburg: Rowohlt, 1983), p. 201. The Germanness of German-made appliances was rarely mentioned specifically in advertisements; to the extent that this did occur, it was a phenomenon of the late 1950s.

12. BBC ad, *Constanze* 14 (29 June) 1955, p. 75.

13. Quoted in Elaine Tyler May, *Homeward Bound: American Families in the Cold War Era* (New York: Basic Books, 1988), p. 17.
14. Vera Bucher, 'Schweinefleisch aus China: Aus dem Alltag einer Leipziger Hausfrau', *Christ und Welt* 13 December 1963, p. 22.
15. Letter from Heike Haeseler in 'Teenager-Briefkasten', *Ihre Freundin* 4 (11 February) 1958, p. 113.
16. Peter Rocholl, 'Die Frau am Steuer', *Ihre Freundin* 1/1950, pp. 8–9.
17. NSU advertisement in *Spiegel* 15 (6 April) 1960, p. 35.
18. *Stimme der Frau* 6 (9 March) 1955, p. 5.
19. *Spiegel* 30 (20 July) 1955, pp. 14–15.
20. Frau P., interview.
21. Frau Ge., interview by author, 27 December 1993.
22. Frau T., interview. On the postwar food situation, see also Manfred J. Enssle, 'The Harsh Discipline of Food Scarcity in Postwar Stuttgart, 1945–1948', *German Studies Review* 10 (October 1987): 481–502.
23. *Constanze* 19/1950, p. 7.
24. 'Kartoffeln werden eingekellert', *Ratgeber* September 1952, p. 393; 'Kleine Vorräte können nie schaden', *Ratgeber* April 1962, p. 364.
25. Michael Wildt, *Am Beginn der 'Konsumgesellschaft': Mangelerfahrung, Lebenshaltung, Wohlstandshoffnung in Westdeutschland in den fünfziger Jahren* (Hamburg: Ergebnisse, 1994).
26. Hans J. Teuteberg, 'Nahrungsmittelverzehr in Deutschland pro Kopf und Jahr 1850–1975', *Archiv für Sozialgeschichte* 19 (1979): 348–9; Michael Wildt, 'Das Ende der Bescheidenheit: Wirtschaftsrechnungen von Arbeitnehmerhaushalten in der Bundesrepublik Deutschland 1950–1963', in Klaus Tenfelde, ed., *Arbeiter im 20. Jahrhundert* (Stuttgart: Klett-Cotta, 1991), pp. 589–600. The decline in potato consumption came despite occasional propaganda in *Ratgeber:* 'In these days of demanding, discriminating [consumers], many people are of the opinion that potatoes belong in the basement', January 1965, p. 40; 'Not only the farmers are sorry that potatoes are not eaten as often as they used to be. Scientists also say that increasing the consumption of potatoes again would not only contribute to a proper and inexpensive diet but also help to keep the population healthy', November 1969, p. 1517.
27. 'Küchenzauber mit Orangen', *Ihre Freundin* 11/1950, p. 31; Ullrich Hellmann, 'Ausgerechnet Bananen', in *Oikos*, pp. 353–62. Bananas were much less available in East Germany. They played a certain symbolic role in depictions of East German lust after Western prosperity in the period of German reunification. On overall fruit consumption, see Teuteberg, 'Nahrungsmittelverzehr in Deutschland', p. 348.

Notes

28. 'Scharf auf Paprika?', *Brigitte* 15 (10 July) 1970, p. 132. See also *Ratgeber* April 1958, pp. 292–3 and September 1962, p. 883. *Constanze* in 1951 still took the position that raw peppers were too hot for anyone not used to them and recommended pouring boiling water on the seeded peppers and letting them sit for half an hour. 'Schoten, scharf wie Pfeffer: Paprika', *Constanze* 19 (12 September) 1951, p. 49.

29. Frau P., interview.

30. 'Für Auge und Zunge: Italienische Leckerbissen', *Ihre Freundin* 10/ 1950, pp. 12–13. Later in the year, the magazine sponsored bus trips to Italy. *Ratgeber* April 1961, p. 386 and July 1969, p. 901.

31. Michael Wildt discusses the 'exotic' recipes of the 1950s in *Am Beginn der 'Konsumgesellschaft'*, pp. 214–39. Wildt notes the frequently symbolic character of names of dishes; for instance, 'French' generally meant only that the dish in question contained wine or cognac and possibly garlic, but was presumably intended to evoke the idea of fine cuisine. 'Das ißt man im Süden', *Ihre Freundin* 16 (26 July) 1960, pp. 70–1, and 'Kochen Sie doch mal indonesisch', *Ihre Freundin* 21 (4 October) 1960, pp. 142–3.

32. Helmut W. Jenkis, *Wohnungswirtschaft und Wohnungspolitik in beiden deutschen Staaten* (Hamburg: Hammonia, 1976), pp. 16, 20.

33. Eva, 10 April 1959, in Jantzen and Niehuss, p. 174.

34. Jenkis, pp. 184–5, and Statistisches Bundesamt, *Bevölkerung und Wirtschaft*, p. 185.

35. Wolfgang Glatzer, 'Ziele, Standards und soziale Indikatoren für die Wohnungsversorgung', in Wolfgang Zapf, ed., *Lebensbedingungen in der Bundesrepublik: Sozialer Wandel und Wohlfahrtsentwicklung* (Frankfurt am Main: Campus, 1977), pp. 610–12.

36. Gabriela Lorenz, *Lebensverhältnisse privater Haushalte in Europa: Sechs Länder im Zahlenvergleich* (Frankfurt am Main: Campus, 1991), p. 119. Overall, only 16.7% of West German households were in such old buildings at that time, compared with 24.6% in Great Britain. Frau Ge.'s mid-nineteenth-century house falls into this category; indoor plumbing was added in the 1960s.

37. Ibid., p. 640.

38. Dr S., interview by author, 14 July 1992.

39. Elisabeth Pfeil, *Die Berufstätigkeit von Müttern* (Tübingen: J.C.B. Mohr, 1961), pp. 86–7.

40. Frau S., interview; Frau P., interview.

41. Rosemarie Nave-Herz *et al.*, *Familiäre Veränderungen seit 1950: Eine empirische Studie: Abschlußbericht*, pt. 1 (Oldenburg: Universität Oldenburg, Institut für Soziologie, n.d. [1985]), p. 109.

42. Glatzer, 'Ziele, Standards und soziale Indikatoren', p. 628.
43. 'Das getarnte Schlafzimmer', *Brigitte* 19 (6 September) 1960, pp. 86–91.
44. 'Die Bettcouch', *Ratgeber* April 1954, pp. 152–3, 'Zwei in einem Zimmer', *Stimme der Frau* 25 (30 November) 1955, pp. 8–9, 'Das müde Haupt zu betten . . . Vorschläge für die Einraumwohnung', *Ihre Freundin* 14 (5 July) 1955, p. 38. See also the illustrations in Jungwirth and Kromschröder, *Die Pubertät der Republik,* pp. 154–8. One author tried to look on the bright side – his wealthy friends, he claimed, had happier marriages now that they were no longer able to have separate bedrooms. Paul C. Prager, 'Das gemeinsame Schlafzimmer: Vom Himmelbett zur Doppelcouch', *Ihre Freundin* 3/1950, p. 10.
45. *Ihre Freundin* 22/1950, p. 2.
46. 'Ein Zimmer, zwei Kinder, drei gute Tips', *Für Sie* 11 (19 May) 1970, pp. 156–65, 'Die gute Kinderstube', *Brigitte* 21 (16 September) 1960, pp. 112–13. See also *Constanze* 42 (12 October) 1965, pp. 134–8.
47. 'Wir haben leider kein Bad', *Ratgeber* September 1954, pp. 389–90.
48. *Constanze* 1/1960, p. 24. Other examples include *Ratgeber* March 1952, p. 105 and June 1959, pp. 544–5 and *Constanze* 8 (11 April) 1951, p. 33. In an interview with a Dortmund woman about her furniture, Heike Fischer noted that perfectly usable furniture was thrown out simply from a desire for change. From the perspective of the present day, that seemed unfortunate: 'the often superior quality of the prewar furniture was no longer appreciated'. Heike Fischer, '+". . . und eines Tages guck ich, da hat er's auch zerhackt." Eine Dortmunder Lebens- und Möbelgeschichte', in Museum für Kunst und Kulturgeschichte der Stadt Dortmund, *Arbeiterwohnen: Ideal und Wirklichkeit* (Dortmund, n.d. [1990]), p. 67.
49. *Brigitte* 21 (4 October) 1960, p. 110. See also *Ratgeber* August 1961, pp. 814–16, *Für Sie* 2 (12 January) 1965, pp. 105–113, and *Constanze* 4 (19 January) 1965, p. 47.
50. *Stimme der Frau* 9 (20 April) 1955, p. 32.
51. Braun ad in *Constanze* 20 (21 September) 1955, p. 139. The *Abitur* is the examination which is required for university study, like the British A-levels or the French *baccalauréat*. At this time, the number of women with this educational qualification was quite small.
52. 'Kleine Möbel – große Wirkung', *Stimme der Frau* 6 (9 March) 1955, pp. 12–13; *Constanze* 13/1950, p. 47; WKS ad, *Constanze* 23/1953,

p. 91, Hülsta furniture ad, *Constanze* 29 (14 July) 1969, p. 7, rug ad, *Ratgeber* October 1961, p. 1101.

53. 'Raum und Möbel . . . In's rechte Licht gerückt', *Stimme der Frau* 2 (12 January) 1955, pp. 12–13.

54. The modern design movement was traditionally associated with the political left, however limited its success in interesting the actually existing working class in its products. It gained a certain political legitimacy in the postwar period from the Nazis' objections to it (as indicated by, for instance, the closure of the Bauhaus). One of the founders of the Hochschule für Gestaltung in Ulm was Inge Aicher-Scholl, the surviving sister of Hans and Sophie Scholl of the Weiße Rose resistance group. See Walter Dirks, 'Das Bauhaus und die Weiße Rose: Über die neueste deutsche Hochschule', *Frankfurter Hefte* 11 (November 1955): 769–73.

55. 'Welche Möbelformen werden heute bevorzugt?', *Ihre Freundin* 22 (18 October) 1960, p. 83. The study was conducted by furniture stores for the Arbeitskreis Deutsche Stilmöbel.

56. Alphons Silbermann, *Vom Wohnen der Deutschen* (Cologne: Westdeutscher Verlag, 1963), pp. 68–9.

57. *Constanze* special issue *Schöner Wohnen* (1955), p. 60.

58. For example, 'Stilmöbel schaffen so viel Behaglichkeit', *Für Sie* 22 (19 October) 1965, pp. 218–22, and 'Neue Möbel im alten Stil', *Brigitte* 5 (23 February) 1960, pp. 62–3.

59. *Constanze* 17 (10 August) 1955, pp. 86–7; the article described a house built in Sweden by an English architect for a wealthy client. See also 'Das getarnte Schlafzimmer', *Brigitte* 19 (6 September) 1960, p. 86.

60. *Brigitte* 23 (1 November) 1960, p. 130.

61. Anna Quehl, 'Stoßseufzer einer unmodernen Frau', *Sie: Die Berliner illustrierte Wochenzeitung* (hereafter *Sie*), 5 November 1950, p. 2.

62. Hans Paul Bahrdt, 'Zwischen Bergmannskotten und Siedlungshaus: Wie Bergleute wohnen, wohnen wollen und wohnen sollen', *Frankfurter Hefte* 7 (September 1952): 683–4.

63. 'Die LDM stellt aus', in *Die Innenarchitektur* 1 no. 5 (1954): 35. On the need for educating consumers, see also Dirks, 'Das Bauhaus und die Weiße Rose', *Frankfurter Hefte* 11 (November 1955): 773.

64. Heike Fischer, pp. 62–7.

65. There was some disagreement about the proper number of *f*s and *t*s.

66. Dr Martha Bode-Schrandt, 'Denken und Planen im Haushalt', *Ihre Freundin* 22/1950, p. 4.

67. Hans-Joachim Friedrich, *Wohnkunde* (Berlin: Ernst Staneck Verlag, 1967), p. 163.

68. Elisabeth Pfeil, ed., *Die Wohnwünsche der Bergarbeiter: Soziologische Erhebung, Deutung und Kritik der Wohnvorstellungen eines Berufes* (Tübingen: J.C.B. Mohr [Paul Siebeck], 1954), p. 81.
69. 'Wir essen in der Küche', *Für Sie* 9 (20 April) 1960, pp. 116–19. See also Simone Hall, 'Soll man in der Küche essen?', *Sie*, 5 November 1950, p. 4.
70. See for example the refrigerator ads in *Constanze*, 17 April 1957, pp. 98–9 and *Ihre Freundin* 7 (21 March) 1961, p. 45, the washing-machine ad in *Brigitte* 2 (13 January) 1970, p. 81, and the dishwasher ad in *Constanze* 16 (6 April)1965, p. 4.
71. See for instance 'Das große 1x1 des richtigen Kühlens', *Für Sie* 16 (27 July) 1960, pp. 40–1.
72. *Für Sie* 9 (21 April) 1970, p. 159.
73. Later, wood veneers would become popular as fashions turned back to nature. Nowadays, the biodegradability of cleaning products is advertised at least as much as their effectiveness.
74. *Für Sie* 9 (21 April) 1970, p. 208.
75. In the US, the figures for both were around 50% at this time. Hans Vogt, *Die Gerätesättigung im Haushalt* (Berlin, 1940), p. 11, cited in Wildt, 'Technik, Kompetenz, Modernität', p. 84.
76. Eva Wagner, *Technik für Frauen: Arbeitszusammenhang, Alltagserfahrungen und Perspektiven der Hausfrauen im Umgang mit technischen Artefakten* (Munich: Profil, 1991), p. 131; Fischer, *Geschichte der Stromversorgung*, pp. 142–3.
77. Ullrich Hellmann, 'Der Keller in der Küche', in Sibylle Meyer and Eva Schulze, eds, *Technisiertes Familienleben: Blick zurück und nach vorn* (Berlin: Edition Sigma, 1993), p. 47.
78. Sibylle Meyer and Eva Schulze, *Von Liebe sprach damals keiner: Familienalltag in der Nachkriegszeit*, (Munich: C.H. Beck, 1985), p. 174.
79. *Ihre Freundin* 22/1950, p. 19.
80. Cited in Silberzahn-Jandt, pp. 20–1. The assumption, clearly, is that laundry is (a) physically strenuous and (b) women's work.
81. See Jungwirth and Kromschröder, pp. 164–7. Motor cycles were also popular.
82. 'Kühl auch ohne Eis', *Ratgeber* August 1952, p. 358; *Ratgeber* May 1952, p. 211; 'Frisch – auch ohne Kühlschrank', *Ratgeber* April 1963, p. 365; *Constanze* 15 (13 July) 1955, p. 79; compare with Cornelia Kopp, *Richtig haushalten: Grundregeln durchdachter Hausarbeit* (Leipzig: Otto Beyer, 1933), p. 54.
83. 'Gekochter Kuchen', *Ihre Freundin* 5/1950, p. 25.

84. Scharpf spin-drier, *Stimme der Frau* 19 (7 September) 1955, p. 25 and 16 (27 July) 1955, p. 39; AEG washer (unheated DM 60 less, without wringer DM 70 less), *Stimme der Frau* 8 (6 April) 1955, p. 8; Zanker Waschbüfett, *Ratgeber* October 1956, p. 649.

85. Frau P., interview. This is probably the same type of device as that shown in Silberzahn-Jandt, pp. 54–5.

86. Letter from Ursula R., *Stimme der Frau* 13/1951, p. 16. This issue of *Stimme der Frau* includes ads for both the Bosch device and a competitor, the Pulsette. See also Orland, *Wäsche waschen*, p. 245.

87. *Constanze* 4/1950, p. 48.

88. AEG water-heater ad, *Stimme der Frau* 19 (7 September) 1955, p. 13; spin-drier ad, *Ihre Freundin* 21 (9 October) 1956, p. 28; *Badische Zeitung* 14/15 May 1960, p. 15.

89. *Ihre Freundin* 6 (15 March)1955, p. 54.

90. Frau Ge., interview. She had a son born in 1945 and a daughter born in 1947.

91. 'Die Bettwäsche ist reparaturbedürftig', *Ratgeber* November 1958, pp. 972–3.

92. 'Keine Angst vor dem Flickkorb!', *Ratgeber* January 1965, pp. 66–9; March 1965, pp. 300–1, 308–9, 312; May 1965, pp. 552–7; June 1965, pp. 648–9, 656–7.

93. 'Bettwäsche kann man auch selbst nähen', *Ratgeber* October 1967, pp. 1204–7, November 1967, pp. 1324–5, December 1967, pp. 1468–71. The series continued through at least the January 1968 issue.

94. Advertisement, *Ratgeber* October 1955, p. 651.

95. Anton Kloss, 'Gar keine Frage: Eine Nähmaschine gehört ins Haus', *Ihre Freundin* 22/1950, p. 20; *Ihre Freundin* 5 (7 March)1951, p. 19; Frau P., interview.

96. Saba ad, *Stimme der Frau* 9 (20 April) 1955, p. 25. Other ads emphasizing economic reasons for purchasing refrigerators include *Ihre Freundin* 20 (3 October)1951, p. 13 and AEG ad, *Constanze* 14 (29 June) 1955, p. 40.

97. 'Jede 10. Mark auf Konto Verderb', *Ratgeber* July 1957, p. 458.

98. 'Der moderne Haushaltskühlschrank', in *Badische Zeitung* supplement *Motor und Maschine*, 28 May 1957. The German expression is '*dienstbare Geister*', ministering spirits, an expression for domestic servants. This article indicated that 34% of the 1.3 million households with some cold-storage equipment still used iceboxes.

99. Bosch ad, *Ihre Freundin* 24 (22 November)1955, p. 33; Hellmann, *Künstliche Kälte*, p. 240.

100. StJ 1956, p. 477.
101. AEG ad, *Ratgeber* June 1969, p. 777; Bauknecht ad, *Constanze* 9 (20 April) 1955, p. 38. The prices listed in the latter ad are: 60 l, DM 385; 80 l, DM 475; 115 l, DM 598; 140 l, DM 750; 160 l, DM 860. In 1959, Bauknecht offered a 190-litre refrigerator for DM 711; in 1961, a tabletop model with 140-litre capacity was available for DM 456, for DM 464 with automatic defrosting. A 155-litre model cost DM 518. Bauknecht ads, *Ratgeber* June 1959, p. 563 and May 1961, p. 575.
102. *Ratgeber* May 1958, p. 379 and May 1969, pp. 609, 687. A BBC automatic washing-machine was available for DM 1090 (*Constanze* 43 (20 October) 1969, p. 35). VW ad, *Ratgeber* September 1969, p. 1169.
103. 'Rabatt-Dämmerung', *Spiegel* 10 (6 March) 1963, pp. 68–71; see also *Ihre Freundin* 4 (7 February) 1961, p. 73.
104. Wagner, *Technik für Frauen*, pp. 136–8.
105. *Ihre Freundin* 4 (7 February) 1961, p. 73.
106. Bruno Tietz, *Konsument und Einzelhandel: Strukturwandlungen in der Bundesrepublik Deutschland von 1960 bis 1985*, 2nd edn, (Frankfurt am Main: Lorch-Verlag, 1973), vol. 1, p. 817. Quelle's particular success with sewing-machines and freezers is probably related to the popularity of these items with rural households.
107. This took place in 1953 or 1954. The machine was a very simple model, which did not heat its own water, but Frau K. found it useful and used it for ten years before getting a more modern one. Frau K., interview by author, 6 December 1993.
108. *Ratgeber* September 1961, pp. 970–1. The washing-machine was of the 'buffet' type with a spin-drier next to the washing compartment.
109. Frau T., interview. The refrigerator cost DM 300 and lasted 27 years – when their furniture was in storage for nine months it got mildew inside and she couldn't get rid of the odour and had to discard it, but it was still functional.
110. *Einkaufsgewohnheiten in Baden-Württemberg*, vol. 1 (Stuttgart: Südwestdeutscher Einzelhandelsverband e.V., 1960), p. 62; Wildt, *Am Beginn der 'Konsumgesellschaft'*, p. 147.
111. See Thomas Fuchs, '"Einst ein mühsam Walten, jetzt ein schnelles Schalten,"' in Andritzky, ed., *Oikos*, pp. 124–132
112. 2nd Bundestag, 89th sess., 21 June 1955, *Stenographische Berichte* (hereafter StB), vol. 25, p. 5044. The topic at issue was the Family Ministry's budget; Ilk was expressing the view that the ministry was not of much practical use.

113. *Spiegel* 41 (5 October)1955, p. 5; Orland, *Wäsche waschen*, pp. 237–8.

114. *Ihre Freundin* 5 (26 February) 1957, p. 105.

115. Klaus Herbert Schuberth, *Konsumentenkredit und wirtschaftliche Entwicklung: Der Einfluß der Kreditfinanzierung des privaten Konsums auf die Struktur der Volkswirtschaft* (Spardorf: René F. Wilfer, 1988), pp. 18–28. As of the early 1990s, credit cards were still relatively little used in Germany, primarily for travel and entertainment expenses (at the upper end of the market – small, inexpensive restaurants and hotels still tended not to accept them) rather than for purchases of consumer goods.

116. Robert Menge, 'Einzelhandel als Träger des Teilzahlungskredits', *Handbuch der Teilzahlungswirtschaft*, pp. 79–81.

117. Robert Menge, 'Der Kundenkredit des Einzelhandels im Jahre 1963', *Die Teilzahlungswirtschaft* 12 (March 1965), p. 52.

118. Wildt, *Am Beginn der 'Konsumgesellschaft'*, p. 148.

119. *Einkaufsgewohnheiten in Baden-Württemberg*, vol. I, pp. 60–1.

120. *Ratgeber* July 1958, p. 563; *Spiegel* 1/1955 (29 December 1954), p. 15. The advertisement suggested that the rebate might be used to buy a Westinghouse electric iron.

121. *Ratgeber* December 1957, p. 923 and January 1958, p. 45. An advertisement from May 1958 (p. 379) announced the reduction of the price of the machine from DM 1780 to DM 1580.

122. Based on an examination of advertisements in the April and October issues of *Constanze* in odd-numbered years. The pattern in *Ratgeber* is similar, though the number of advertisements which mention credit is much smaller. Advertisements in *Der Spiegel* tended not to mention the possibility of credit.

123. Nave-Herz *et al.*, *Familiäre Veränderungen seit 1950*, p. 113.

124. Freidank, pp. 123–33.

125. 'Natürlich werden wir jetzt heiraten!', *Stimme der Frau* 5/1951, pp. 8–9.

126. Frau Ge.'s mother started buying her sheets when she was fifteen – a good thing, as it turned out, since at the time she did marry (1944) such things were unavailable. Frau Ge., interview.

127. 'Junge Ehe – gut ausgesteuert', *Constanze* 27 (30 June) 1969, p. 52.

128. Frau P., interview; Oberlandesgericht Frankfurt, 9 July 1964, cited in Hellmann, 'Der Keller in der Küche', p. 48.

129. Statistisches Bundesamt, *Fachserie M, Reihe 18, 1969*, pp. 74–6, 148–9.

130. See Schuberth, p. 74. This type of credit accounted for only part of the total consumer credit, but it is the type for which the most reliable statistics are available. See also Günter Hobbensiefken, 'Statistik der Teilzahlungsfinanzierung', in Wirtschaftsverband Teilzahlungsbanken e.V., *Handbuch der Teilzahlungswirtschaft* (Frankfurt am Main: Fritz Knapp, 1959), pp. 257–96.
131. *Faust*, part 2, act 1, lines 4873–5 (translation by Miss Swanwick (New York: Thomas Y. Crowell, 1882)), quoted in Wilhelm Röpke, *Vorgegessen Brot: Kritische Nachlese zur Diskussion über das Borgkaufwesen* (Cologne: Carl Heymanns Verlag, 1955), p. 7. Karl Ockel used the same quotation in his 1961 dissertation which, however, took a more positive view of consumer credit. 'Zur volkswirtschaftlichen Problematik des Teilzahlungskredites: Eine vergleichende Untersuchung der Verhältnisse in den USA und der BRD unter besondere Berücksichtigung der Möglichkeiten einer Einflußnahme auf das Teilzahlungskreditgeschäft' (diss., Frankfurt am Main, 1961).
132. See George Katona, Burkhard Strumpel and Ernest Zahn, *Aspirations and Affluence: Comparative Studies in the United States and Western Europe* (New York: McGraw-Hill, 1971), pp. 94–9.
133. 'Nur ein Drittel Anzahlung', *Ratgeber* July 1953, p. 293.
134. 'Für die, die in der Kreide sitzen', *Ratgeber* September 1954, pp. 385–6.
135. According to a 1955 survey, 70% of West Germans ate meat three times a week, 27% daily. Michael Wildt, 'Plurality of Taste: Food and Consumption in West Germany during the 1950s', *History Workshop Journal* 39 (spring 1995): 29.
136. See for example Curt Bley, *Tatsachen über Kredit und Kreditmißbrauch* (Cologne: Carl Heymanns Verlag, 1954), pp. 16–20, and 'Weihnachts-Raten im April', *Spiegel* 10 (2 March) 1955, p. 19.
137. Bundestag, Representative Schmitt (SPD), written statement in support of the reform of the law regulating payment by instalment, appended to StB, 2nd Bundestag, 14th sess., 11 Feb. 1954, p. 469. All attempts to reform the law in the 1950s were unsuccessful; a new law took effect in 1969.
138. Günter Schmölders with G. Scherhorn and G. Schmidtchen, *Der Umgang mit Geld im privaten Haushalt* (Berlin: Duncker & Humblot, 1969), pp. 132–6.
139. *Ihre Freundin* 8 (12 April) 1955, p. 11.
140. Walter Dirks, 'Der Neid auf den Kühlschrank', *Frankfurter Hefte* 10 (April 1955), pp. 285–6.

141. Sigrid-Esther Mayer, 'Die Hauptursachen der tendenziellen Gestaltung der deutschen Lebenshaltung in der Nachkriegszeit (ab 1950)' (diss., Göttingen, 1960), p. 68.

142. *Sonntagsblatt*, 29 January 1956, in *Ludwig Erhard: Gedanken aus fünf Jahrzehnten: Reden und Schriften,* edited by Karl Hohmann (Düsseldorf: Econ-Verlag, 1988), p. 467.

143. 'Wir haben keine Zeit für uns!', *Brigitte* 2/1956, pp. 3–5.

144. StJ 1963, 53 and 1971, 46. In the US, the median age at first marriage for women was between 20 and 21 throughout the period 1950–70 (for grooms, it was about 23) (*Statistical Abstract of the United States* (Washington: Government Printing Office, 1971), p. 60).

145. Hagena, p. 20.

146. Ibid., p. 21.

147. Around 36%, compared with 33.7% in 1907. Calculated from Statistisches Bundesamt, *Bevölkerung und Wirtschaft,* p. 140. See also Gerd Hardach, *Deutschland in der Weltwirtschaft 1870–1970* (Frankfurt am Main: Campus, 1977), pp. 17–18.

148. Willms, p. 35.

149. Statistisches Bundesamt, *Bevölkerung und Wirtschaft*, p. 145.

150. Elisabeth Noelle and Erich Peter Neumann, eds, *The Germans: Public Opinion Polls, 1947–1966* (Allensbach: Verlag für Demoskopie, 1967), p. 358.

151. StJ 1971, 48.

152. Frevert, p. 270.

153. Peter Marschalck, 'Demographische Anmerkungen zur Rolle der Flüchtlinge und Vertriebenen in der westdeutschen Nachkriegsgeschichte', in Schulze *et al.*, eds, *Flüchtlinge und Vertriebene,* p. 166.

154. Duchen, p. 97.

155. W. Hubbard, *Familiengeschichte: Materialien zur deutschen Familie seit dem Ende des 18. Jahrhunderts* (Munich, 1983), p. 101, cited in Frevert, p. 284, n. 55.

156. StJ 1966, p. 45 and 1971, p. 128.

157. Frau K., interview.

158. Frau Ga., Frau Ma. and Frau T. all reported that their husbands wanted them to stay at home.

159. Walther von Hollander, 'Schade, der Haushalt ist doch heilig', *Constanze* 17 (20 April) 1965, p. 7, responding to reactions to his article, 'Ist der Haushalt heilig?' in issue 2 (5 January). Hollander referred to women whose children were '*aus dem Gröbsten heraus*', out of the worst of it.

160. Frau Ma., interview by author, 6 December 1993.
161. 'Francine', 'Ich langweile mich zu Hause!', *Ihre Freundin* 5 (25 February) 1958, p. 15.
162. One example of this attitude, which also cropped up in articles on marriage, is an advertisement for Camelia disposable nappies, which presented the mother as protecting the father from sleepless nights through her knowledge of modern baby care – i.e. disposable nappies. *Ihre Freundin* 2 (11 January) 1960, p. 45.
163. 'Ein ernstes Problem: "Schlüsselkinder" sind immer im Nachteil', *Ratgeber* November 1958, pp. 885–7. 'Asocial' is a rather loosely defined expression for the delinquent and disobedient which was popular in the Third Reich. On *Ratgeber*'s criticism of women working outside the home in pursuit of an excessive standard of living, see also 'Ein ernstes Wort: Berufstätige Hausfrau – ist es nötig?', *Ratgeber* March 1954, pp. 97–9. See also H[ubert] H[abicht], 'Der Alltag der Kinder', *Frankfurter Hefte* 11 (January 1956), p. 48 and Otto Speck, *Kinder erwerbstätiger Mütter* (Stuttgart: Ferdinand Enke, 1956).
164. 'Beruf und Ehe: Wie verträgt sich das?', *Brigitte* 17 (17 August) 1965, pp. 100–3.
165. Frau K., interview ; Frau Ma., interview.
166. *Ratgeber* November 1958, p. 948. The same issue contained an article on latchkey children in West Germany: 'Ein ernstes Problem: "Schlüsselkinder" sind immer im Nachteil', pp. 885–7. See also Klaus-Jörg Ruhl, 'Familie und Beruf: Weibliche Erwerbstätigkeit und katholische Kirche in den 50er Jahren', *Aus Politik und Zeitgeschichte* 93 (23 April 1993): 30–8. On the youth culture of the late 1950s, see Kaspar Maase, *BRAVO Amerika: Erkundungen zur Jugendkultur der Bundesrepublik in den fünfziger Jahren* (Hamburg: Junius, 1992).
167. Hermann Schubnell, 'Die Erwerbstätigkeit von Frauen und Müttern und die Betreuung ihrer Kinder', *Wirtschaft und Statistik* 8 (August) 1964, p. 454, p. 459*. Virtually all of the children under two were cared for by individuals. This 1961 study included mothers of children under fourteen who were employed outside the agricultural sector.
168. Pfeil, *Berufstätigkeit von Müttern*, p. 337. Pfeil's study is much less tendentious than that of Otto Speck. An article in *Für Sie* painted a much more positive view of day care, while still taking the position that the 'ideal case' was for mothers to be with their children full time. 'Müssen "Schlüsselkinder" sein?', *Für Sie* 22 (19 October) 1960, pp. 32–9.

169. Alfred Horné, 'Frauen in Fabrik und Büro', *Frankfurter Hefte* 11 (November 1955), p. 813.

170. 'Die Betreuung der Kinder erwerbstätiger und nichterwerbstätiger Mütter: Ergebnis der Mikrozensus-Zusatzbefragung 1969', *Wirtschaft und Statistik* 3 (March) 1971, p. 162.

171. 'Frauen-Mosaik', *Ihre Freundin* 23 (1 November) 1960, p. 88. See also Robert G. Moeller, *Protecting Motherhood: Women and the Family in the Politics of Postwar West Germany* (Berkeley and Los Angeles: University of California Press, 1993), pp. 175–6.

172. Dr S., interview.

173. Pfeil, *Berufstätigkeit von Müttern,* p. 181. The study does not distinguish educational levels beyond the *Abitur.*

174. Walter Müller, 'Frauenerwerbstätigkeit im Lebenslauf', in Müller, Willms and Handl, *Strukturwandel der Frauenarbeit,* p. 77; categorized by husband's educational level.

175. On women's employment, see Müller, Willms and Handl, *Strukturwandel der Frauenarbeit.*

176. Frau Pr., interview by author, 6 December 1993.

177. StJ 1972, p. 125.

178. Frau P., interview.

179. Dr S., interview.

180. Pfeil, *Berufstätigkeit von Müttern,* pp. 192–8, 200–7.

181. Frau Ma., interview.

182. Erica Carter, *How German is She? Postwar West German Reconstruction and the Consuming Woman* (Ann Arbor: University of Michigan Press, 1997).

183. Schmölders *et al.* In her study of working-class Englishwomen, Elizabeth Roberts notes that women lost their traditional control of the family finances when their husbands began to be paid by cheque, deposited either in joint accounts or in accounts in the husband's name, rather than in cash, which they turned over to their wives. Elizabeth Roberts, *Women and Families: An Oral History, 1940– 1970* (Oxford: Blackwell, 1995), pp. 91–2.

184. *Für Sie* 16 (27 July) 1960, p. 15. On the subject of men's concealing important financial matters from their wives see also Sonja Pape, 'Warum das Haushaltsgeld nicht reicht', *Für Sie* 9 (21 April) 1970, pp. 83–9.

185. 'Wieviel Taschengeld braucht eine Ehefrau?', *Brigitte* 14 (26 June) 1970, pp. 108–15. On allowances for housewives, see also 'Taschengeld für die Ehefrau', *Ihre Freundin* 9 (26 April) 1955, pp. 3, 48.

186. See for instance 'Das knappe Haushaltsgeld', *Ratgeber* March 1952,

pp. 97–8 and 'Leser-Forum: Warum das Haushaltsgeld nicht reicht', *Für Sie* 13 (12 June) 1970, pp. 104–8.
187. *Constanze* 23 (1 June) 1965, p. 143.
188. *Constanze* 21 (5 October) 1955, pp. 48–9.
189. 'Fleischgerichte, die nicht zu teuer sind', *Ratgeber* March 1954, p. 109.
190. 'Krise am Kochtopf', *Spiegel* 30 (17 July) 1967, pp. 55–6.
191. Noelle and Neumann, p. 152. 'Good looks' was chosen by 38%, 'intelligence' by 29%. Women valued 'faithfulness' (71%) and 'diligence' (63%) in men; 'intelligence' was listed by 46% and 'good appearance' by 20%.
192. Frau M., interview by author, 21 July 1992.
193. Lilo Aureden, 'Zur Diskussion gestellt: Mein Mann verdient nicht genug!', *Ihre Freundin* 8 (12 May) 1955, pp. 22–3, 40.
194. Letter from Annemarie A., *Ihre Freundin* 12 (7 July) 1955, p. 2.
195. See for example *Ihre Freundin* 9 (18 April) 1961, pp. 66–8 and 10 (2 May) 1961, pp. 100–1.
196. 'Ist das Leben wirklich so teuer?', *Ratgeber* January 1956, pp. 6–9.
197. 'Sind 600 DM nur 280?', *Stimme der Frau* 25 (30 November) 1955, p. 39.
198. Dr Reischl (SPD), speaking for the SPD's proposed reform of the law on payment by instalments, 5th Bundestag, 143rd sess., 13 Dec. 1967, StB, p. 7428.
199. 'Wenn die Wünsche davonlaufen', *Ratgeber* April 1959, p. 291; *Ihre Freundin* 1 (1 January) 1957, p. 2. The particular reference to *Koteletts* and cauliflower is not in the article this writer is responding to, so she must have it from some other source.
200. 'Claudia', 'Sündenbock Hausfrau', *Ihre Freundin* 22 (23 October) 1956, pp. 54–6.
201. Wildt, *Am Beginn der 'Konsumgesellschaft'*, p. 236. Wildt adds, 'Husbands appear in the other interviews as well as advocates of the good, comfortable life, who strain the household budget with the statement that [the family] could afford to eat better now.'
202. Katja Koelle, 'Endstation Supermarkt?', *Ihre Freundin* 2 (10 January) 1961, pp. 22–4; *Ihre Freundin* 4 (7 February) 1961, p. 46.
203. For a discussion of self-service shops, see Wildt, *Am Beginn der 'Konsumgesellschaft'*, pp. 176–211.
204. 'Selbstbedienung ist verführerisch: Neue Probleme beim täglichen Einkauf', *Ratgeber* February 1965, pp. 104–6; 'Selbstbedienung verführt Jugendliche', *Ratgeber* September 1961, pp. 888–9.
205. Wildt, *Am Beginn der 'Konsumgesellschaft'*, p. 179.

206. On the role of doctors and other experts in the campaign against married women's work, see Ruhl.

207. Grete Boruttau, *Das bürgerliche Kochbuch* (Marbach/Neckar: Süd-West Verlags- und Vertriebs-GmbH, n.d. [1958]), p. 41.

208. *Ratgeber* July 1954, p. 322. See also *Ihre Freundin* 3/1950, pp. 24–6 and *Ratgeber* July 1961, p. 766.

209. Heinz Schröter, 'Rückblick auf ein Jahrzehnt: Die tollen fünfziger Jahre', *Ihre Freundin* 1/1960 (28 December 1959), pp. 8–15. For an example of the depiction of the 'Freßwelle' in the 1950s-nostalgia literature, see Jungwirth and Kromschröder, pp. 120–7.

210. *Ratgeber* July 1962, p. 655; 'Wenn die Wünsche davonlaufen', *Ratgeber* April 1959, p. 291.

211. *Ratgeber* June 1954, p. 243 and April 1959, p. 291; *Ratgeber* August 1958, p. 603; 'Nachrichten für die Frau', May 1961, p. 477, and July 1961, p. 713. The latter notice blamed an increase on the number of premature births in the USA on high employment rates for married women there. On health dangers from women's overwork, see also Alfred Horné, 'Frauen in Fabrik und Büro', *Frankfurter Hefte* 11 (November 1955), pp. 812–13.

212. Heinz-Dietrich Ortlieb, 'Unsere Konsumgesellschaft: Glanz und Elend des deutschen Wirtschaftswunders', in Ortlieb, ed., *Hamburger Jahrbuch für Wirtschafts- und Gesellschaftspolitik, Festausgabe für Eduard Heimann zum 70. Geburtstage* (Tübingen: J.C.B. Mohr [Paul Siebeck], 1959), p. 240.

213. 'Keine Zeit für Liebe?', *Brigitte* 13 (6 June) 1956, pp. 3–5. The term 'Zusammenbruch' was a popular euphemism for the defeat and extensive destruction of Germany in the Second World War, making it seem like an unfortunate accident.

214. 'Die Gefangenschaft der Karriere', *Ratgeber* July 1962, pp. 652–3. The wife envied the neighbours, one of whom had a fur coat, another a washing-machine. In a reflective article looking back at the year 1957, *Ratgeber* also warned of the possible health consequences of the 'frantic chase after the notorious "standard of living"'. '1957: Jahresrückblick für die Frau', *Ratgeber* December 1957, p. 871. A 1950 article in the Berlin magazine *Sie* criticized American wives for working their husbands to death: 'she has the habit of pushing him to ever higher earnings, so that she can keep up with the "Johnsons", the legendary neighbours ... Most of the wealth in America is controlled by women, inherited from the men who earned it.' Gerte Noetzel, 'Es gibt drei Arten von Frauen ...', *Sie* 14 (2 April) 1950.

215. *Spiegel* 6 (2 February) 1955, pp. 35–6. RM stands for *Reichsmark*, the currency in use before the postwar currency reform. The article quotes Max Grundig as describing his firm's 43-cm TV, which sold for DM 698, as the 'new *Volksempfänger*'. Sibylle Meyer and Eva Schulze, 'Fernseher contra Waschmaschine – Wie Familienstrukturen auf Technik wirken', in Gert Wagner, Notburga Ott and Hans-Joachim Nowotny, eds, *Familienbildung und Erwerbstätigkeit im demographischen Wandel* (Berlin: Springer, 1989), p. 261.

216. 'Fernsehen pro und contra', *Ratgeber* November 1954, p. 488.

217. 'Problemkinder: Fernsehen macht dumm', *Spiegel* 15 (13 April) 1950, pp. 38–9. A 1952 item in the same magazine reported that, in one week, 167 murders, 112 suicides and 356 attempted murders were committed in television programmes, two-thirds of them in children's programmes. *Spiegel* 27 (2 July) 1952, 'Hohlspiegel', p. 2. The first television stations in West Germany, their range limited to a few small areas in the north-west, began regular broadcasts on 25 December 1952.

218. 'Ein Problem: Kinder vor dem Bildschirm', *Ratgeber* June 1961, pp. 592–3. See also 'Eine Warnung an alle Eltern: Vorsicht, unsere Kinder werden fernsehkrank!', *Für Sie* 12 (1 June) 1960, pp. 18–21.

219. 'Frauen und Rundfunk', *Ratgeber* October 1958, p. 774. See also *Ratgeber* January 1953, p. 6.

220. 'Die Gefährdung des jungen Menschen durch den Film', *Ratgeber* June 1956, pp. 349–50.

221. 'Fernsehen pro und contra', *Ratgeber* November 1954, p. 489.

222. *Ratgeber* November 1958, p. 923.

223. Ad for Adler Käse-Creme, *Ratgeber* April 1958, p. 255. Another advertisement from the same campaign featured the principal chef at Lufthansa. *Ratgeber* October 1958, p. 777.

224. *Stimme der Frau* 13/1951, p. 6.

Chapter 4 Men, Women and Machines

1. The guarantee of equal rights is Article 3, Paragraph 2; the protection of the family is Article 6. For a discussion of Selbert's efforts see Moeller, *Protecting Motherhood,* pp. 50–61.

2. This provision is contained in Article 117, Paragraph 1.

3. On legislation affecting women's position in West Germany in the 1950s see Moeller, *Protecting Motherhood*, Angela Delille and Andrea Grohn, *Blick zurück aufs Glück: Frauenleben und Familienpolitik in den 50er Jahren* (Berlin: Elefanten Press, 1985), esp. pp. 138–41, and Georg Thielmann, 'Die Entwicklung des Familienrechts im Bundesgebiet mit Berlin (West) seit 1949', in *Das Familienrecht in beiden deutschen Staaten: Rechtsentwicklung, Rechtsvergleich, Kollisionsprobleme* (Cologne: Carl Heymanns Verlag, 1983), pp. 13–40.

4. Duchen, p. 98.

5. In 'Kurzmeldungen für die Frau', *Ratgeber* December 1952, p. 537.

6. Paragraph 1356 of the Civil Code. In keeping with the decision that the husband did not have final say in questions relating to the marriage, the wife's conduct of the household was stated to be 'in eigener Verantwortung', not subject to the husband's control.

7. This had previously existed under Paragraph 1358.

8. Paragraph 1360 a. A reform of marriage law in 1976 (effective 1 July 1977) introduced gender-neutral language and left the division of responsibilities up to the couple themselves.

9. See Angela Seeler, 'Ehe, Familie und andere Lebensformen in den Nachkriegsjahren im Spiegel der Frauenzeitschriften', in Anna-Elisabeth Freier and Annette Kuhn, eds, *Frauen in der Geschichte V: 'Das Schicksal Deutschlands liegt in der Hand seiner Frauen':* *Frauen in der deutschen Nachkriegsgeschichte* (Düsseldorf: Schwann, 1984), pp. 90–121, and Lott, *Frauenzeitschriften*, pp. 624–5.

10. *Constanze,* 8 April 1953, p. 3.

11. 'Vier Fälle, vier Schicksale: Die Röntgenärztin hat Sprechstunde', *Ihre Freundin* 1/1950, pp. 6–8.

12. *Constanze*, 25 March 1953, pp. 72–3.

13. 'Welchen Beruf soll unsere Tochter wählen?', *Ratgeber* March 1956, p. 149. The emphasis on 'women's jobs' in the magazines was only a pale reflection of the actual sex segregation of apprenticeships.

14. Bosch ad, *Ihre Freundin* 12 (4 June) 1957, p. 45.

15. 'Im Büro ein Star – am Herd eine Niete', *Constanze* 3 (2 February) 1960, pp. 2–7.

16. Langer-El Sayed, p. 60.

17. *Stimme der Frau* 16 (27 July) 1955, p. 26.

18. Richard Tom, 'Ich finde keinen Mann ...', *Für Sie* 1/1965 (29 December 1964), pp. 40–3.

19. Stefan Moves, 'Frauen in Israel', *Ihre Freundin* 9 (18 April) 1961,

p. 10. Men, on the other hand, were often referred to, with varying degrees of irony, as 'the lords of creation'.

20. 'Gleichberechtigung?', *Brigitte* 26 (11 December) 1970, p. 69.
21. Susanne von Paczensky, 'Wo fehlt es heute denn noch?', *Für Sie* 9 (21 April) 1970, pp. 114–24.
22. *Constanze* 50 (1 December) 1969, p. 6.
23. Dieter Bochow, 'Das Tischgespräch mit Dr Ursula Krips', *Constanze* 16 (14 April) 1969, pp. 102ff.
24. Frau K., interview.
25. Frau Ge., interview. She lived with her parents in a single household and before her father's retirement did most of the shopping herself.
26. Frau Ma., interview. The word *Hausmann* also came up in the interview with Frau K., and also in reference to a man participating in housework but at a level far removed from that of a *Hausfrau*: she described her son as a *Hausmann* because he watched the children when her daughter-in-law was away.
27. Frau Ga., interview by author, 6 December 1993.
28. 'Für die Männerwelt', *Ratgeber* October 1958, p. 788.
29. *Constanze* 25 (6 December) 1960, pp. 3–7; see also Irmgard Keun, 'Männer haben es viel besser', *Für Sie* 3 (26 January) 1965, p. 51. Keun stated that, while it was not degrading to her to clean her husband's shoes, she didn't see why he shouldn't make the bed occasionally – provided that they both needed to work to earn money.
30. 'Von wegen: Ist das Männerarbeit?', *Ratgeber* September 1956, pp. 552–3.
31. See for example Kurt Kuberzig, 'So erzieht man Junggesellen', *Stimme der Frau* 15 (13 July) 1955, pp. 8–9.
32. 'Sollen Männer im Haushalt helfen?', *Brigitte* 5 (24 February) 1970, pp. 164–5.
33. Christel Eckart, Ursula Jaerisch and Helgard Kramer, *Frauenarbeit in Familie und Fabrik: Eine Untersuchung von Bedingungen und Barrieren der Interessenwahrnehmung von Industriearbeiterinnen* (Frankfurt am Main: Campus, 1979), p. 211.
34. 'Hauswirtschaftsunterricht in den großen Ferien', *Ratgeber* July 1952, pp. 326–7.
35. Elisabeth Lippert, *Hauswirtschaftliche Bildung in der Bundesrepublik Deutschland* (Bonn: Bundesministerium für Wirtschaft, 1966). Lippert stressed the important role still played in home economics training by nineteenth-century notions of womanliness.
36. 'Ein freudiges Ereignis steht bevor', *Ratgeber* May 1961, p. 538.
37. *Brigitte* 15 (15 July) 1960, pp. 60–1. Some recipes in *Ihre Freundin* were described as so easy that 'even single persons of the male sex'

could prepare them 'without risk'. *Ihre Freundin* 3 (24 January) 1961, p. 70.

38. Duchen, p. 79.
39. Text from Ernst Moritz Arndt, 'Vaterlandslied' (1812).
40. *Constanze*, 14 October 1959, p. 155. Male incompetence in domestic tasks, especially cooking, was also a popular subject for cartoonists; see for example *Constanze*, 19 October 1955, p. 146, 3 April 1957, p. 146, 2 October 1957, p. 110.
41. Initial letter in *Ihre Freundin* 13 (17 June) 1958, pp. 22–3, responses in 19 (9 September), pp. 46–9.
42. Hermann Scheffauer, *Das geistige Amerika von heute* (Berlin: Wege zum Wissen, 1925), quoted in Hammond, p. 98.
43. *Stimme der Frau* 8 (6 April) 1955, p. 8. In a 1955 article on American cars, *Der Spiegel* quoted a British journalist as attributing the American preference for large, powerful cars to 'Her Majesty, the American housewife'. 'Die PS-Protze von Detroit', *Spiegel* 13 (23 March) 1955, p. 41.
44. The three-part series began with 'Amerika beneidet Deutschlands Frauen', *Constanze* 31 (27 July) 1965, pp. 44–50, 67. Habe mentioned dishwashing American husbands in at least two of the three articles.
45. Hans Habe, 'Das Bund der Ehe ist ihr lieber', *Constanze* 32 (3 August) 1965, p. 42.
46. Hans Habe, 'Von A–Z alles über die deutsche und die amerikanische Frau: Die eine liebt, die andere lebt besser', *Constanze* 33 (10 August) 1965, pp. 50–60. Guess which appears under Xanthippe in this alphabet.
47. 'Wie lebt die Hausfrau in anderen Ländern? Die Amerikanerin', *Ratgeber* January 1959, pp. 35–7.
48. Dr Hermann Schulz, 'Die Vielgeplagte', *Ihre Freundin* 19/1950, p. 3.
49. 'Wie lebt die Hausfrau in anderen Ländern? Die Engländerin', *Ratgeber* May 1958, pp. 386–7.
50. 'Höchste Dringlichkeitsstufe: Mehr Maschinen im Haushalt!', *Ihre Freundin* 16/1950, p. 4.
51. Judith Crist, 'Do European Women Make Better Wives?', *Reader's Digest* 66/398 (June 1955), pp. 69–72, condensed from *Redbook*, March 1955.
52. Russell Lynes, 'Husbands: The New Servant Class', *Reader's Digest* 66/395 (March 1955), pp. 85–7, condensed from *Look*, 14 December 1954.
53. 'Benimm dich schlecht!', *Ihre Freundin* 5 (21 February) 1961, p. 82.

54. Alfred Sterzel, 'Ehe auf schwedisch', *Constanze* 17 (17 April) 1967, pp. 14–25.
55. Nowadays, one does occasionally see the word *Hausmann* used to mean 'househusband', though the need for such a term remains rather rare. My German–English dictionary (Langenscheidt Pocket Books edition, 1970) goes straight to *Hausmannskost* (plain cooking, understood as for, not by, the man of the house) without listing *Hausmann*. In the interviews, the term was used occasionally for men who participated in housework without having primary responsibility for it.
56. 'Sind wir wirklich so? Sechs Ausländerinnen urteilen Über die deutsche Frau', *Für Sie* 2 (13 January) 1970, pp. 26–9; 'Sind die deutschen Frauen unterdrückt?', *Ihre Freundin* 6 (15 March) 1955, pp. 12–13. See also the criticism of an article which appeared in *Elle* (3 August 1953) in *Constanze* 21 (7 October) 1953, pp. 7, 36–40.
57. *Ihre Freundin* 22/1950, p. 33. Miele had used the same slogan in a 1932 advertisement; see Orland, *Wäsche waschen,* p. 213.
58. *Constanze* 7 (23 March) 1955, p. 35.
59. *Brigitte* 8 (13 April) 1965, p. 86. One example of the portrayal of a male professional chef is in an Esge ad, *Ihre Freundin* 4 (7 February) 1961, p. 52.
60. Fewa ad, *Constanze,* 2 October 1957, p. 67; *Ratgeber* April 1958, p. 269.
61. Esge ad, *Constanze* 8 (11 April) 1961, p. 78. See also the Constructa ad, *Ratgeber* July 1958, p. 538, featuring a boy and a washing-machine: 'Nobody home! Except me. And it's my washday! That is, I'm just watching. You don't need to do anything yourself any more. Constructa does it alone, from A to Z. When Mummy comes back, everything will be done.'
62. Advertisement for Dor, *Constanze* 8 (11 April) 1961, p. 50.
63. See for example *Ihre Freundin* 4 (11 February) 1958, p. 51.
64. See Erving Goffman, *Gender Advertisements* (Cambridge: Harvard University Press, 1979), pp. 29–30.
65. *Ratgeber* May 1956, p. 333, (also March 1957, p. 191) and October 1956, p. 649.
66. The photo of the two children was also used in another Seiblank ad.
67. *Ratgeber* May 1969, p. 644.
68. The text gives no explanation for the enormous number of dishes – did she do dishes only once a month? did they have the Bundeswehr over for lunch? Presumably, a woman with only a normal amount of washing-up to do would have even less need of help from her husband.

69. Osram advertisement in *Ratgeber* January 1969, p. 31. An advertisement in *Der Spiegel* for scales also carried this theme that the husband should provide his wife with technical aids similar to those he enjoyed in the workplace. *Spiegel* 9 (24 February) 1965, p. 7.

70. *Brigitte*, 21 (4 October) 1960, p. 41, also *Ihre Freundin* 22 (18 October) 1960, p. 65.

71. *Ratgeber* December 1969, p. 1629. Another dishwasher advertisement suggested, though more subtly, that the dishwasher could substitute for child labour: the photo showed a little boy triumphantly holding up a clean saucer, evidently taken from the dishwasher, to his mother. Siemens advertisement, *Constanze* 42 (9 October) 1967, p. 77.

72. Jockey advertisement, *Constanze,* 22 April 1953; socks in *Spiegel* 12 (16 March) 1955, p. 29. The sock advertisement suggested that women could otherwise spend their time being nice to their husbands or reading *Der Spiegel* themselves.

73. Meyer and Schulze, 'Fernseher contra Waschmaschine'.

74. The earliest 'crystal detectors', which did not feature amplifiers and consequently required the use of headphones, did not require an electrical connection. *Brockhaus Enzyklopädie,* 19th edn, s.v. 'Rundfunk'.

75. 'So ist es bei den Deutschen', *Brigitte* 14 (26 June) 1970, pp. 90–6.

76. 'Geschirrspüler im Examen', *Für Sie* 22 (18 October) 1970, p. 134.

77. 'Höchste Dringlichkeitsstufe: Mehr Maschinen im Haushalt!', *Ihre Freundin* 16/1950, p. 4.

78. 'Hausfrau, Dir soll's besser gehen!', *Ihre Freundin* 3 (1 February) 1955, pp. 3, 42.

79. Charles A. Thrall, 'The Conservative Use of Modern Household Technology', *Technology and Culture* 23 (April 1982): 175–94.

80. Wolfgang Glatzer, Gisela Dörr, Werner Hübinger, Karin Prinz, Mathias Bös and Udo Neumann, eds, *Haushaltstechnisierung und gesellschaftliche Arbeitsteilung* (Frankfurt am Main: Campus Verlag, 1991), pp. 292–3. Wolfgang Zapf, Jürgen Hampel, Heidrun Mollenkopf and Ursula Weber, on the other hand, see the factors of female employment outside the home and family structure (men with children help less around the house) as more important than equipment in determining the division of labour in the family. 'Technik im Alltag von Familien', in Burkart Lutz, ed., *Technik in Alltag und Arbeit: Beiträge der Tagung des Verbands Sozialwissenschaftliche Technikforschung* (Berlin: Edition Sigma, 1989).

81. Wildt, 'Technik, Kompetenz, Modernität', p. 85. The remaining women had assistance from relatives.

Notes

82. Willms, p. 54.

83. On the housewives' movement in the Weimar Republic, see Bridenthal.

84. 'Gedanken zum Tarifvertrag: Minna geht ... Es lebe Fräulein Else', *Stimme der Frau* 22 (19 October) 1955, pp. 16–17. *Ratgeber* noted in its news column, April 1952, p. 150, that such a contract had been under consideration for some time and that the Ministry of Labour was working on guidelines. For further discussion of the servant problem and the question of the labour contract, see 'Fini Pfannes: Die Perle in der Muschel', *Spiegel* 51 (14 December)1955, pp. 22–31; 'Hausarbeit nach Tarif?', *Constanze* 1/1955 (29 December 1954), pp. 24–5; Martha Maria Gehrke and Walther von Hollander, 'Hausgehilfin nach Tarif', *Constanze* 21 (5 October) 1955, p. 34; 'Zwischen Minna und "Fräulein": Acht-Stunden-Tag für Hausgehilfinnen?', *Ihre Freundin* 1 (2 January) 1956, pp. 3, 46; 'Hauspersonal– ein Mangelberuf', *Ratgeber* August 1958, pp. 594–6; *Ratgeber* December 1959, p. 1173; *Ratgeber* March 1961, p. 211.

85. 'Auch ein halbes Zimmer ist ein ganzer Raum', *Stimme der Frau* 3 (26 January) 1955, p. 12. The rooms described in the article measured 2 x 2 and 2 x 4 metres, which gives a further suggestion of why this wasn't a very attractive job.

86. 'Deutsches Mädchen im schwedischen Haushalt', *Ihre Freundin* 4 (15 February) 1955, p. 42.

87. 'Auch "Zimmer mit Bad" uninteressant', *Badische Zeitung* 10 May 1960, p. 9.

88. Moulinex ad, *Constanze* 43 (14 October) 1969, p. 131. A steel-wool pad could also be a 'pearl': Abrazo-Flip ad, *Ratgeber* October 1961, p. 1025. One advertisement compared a water-heater to a slave (in ancient Phoenicia): Vaillant ad, *Ihre Freundin* 20/1951, p. 22.

89. 'Hausgehilfin: Küchentechnik', *Für Sie* 10 (4 May) 1960, pp. 66–76.

90. 'Frühjahrsputz – leicht gemacht', *Ratgeber* March 1967, p. 246.

91. Cited in *Constanze* 15 April 1959, p. 140. The complete list of appliances: cooker, refrigerator, washer, spin-drier, water-heaters for kitchen and bath, vacuum cleaner, food processor, iron, coffee grinder, hotplate, toaster, space heater, heating pad, hair-drier. This was supposed to come to DM 3600, with the most expensive item being the washer for DM 900.

92. See Sibylle Meyer, *Das Theater mit der Hausarbeit: Bürgerliche Repräsentation in der Familie der wilhelminischen Zeit* (Frankfurt am Main: Campus, 1982).

93. Orland, 'Emanzipation durch Rationalisierung?', p. 232.

94. Dolores Hayden, *The Grand Domestic Revolution: A History of Feminist Designs for American Homes, Neighborhoods, and Cities* (Cambridge, Mass.: MIT Press, 1981), pp. 282–3.

95. For an account of the political struggle over *Kinderläden* (literally children's shops – shop-front day-care centres originally organized by parents' groups) between women wanting liberation from child care and men wanting experiments in anti-authoritarian education, see Helke Sander, 'Mütter sind politische Personen', *Courage* 3 (October 1978), pp. 38–45, translated and excerpted in Edith Hoshino Altbach, Jeanette Clausen, Dagmar Schulz and Naomi Stephan, eds, *German Feminism: Readings in Politics and Literature* (Albany: State University of New York Press, 1984), pp. 240–5.

96. H. von Feldmann, 'Eine revolutionäre Frage: Hausfrauenarbeit gegen Lohn?', *Ihre Freundin* 22/1950, p. 21. Feldmann was against pay for housework, but thought it ought to be appreciated more.

97. *Ratgeber*, June 1957, p. 349.

98. See Altbach *et al.*, eds, *German Feminism*, pp. 233–74, for an introduction to the German debate on wages for housework. On the international movement, see also Ellen Malos, introduction to Malos, ed., *The Politics of Housework* (London: Allison & Busby, 1980), pp. 7–43, and Pieke Biermann, *Das Herz der Familie: Lohn für Hausarbeit: Materialien für eine internationale feministische Strategie Nr. 1* (Berlin: privately published, 1977). Alice Schwarzer, *So fing es an! Die neue Frauenbewegung* (Munich: Deutscher Taschenbuch Verlag, 1983), p. 49.

99. Irmgard Becht, 'Ich bin gern eine Hausfrau', *Ihre Freundin* 18 (23 August) 1960, p. 77.

100. *Ratgeber* April 1956, p. 212. Roughly, this meant saying a woman was 'fully' rather than 'just' a housewife.

101. 'Das Lied von der Glocke' (1799), lines 116–132.

102. See also 'Rekorde der Hausfrau', *Ihre Freundin* 22/1950, pp. 24–5, and *Ihre Freundin* 8 (4 April) 1961, p. 56. The latter article gives the German Housewives' League as the source of the information. The same organization may well have provided the data for the earlier articles as well.

103. *Constanze* 22 April 1953, p. 33.

104. Frau Sch., interview by author, 17 October 1993. In her case, the final year of practical training, in Mecklenburg, was cut short by the approach of the Soviet army; then the school was destroyed in the big Freiburg air raid of 27 November 1944. Frau Sch. remained without a degree.

105. See for instance Joachim Senchpiehl, 'Bräute auf der Schulbank', *Ihre Freundin* 9 (23 April) 1957, pp. 78–9 and 'Die Schule der perfekten Hausfrauen', *Ihre Freundin* 2 (15 January) 1957, pp. 22–3. The second article described a rather expensive-sounding finishing-school for housewives with a one-year course of study, while the first described a five-week course.

106. *Stimme der Frau* 4/1951, p. 29 describes one such, in North Rhine-Westphalia. Classes met one afternoon a week for two years, at the end of which there was an examination.

107. 'Stirbt die perfekte Hausfrau aus?', *Stimme der Frau* 16 (27 July) 1955, pp. 8–9. *Ratgeber* also cited divorce lawyers on this subject: 'Hübsch sein allein genügt nicht', June 1959, p. 531.

108. See Ann Oakley, *The Sociology of Housework* (New York: Pantheon, 1974), pp. 104–6, and Helge Pross, *Die Wirklichkeit der Hausfrau* (Reinbek bei Hamburg: Rowohlt, 1976).

109. Bärbel Kuhn, *Haus Frauen Arbeit 1915–1965: Erinnerungen aus fünfzig Jahren Haushaltsgeschichte* (St. Ingbert: Röhrig, 1994), pp. 61–2. Frau Brosowski, in Kuhn's study, spoke of a sparkling clean stove as 'obligatory' if one wanted to be considered a good house-wife, and, as she recalled it, every woman wanted to be one, or at least give that impression. The study was done in the Saarland, where an unusually high proportion of the population owned their own (single-family) homes, which may have had an impact on the amount of visiting.

110. Silberzahn-Jandt, p. 49, quotes Frau H. to the effect that women felt obligated to hang their washing in categories: sheets here, underwear there – and would have found it embarrassing to have disorderly washing.

111. 'Reinigung des Bettzeuges', *Ratgeber* May 1954, pp. 200–2.

112. *00* ad, *Ratgeber* March 1967, p. 313; Sidolin ad, *Ihre Freundin* 13 (14 June) 1960, p. 67.

113. *Ratgeber* March 1958, p. 211; *Constanze,* 3 April 1957, p. 14.

114. Gudrun Silberzahn-Jandt reproduces one of these rather entertaining advertisements: *Wasch-Maschine,* p. 75.

115. Anker ad, *Ihre Freundin* 8 (4 April) 1961, p. 106.

116. *Ihre Freundin* 14 (3 July) 1956, p. 26.

117. AEG ad, *Ratgeber* March 1962, p. 283.

118. Siemens ad, *Ratgeber* October 1961, p. 1049.

119. *Ratgeber*, October 1956, p. 641.

120. *Ratgeber,* May 1956, p. 307.

121. Bosch ad, *Ratgeber* November 1956, p. 713. According to another

ad from the same campaign, the refrigerator would also produce food and beverages for unexpected guests. *Ratgeber* May 1956, p. 291.

122. See Silberzahn-Jandt, *Wasch-Maschine,* pp. 75–9. See also Constructa ads, *Ratgeber* May 1969, p. 687 and June 1969, p. 869.

123. *Constanze* 25 March 1953, p. 79. An advertisement for an ordinary vacuum cleaner proclaimed the necessity of removing even 'invisible dirt'. Miele ad, *Ihre Freundin* 6 (11 March) 1958, p. 56.

124. Advertisement for Pre laundry detergent, *Constanze* 2 October 1957, p. 53.

125. With the growth of the environmental movement from the 1970s would come a trend away from the proliferation of specialized, non-biodegradable cleaning products in non-reusable containers, in some cases back to more traditional products.

126. Sanella ad, *Constanze* 21 (5 October) 1955, p. 12.

127. Bonnie J. Fox, 'Selling the Mechanized Household: 70 Years of Ads in *Ladies Home Journal*', *Gender and Society* 4 (March 1990): 25–40.

128. See Meyer, *Das Theater mit der Hausarbeit.*

129. 'Sybill', 'Das große *Freundin* Schönheits-ABC: M: Managerkrankheit der Frauen', *Ihre Freundin* 24 (20 November) 1956, p. 42. The poet is Schiller ('Würde der Frauen').

130. 'Schön auch beim Hausputz', *Ratgeber* March 1961, p. 292. See also 'Hausputz contra Gemütlichkeit', *Ihre Freundin* 6 (15 March) 1955, pp. 3, 15.

131. 'Frauen, die zu tüchtig sind', *Ratgeber* January 1952, pp. 3–4.

132. Zaren-Kaffee ad, *Ihre Freundin* 18 (23 August) 1960.

133. *Stimme der Frau* 8 (6 April) 1955, p. 8. See also *Stimme der Frau* 6 (9 March) 1955, p. 23.

134. Zanker ad, *Ratgeber* January 1957, p. 41.

135. Glänzer ad, *Ihre Freundin* 7 (22 March) 1960, p. 95.

136. Henko ad, *Badische Zeitung* 24 May 1960, p. 10.

137. 'Hausfrau, Dir soll's besser gehen!', *Ihre Freundin* 3 (1 February) 1955, p. 3. This may well refer to the same study which *Ratgeber* reported in its July 1953 issue, p. 292.

138. *Ihre Freundin* 25 (4 December) 1956, p. 30.

139. *Ihre Freundin* 22 (23 October) 1956, p. 32.

140. 'Sie fragen – Vera antwortet', *Ihre Freundin* 21 (4 October) 1960, p. 100. See also advice to Charlotte M. in the same column: 'Furthermore, you made a gigantic mistake in running around in excessively plain clothing and putting everything into your

husband's wardrobe. Now he sees only an unattractive, faded woman and the other woman has an easy time of it.'

141. *Ratgeber* June 1958, p. 455. Another Constructa ad emphasizing time for children is in *Spiegel* 16 (13 April) 1960, p. 43.

142. *Constanze,* 2 October 1957, p. 126.

143. *Ratgeber* March 1961, p. 241.

144. Wolfgang Fischer, 'Sozial-Ökonomische Aspekte der Entwicklung der privaten Haushalte' (diss., Bonn, 1972), p. 149.

145. See Maria S. Rerrich, 'Veränderte Elternschaft: Entwicklungen in der familialen Arbeit mit Kindern seit 1950', *Soziale Welt* 34 no. 4 (1983): 420–49, and Josef Mooser, *Arbeiterleben in Deutschland 1900–1970* (Frankfurt am Main: Suhrkamp, 1984), p. 159.

146. See Kuhn, *Haus Frauen Arbeit,* p. 63.

147. This did not escape criticism. Walther von Hollander argued that it was unfair of the schools to shift their responsibilities on to unpaid, untrained mothers. 'Schade, der Haushalt ist doch heilig', *Constanze* 17 (20 April) 1965, p. 7. Helge Pross was also very critical of the short school day in *Die Wirklichkeit der Hausfrau* (Reinbek bei Hamburg: Rowohlt, 1976). The occasional passing references in women's magazines to the longer school day and the provision of school meals in other countries were generally positive. The authorities could always argue (and continue to do so), however, that constructing cafeteria facilities and hiring additional personnel would be simply too expensive.

148. See for instance '5-Tage-Woche für die Hausfrau?', *Ratgeber* June 1958, pp. 432–3. The article takes the position that the seven-day working week is inevitable and that it's better to spread out the work than to hurry to get done early in order to have leisure time and then be too wound up to relax. It also reports a sketch by the Berlin cabaret Die Insulaner portraying the chaos which results when a housewife decides she'll only work five days a week. But there are also critical notices in *Ratgeber*'s miscellaneous-news column reporting on studies of housewives' working hours and indicating that something needed to be done about the situation (without making any specific suggestions). 'Nachrichten für die Frau', August 1957, p. 523 and February 1958, p. 85.

149. Miele ad, *Ratgeber*, June 1958, p. 447. An advertisement for Siemens household appliances promised 'Mehr Zeit für Freizeit'. *Ihre Freundin* 6 (11 March) 1958, p. 79. *Ratgeber* August 1959, p. 732; *Ratgeber* August 1959, p. 774.

150. 'Ist denn das sooo wichtig?', *Ratgeber* July 1956, pp. 416–18. See

also 'Die "Glücklichen Inseln" der Hausfrau', *Ratgeber* March 1958, pp. 156–7, and 'Auch die Frau möchte einmal allein sein', October 1956, pp. 616–17. The miscellaneous-news column on p. 617 also reported that more than 60,000 mothers had enjoyed rest cures in the homes operated by the Deutsche Müttergenesungswerk, a charitable organization devoted to providing women with vacations from home and family responsibilities.

151. See Hans Jürgen Teuteberg, 'Studien zur Volksernährung unter sozial- und wirtschaftsgeschichtlichen Aspekten', in Hans Jürgen Teuteberg and Günter Wiegelmann, *Der Wandel der Nahrungsgewohnheiten unter dem Einfluß der Industrialisierung* (Göttingen: Vandenhoeck & Ruprecht, 1972), pp. 78–85, and Hans P. Mollenhauer, *Von Omas Küche zur Fertigpackung: Aus der Kinderstube der Lebensmittelindustrie* (Gernsbach: Casimir Katz, 1988).

152. *Constanze* 7 (23 March) 1955, p. 110. *Stimme der Frau* also saluted cake mixes as a great convenience in 1955 (7 (3 March) 1955, p. 30); *Brigitte* seems to have found out about them ten years later (14 (6 July) 1965, p. 71).

153. West German consumption of frozen foods rose rapidly in the 1960s, from very low levels, but remained well behind consumption in the United States, Switzerland, Great Britain and the Scandinavian countries except for Finland, while ahead of consumption in France and Italy. As of 1970, it had reached about 5 kg per capita per year, while Americans consumed more than 30 kg, Swedes over 15 kg and Britons about 10 kg. Figures from Lennart Bäck, *Studies on the Development of Consumption and Market Structure for Quick Frozen Foods* (Uppsala: Kulturgeografiska Institutionen, 1975), p. 33.

154. *Constanze* 13/1950, p. 55. Pudding manufacturers were evidently also concerned that their product was seen as 'kids' stuff' which red-blooded men did not care for; see the Dr Oetker ad in the same issue, p. 32.

155. *Brigitte* 22 (16 October) 1970, pp. 274–5.

156. *Ratgeber* January 1956, p. 30. See also March 1956, p. 170 and April 1956, p. 230.

157. *Ratgeber* August 1957. See also January 1957, p. 18.

158. 'Vitamine in Blech. Ein Trost für die Wintermonate', *Stimme der Frau* 22 (19 October) 1955, pp. 14–15; Teuteberg, 'Nahrungsmittelverzehr in Deutschland', p. 339.

159. Wolfgang Fischer, pp. 132–7.

160. *Constanze* 29 (13 July) 1965, p. 72. The recipe gave the preparation

time as 12 minutes and the price as DM 5. Dessert consisted of a pound of fresh cherries.

161. 'Wer wird Freizeit-Kochkönigin 1970?', *Für Sie* 15 (10 July) 1970, p. 69.

162. My calculations from StJ 1961, pp. 526–7 and 1971, p. 480. The figures for vegetables do not include potatoes, which were counted separately.

163. Fischer, 'Sozial-Ökonomische Aspekte', pp. 133–4.

164. *Constanze* 17 (20 April) 1965, pp. 140–3, 'Phantasien mit Fertigsuppen'. Some of the recipes call for frozen vegetables. See also *Ratgeber* April 1955, p. 228. Prepared sauce mixes seem also to have been widely used, though a *Brigitte* article in 1960 talks about using them to stretch the sauce from a roast for more people, rather than as a substitute for home-made sauce. *Brigitte* 21 (4 October) 1960, p. 109. It does also list sauces nobody makes at home, like ketchup, soy sauce, Worcestershire sauce.

165. *Constanze* 1/1960, p. 46. See also the similar article in *Ratgeber* July 1969, pp. 925–8.

166. 'Ich empfehle: Amerikanische Spezialitäten', *Ihre Freundin* 5 (1 March) 1955, p. 70.

167. *Ihre Freundin* 23 (8 November) 1955, p. 47.

168. *Ratgeber* July 1955, p. 418.

169. 'Nestlé: Magd in der Tüte' (cover story), *Spiegel* 30 (24 July) 1963, p. 29. According to this article, in 1962, West German consumption of frozen foods was only one kilogram per person and year, compared with twenty-two in the US and four in Sweden and England.

170. *Ratgeber* May 1959, p. 407.

171. *Spiegel* 47 (15 November) 1961, p. 88. *Ihre Freundin* gave a more positive assessment of the TV dinner, as a boon for bachelors. 14/ 1950, p. 28.

172. Chapter title in Betty Friedan, *The Feminine Mystique* (New York: W.W. Norton, 1963).

173. *Ihre Freundin* 9 (19 April) 1960, p. 33.

174. Joann Vanek, 'Time Spent in Housework', *Scientific American* 231 (November 1974), pp. 116–20. Vanek found that women who worked outside the home cut back on the time they spent on housework, even spending less time on housework at the weekends than women who did not have outside jobs.

175. Irmhild Kettschau, 'Wieviel Arbeit macht ein Familienhaushalt? Zur Analyse von Inhalt, Umfang und Verteilung der Hausarbeit heute'

(diss., PH Dortmund, 1980). See especially pp. 166, 189. Of course, time spent on housework is difficult to measure accurately.

176. Meyer and Schulze, 'Technisiertes Familienleben', p. 27; Karin Hausen, 'Große Wäsche: Technischer Fortschritt und sozialer Wandel in Deutschland vom 18. bis ins 20. Jahrhundert', *Geschichte und Gesellschaft* 13 (1987): 273–303. On changing standards of cleanliness, see also Silberzahn-Jandt, pp. 66–86.

177. German housewives differentiated between the '*große Wäsche*', which included household linen and was traditionally done on Monday and the '*kleine Wäsche*', done by hand as needed, especially for coloured and delicate items. Often, the *große Wäsche* was done commercially. The distinction has become more or less obsolete with the use of the washing-machine.

178. 'Der Waschtag eine Strapaze? Moderne Maschinen erleichtern die Arbeit', *Ihre Freundin* 22/1950, p. 45.

179. Dr S., interview.

180. Frau M., interview. The installation of central heating tended both to reduce and to warm cellar space, since the cellar was the logical place to put the boiler and the fuel storage.

181. A pram offered some possibility of wheeled transportation. I do not know whether the small two-wheeled carts so much in evidence now were around in the 1950s and 1960s or not. Bicycles were less popular then than now.

182. Frau Pr., interview by author, 6 December 1993.

183. Frau Sch., interview.

184. One advertisement for a new floor-polish listed eight brand-name and five generic types of flooring for which the product was suitable. Glänzer ad, *Ratgeber* November 1959, p. 1133.

185. StJ 1962, p. 278. These figures exclude basement and attic flats.

186. StJ 1970, p. 241.

187. *Constanze* 22 (19 October) 1955, pp. 130–3.

188. 'Heizen mit Öl', *Ihre Freundin* 22 (25 October) 1955, p. 55.

189. Blinker ad, *Constanze* 15 (3 April) 1967, p. 139.

190. *Ihre Freundin* 23 (1 November) 1960, p. 61.

191. Sidolin ad, *Ratgeber* March 1965, p. 299.

192. *Ratgeber*, January 1959, pp. 42–3.

193. *Ratgeber* December 1958, p. 1037.

194. Glänzer ad, *Ratgeber* May 1961, p. 499, also *Ihre Freundin* 8 (4 April) 1961, p. 41. A later advertisement proclaimed that waxing the floor had become old-fashioned due to the advent of the new and improved Glänzer Neu. *Ratgeber* April 1965, pp. 446–7.

195. On the wax issue, see *Ratgeber*, 'Die Behandlung der Fußböden', January 1954, pp. 9–11, 'Die Pflege des Fußbodens', January 1957, pp. 8–9, and 'Bodenpflege – so oder so', April 1961, pp. 350–1.

196. 'Dreikampf im Bottich', *Spiegel* 11 (10 March) 1965, pp. 113–15.

197. For a photograph of the freezer in question, see Hellmann, *Künstliche Kälte*, p. 228. He gives the date as about 1986. Frau P. had one.

198. Friedrich, *Wohnkunde* , p. 163.

199. W[alter] D[irks], 'Zeichen und Wunder', *Frankfurter Hefte* 10 (November 1955), p. 816.

200. Gritzner-Kayser ad, *Ratgeber* November 1956, p. 721; 'Nähmaschine unter der Tarnkappe', *Ratgeber* August 1958, p. 601.

201. Adrian Forty, *Objects of Desire* (New York: Pantheon, 1986), p. 219.

202. AEG Lavamat ad, *Ihre Freundin* 13 (13 June) 1961, p. 81. The advertisement also praised the machine's quietness.

203. Thomas ad, *Ratgeber*, September 1959, p. 819.

204. Bauknecht ad, *Ratgeber* January 1951, p. 32.

205. The mixer is clearly placed backwards, with the cord visible at the lower left and the control dial nowhere to be seen. For a comparison, see the Braun advertisement from the same year, *Ihre Freundin* 2 (12 January) 1960, p. 21.

206. Bosch ad, *Ratgeber* June 1956, p. 373; AEG ad, *Ratgeber* October 1959, p. 1006.

207. George F. Taubeneck, 'The Development of the American Household Electric Refrigeration Industry', in *Proceedings of the VIIth International Congress of Refrigeration*, 1936, quoted in Giedion, p. 608.

208. AEG ad, *Ratgeber*, June 1969, p. 777.

209. Neff ads, *Ratgeber* October 1958, p. 803 and *Ratgeber*, August 1958, p. 641.

210. Linde ad, *Ihre Freundin* 14 (5 July) 1955, p. 46.

211. Constructa ad, *Ratgeber* September 1957, p. 617.

212. Outside the household, the world of machines was decidedly male. A 1965 poll indicated that 44% of men but only 17% of women drove cars; the gender imbalance was greater (though the total numbers involved were smaller) for lorries, buses and vans, motor cycles and mopeds but less for tractors (3% of women and 5% of men). Noelle and Neumann, p. 325.

Chapter 5 Conclusions

1. On discontent with the housewife role, see Pross, *Die Wirklichkeit der Hausfrau*.
2. In 1972, the birth rate fell below the death rate. As of 1982, over half of all families with children under fifteen had only one child, and most of the remainder had two. Frevert, pp. 299–300, and Kolinsky, pp. 81–3.
3. Kolinsky, p. 174 and pp. 86–8. A 1983 survey in Baden-Württemberg indicated that 20% of husbands of women with full-time jobs helped with the housework (Frevert, p. 287).
4. Frevert, pp. 287–303; Schwarzer; and Altbach *et al.*

Bibliography

Periodicals:

Badische Zeitung
Brigitte
Constanze
Ihre Freundin
Frankfurter Hefte
Für Sie (before 1957 *Stimme der Frau*)
Ratgeber für Haus und Familie
Reader's Digest
Sie: Die Berliner illustrierte Wochenzeitung
Der Spiegel

Books and articles

Abelshauser, Werner. *Wirtschaftsgeschichte der Bundesrepublik Deutschland, 1945-1980*. Frankfurt am Main: Suhrkamp, 1983.
——. *Die langen Fünfziger Jahre: Wirtschaft und Gesellschaft der Bundesrepublik Deutschland, 1949-1966*. Düsseldorf: Schwann, 1987.
Agassi, Judith Baker, ed. *Women on the Job: The Attitudes of Women to their Work*. Lexington, Massachusetts: Lexington Books, 1979.
Albisetti, James C. *Schooling German Girls and Women: Secondary and Higher Education in the Nineteenth Century*. Princeton: Princeton University Press, 1988.
Altbach, Edith Hoshino, Jeanette Clausen, Dagmar Schultz and Naomi Stephan, eds. *German Feminism: Readings in Politics and Literature*. Albany: State University of New York Press, 1984.
Andritzky, Michael, ed. *Oikos: Von der Feuerstelle zur Mikrowelle: Haushalt und Wohnen im Wandel*. Gießen: Anabas, 1992.
Andritzky, Michael. 'Gemeinsam statt einsam: Otl Aicher und die Küchenphilosophie von bulthaup'. In *Oikos: Von der Feuerstelle zur Mikrowelle: Haushalt und Wohnen im Wandel,* edited by Michael Andritzky. Gießen: Anabas, 1992.

———. 'Eine Küche für den neuen Lebensstil'. In *Oikos: Von der Feuerstelle zur Mikrowelle: Haushalt und Wohnen im Wandel,* edited by Michael Andritzky. Gießen: Anabas, 1992.

Arbeiterwohnen: Ideal und Wirklichkeit. Dortmund: Museum für Kunst und Kulturgeschichte der Stadt Dortmund, n.d. [1990].

Auflagenmeldungen erstattet der Informationsgemeinschaft zur Feststellung der Verbreitung von Werbeträgern e.V. Bad Godesberg: Zeitungs-Verlag und Zeitschriften-Verlag GmbH, n.d. [1961].

Avdem, Anna Jorunn, and Kari Melby. *Oppe først og sist i seng: Husarbeid i Norge fra 1850 til i dag.* Oslo: Universitetsforlaget, 1985.

Bab, Bettina. 'Frauen helfen siegen'. In *Frauenleben im NS-Alltag,* edited by Annette Kuhn. Pfaffenweiler: Centaurus, 1994.

Bäck, Lennart. *Studies on the Development of Consumption and Market Structure for Quick Frozen Foods.* Uppsala: Kulturgeografiska Institutionen, 1975.

Bark, Georg R. 'Energiewirtschaft als Träger des Teilzahlungskredits'. In Wirtschaftsverband Teilzahlungsbanken e.V., *Handbuch der Teilzahlungswirtschaft,* pp. 70–6. Frankfurt am Main: Fritz Knapp, 1959.

Barthes, Roland. *Mythologies.* Selected and translated by Annette Lavers. New York: Hill & Wang, 1972.

———. 'Rhetoric of the Image'. In *Image Music Text,* pp. 32–51. Translated by Stephen Heath. New York: Hill & Wang, 1977.

Baumert, Gerhard, and Edith Hünninger. *Deutsche Familien nach dem Kriege.* Darmstadt: Eduard Roether, 1954.

Benz, Wolfgang, ed. *Die Geschichte der Bundesrepublik Deutschland,* vol. 3: *Gesellschaft.* Frankfurt am Main: Fischer Taschenbuch Verlag, 1989.

Berman, Ronald. *Advertising and Social Change.* Beverly Hills: SAGE, 1981.

Biermann, Pieke. *Das Herz der Familie: Lohn für Hausarbeit: Materialien für eine internationale feministische Strategie Nr. 1.* Berlin: privately published, 1977.

Bley, Curt. *Tatsachen über Kredit und Kreditmißbrauch.* Cologne: Carl Heymanns Verlag, 1954.

Bock, Gisela, and Barbara Duden. 'Arbeit aus Liebe—Liebe als Arbeit: Zur Entstehung der Hausarbeit im Kapitalismus'. In Gruppe Berliner Dozentinnen, *Frauen und Wissenschaft: Beiträge zur Berliner Sommeruniversität für Frauen, Juli 1976.* Berlin: Courage, 1977.

Bocock, Robert. *Consumption.* London: Routledge, 1993.

Bohrer, Robert. 'Die Wahlbedarfe westdeutscher Arbeitnehmerhaushalte an hochwertigen Gebrauchsgütern und Immobilien in ihrer Bedeutung für das elastische Arbeitsangebot und private Sparaufkommen'. Dissertation, Gießen, 1974.

Borchardt, Knut. 'Zäsuren in der wirtschaftlichen Entwicklung'. In *Zäsuren nach 1945: Essays zur Periodisierung der deutschen Nachkriegsgeschichte*, edited by Martin Broszat. Munich: R. Oldenbourg, 1990.

Boruttau, Grete. *Das bürgerliche Kochbuch*. Marbach/Neckar: Süd-West Verlags- und Vertriebs-GmbH, n.d. [1958].

Bourdieu, Pierre. *Distinction: A Social Critique of the Judgement of Taste*. Translated by Richard Nice. Cambridge: Harvard University Press, 1984.

Braun, Hans. 'Helmut Schelskys Konzept der "nivellierten Mittelstandsgesellschaft" und die Bundesrepublik der 50er Jahre'. *Archiv für Sozialgeschichte* 29 (1989): 199–223.

Braun, Ingo. *Stoff, Wechsel, Technik: Zur Soziologie und Ökologie der Waschmaschinen*. Berlin: Edition Sigma, 1988.

Brech, Joachim, ed. *Wohnen zur Miete: Wohnungsversorgung und Wohnungspolitik in der Bundesrepublik*. Weinheim/Basel: Beltz, 1981.

Bridenthal, Renate. '"Professional" Housewives: Stepsisters of the Women's Movement'. In *When Biology Became Destiny: Women in Weimar and Nazi Germany*, edited by Renate Bridenthal, Atina Grossmann and Marion Kaplan. New York: Monthly Review Press, 1984.

Bridenthal, Renate and Claudia Koonz. 'Beyond *Kinder, Küche, Kirche*: Weimar Women in Politics and Work'. In *When Biology Became Destiny: Women in Weimar and Nazi Germany*, edited by Renate Bridenthal, Atina Grossmann and Marion Kaplan. New York: Monthly Review Press, 1984.

Broszat, Martin, ed. *Zäsuren nach 1945: Essays zur Periodisierung der deutschen Nachkriegsgeschichte*. Schriftenreihe der Vierteljahreshefte für Zeitgeschichte, no. 61. Munich: R. Oldenbourg, 1990.

'Bs'. 'Die Betreuung der Kinder erwerbstätiger und nichterwerbstätiger Mütter: Ergebnis der Mikrozensus-Zusatzbefragung 1969'. *Wirtschaft und Statistik* 3 (March) 1971: 161–5.

Burke, Joanna. 'Housewifery in Working-Class England, 1860–1914'. *Past and Present* 143 (May 1994): 167–97.

Carter, Erica. 'Alice in the Consumer Wonderland: West German Case Studies in Gender and Consumer Culture'. In *Gender and Generation*, edited by Angela McRobbie and Mica Neva. London: Macmillan, 1984.

——. *How German is She? Postwar West German Reconstruction and*

Bibliography

the Consuming Woman. Ann Arbor: University of Michigan Press, 1997.

Charles, Nickie, and Marion Kerr. *Women, Food and Families.* Manchester: Manchester University Press, 1988.

Cowan, Ruth Schwartz. *More Work for Mother: The Ironies of Household Technology from the Open Hearth to the Microwave.* New York: Basic Books, 1983.

Craig, Gordon A. *Germany, 1866–1945.* New York: Oxford University Press, 1978.

Cross, Gary. *Time and Money: The Making of Consumer Culture.* London: Routledge, 1993.

Cumberbatch, Guy, and Dennis Howitt. *A Measure of Uncertainty: The Effects of the Mass Media.* London: John Libbey, 1989.

Curran, James, Michael Gurevitch and Janet Woollacott. 'The Study of the Media: Theoretical Approaches'. In *Culture, Society and the Media*, edited by Michael Gurevitch, Tony Bennett, James Curran and Janet Woollacott. London: Methuen, 1982.

Davidson, Caroline. *A Woman's Work is Never Done: A History of Housework in the British Isles 1650–1950.* London: Chatto & Windus, 1982.

de Certeau, Michel. 'Reading as Poaching'. In *The Practice of Everyday Life*, pp. 165–76. Translated by Steven F. Rendall. Berkeley and Los Angeles: University of California Press, 1984.

de Jong, Jutta, '"Sklavin" oder "Hausdrache"? Frauen in Bergarbeiter-familien'. In *Eine Partei in ihrer Region: Zur Geschichte der SPD im Westlichen Westfalen*, edited by Bernd Faulenbach and Günther Högl. Essen: Klartext Verlag, 1988.

Delille, Angela, and Andrea Grohn. *Blick zurück aufs Glück: Frauenleben und Familienpolitik in den 50er Jahren.* Berlin: Elefanten Press, 1985.

———. *Perlonzeit: Wie die Frauen ihr Wirtschaftswunder erlebten.* Berlin: Elefanten Press, 1985.

———, eds. *Geschichten der Reinlichkeit: Vom römischen Bad zum Wasch-salon.* Frankfurt am Main: Eichborn, 1986.

Dörhöfer, Kerstin, and Ulla Terlinden, eds. *Verbaute Räume: Auswirk-ungen von Architektur und Stadtplanung auf das Leben von Frauen.* Cologne: Pahl-Rugenstein, 1985.

Dörner, Renate. 'Zum Frauenbild der Illustrierten'. *Das Argument* 4(3) (1962): 41–8.

Duchen, Claire. *Women's Rights and Women's Lives in France, 1944–1968.* London: Routledge, 1994.

Dunckelmann, Henning. *Die erwerbstätige Ehefrau im Spannungsfeld von Beruf und Konsum: Dargestellt an den Ergebnissen einer Befragung.* Tübingen: J.C.B. Mohr (Paul Siebeck), 1961.

Eckart, Christel, Ursula Jaerisch and Helgard Kramer. *Frauenarbeit in Familie und Fabrik: Eine Untersuchung von Bedingungen und Barrieren der Interessenwahrnehmung von Industriearbeiterinnen.* Frankfurt am Main: Campus, 1979.

Egner, Erich, ed. *Aspekte der hauswirtschaftlichen Strukturwandels.* Berlin: Duncker & Humblot, 1967.

Einfeldt, Anne-Katrin, 'Zwischen alten Werten und neuen Chancen. Häusliche Arbeit von Bergarbeiterfrauen in den fünfziger Jahren'. In *'Hinterher merkt man, daß es richtig war, daß es schiefgegangen ist': Nachkriegserfahrungen im Ruhrgebiet,* edited by Lutz Niethammer. Bonn: J.H.W. Dietz Nachf., 1983.

Einkaufsgewohnheiten in Baden-Württemberg, vols. 1 and 2. Stuttgart: Südwestdeutscher Einzelhandelsverband e.V., 1960–1.

Eldridge, John, Jenny Kitzinger and Kevin Williams. *The Mass Media and Power in Modern Britain.* Oxford: Oxford University Press, 1997.

Enssle, Manfred J. 'The Harsh Discipline of Food Scarcity in Postwar Stuttgart, 1945–1948'. *German Studies Review* 10 (October 1987): 481–502.

Erd-Küchler, Heide. *Die Aufgabenteilung der Ehegatten bei der Hausarbeit: Ökonomische, ideologische und psychische Funktionsbestimmung privater, vorrangig von Frauen geleisteter Hausarbeit.* Frankfurt am Main: Peter Lang, 1981.

Erdmann, Karl Dietrich. *Der Zweite Weltkrieg. Gebhardt Handbuch der deutschen Geschichte,* 9th edn, vol. 21. Munich: Deutscher Taschenbuch Verlag, 1980.

Erhard, Ludwig. *Wohlstand für alle.* Düsseldorf: Econ-Verlag, 1957.

——. *Ludwig Erhard: Gedanken aus fünf Jahrzehnten: Reden und Schriften.* Edited by Karl Hohmann. Düsseldorf: Econ-Verlag, 1988.

Ewen, Stuart. *Captains of Consciousness: Advertising and the Social Roots of the Consumer Culture.* New York: McGraw-Hill, 1976.

Ferguson, Marjorie. *Forever Feminine: Women's Magazines and the Cult of Femininity.* London: Heinemann, 1983.

Fischer, Heike. '"... und eines Tages guck ich, da hat er's auch zerhackt". Dortmunder Lebens- und Möbelgeschichte'. In *Arbeiterwohnen: Ideal und Wirklichkeit.* Dortmund: Museum für Kunst und Kulturgeschichte der Stadt Dortmund, n.d. [1990].

Fischer, Wolfgang. 'Sozial-Ökonomische Aspekte der Entwicklung der privaten Haushalte'. Dissertation, Bonn, 1972.

Fischer, Wolfram, ed. *Die Geschichte der Stromversorgung.* Frankfurt

Bibliography

am Main: Verlags- und Wirtschaftsgesellschaft der Elektrizitätswerke m.b.H., 1992.

Forty, Adrian. *Objects of Desire*. New York: Pantheon, 1986.

Fox, Bonnie J. 'Selling the Mechanized Household: 70 Years of Ads in *Ladies Home Journal*'. *Gender and Society* 4 (March 1990): 25–40.

Freidank, Michael. 'Langfristige Entwicklungstendenzen auf den Märkten ausgewählter Haushaltsmaschinen'. Dissertation, St Gallen, 1966.

Freier, Anna-Elisabeth, and Annette Kuhn, eds. *Frauen in der Geschichte V: 'Das Schicksal Deutschlands liegt in der Hand seiner Frauen': Frauen in der deutschen Nachkriegsgeschichte*. Düsseldorf: Schwann, 1984.

Frevert, Ute. *Women in German History: From Bourgeois Emancipation to Sexual Liberation*. Translated by Stuart McKinnon-Evans. Oxford: Berg, 1989.

Friedan, Betty. *The Feminine Mystique*. New York: W.W. Norton, 1963.

Friedrich, Hans-Joachim. *Wohnkunde*. Berlin: Ernst Staneck Verlag, 1967.

Frost, Robert L. 'Machine Liberation: Inventing Housewives and Home Appliances in Interwar France'. *French Historical Studies* 18 (spring 1993): 109–130.

Fuchs, Thomas. '"Einst ein mühsam Walten, jetzt ein schnelles Schalten"'. In *Oikos: Von der Feuerstelle zur Mikrowelle: Haushalt und Wohnen im Wandel,* edited by Michael Andritzky. Gießen: Anabas, 1992.

Fuchs, Werner. *Biographische Forschung: Eine Einführung in Praxis und Methoden*. Opladen: Westdeutscher Verlag, 1984.

Gerstein, Hannelore. *Studierende Mädchen: Zum Problem des vorzeitigen Abgangs von der Universität*. Munich: R. Piper, 1965.

Giedion, Sigfried. *Mechanization Takes Command*. New York: Oxford University Press, 1948.

Glaser, Hermann. *Die Kulturgeschichte der Bundesrepublik Deutschland,* vol. 2, *Zwischen Grundgesetz und Großer Koalition, 1949–1967.* Frankfurt am Main: Fischer Taschenbuch Verlag, 1990.

Glatzer, Wolfgang. 'Ziele, Standards und soziale Indikatoren für die Wohnungsversorgung'. In *Lebensbedingungen in der Bundesrepublik: Sozialer Wandel und Wohlfahrtsentwicklung*, edited by Wolfgang Zapf. Frankfurt am Main: Campus, 1977.

Glatzer, Wolfgang, Gisela Dörr, Werner Hübinger, Karin Prinz, Mathias Bös and Udo Neumann. *Haushaltstechnisierung und gesellschaftliche Arbeitsteilung*. Frankfurt am Main: Campus, 1991.

Godau, Marion. 'Vom guten und schlechten Geschmack: Arbeiter- und Intellektuellenästhetik'. In *Arbeiterwohnen: Ideal und Wirklichkeit*, pp. 87–102. Dortmund: Museum für Kunst und Kulturgeschichte der Stadt Dortmund, n.d. [1990].

Bibliography

Goffman, Erving. *Gender Advertisements*. Cambridge: Harvard University Press, 1979.

Goldman, Robert. *Reading Ads Socially*. London: Routledge, 1992.

Die Große Wäsche. Exhibition catalogue published by Landschaftsverband Rheinland/Rheinisches Museumsamt. Cologne: Rheinland-Verlag, 1988.

Grossmann, Atina. 'Abortion and Economic Crisis: The 1931 Campaign Against Paragraph 218'. In *When Biology Became Destiny: Women in Weimar and Nazi Germany,* edited by Renate Bridenthal, Atina Grossmann and Marion Kaplan. New York: Monthly Review Press, 1984.

Grube, Frank, and Gerhard Richter, eds. *Das Wirtschaftswunder: Unser Weg in den Wohlstand*. Hamburg: Hoffmann & Campe, 1983.

Hachtmann, Rüdiger. '"Die Begründer der amerikanischen Technik sind fast lauter schwäbisch-allemannische Menschen": Nazi-Deutschland, der Blick auf die USA und die "Amerikanisierung" der industriellen Produktionsstrukturen im "Dritten Reich"'. In *Amerikanisierung: Traum und Alptraum im Deutschland des 20. Jahrhunderts,* edited by Alf Lüdtke, Inge Marßolek and Adelheid von Saldern. Stuttgart: Franz Steiner, 1996.

Haensch, Dietrich. *Repressive Familienpolitik: Sexualunterdrückung als Mittel der Politik*. Reinbek bei Hamburg: Rowohlt, 1969.

Hagberg, Jan-Erik. *Tekniken i kvinnornas händer: Hushållsarbete och hushållsteknik under tjugo- och trettiotalen*. Malmö: Liber, 1986.

Hagemann, Karen. *Frauenalltag und Männerpolitik: Alltagsleben und gesellschaftliches Handeln von Arbeiterfrauen in der Weimarer Republik*. Bonn: J.H.W. Dietz Nachf., 1990.

Hagena, Jörg. 'Die berufstätige Frau in illustrierten Zeitschriften'. Dissertation, Erlangen-Nuremberg, 1974.

Hall, Stuart. 'Encoding, decoding'. In *The Cultural Studies Reader*, edited by Simon During. London: Routledge, 1993.

Hamilton, Richard F. 'Affluence and the Worker: The West German Case'. *American Journal of Sociology* 71 (September 1965): 144–52.

Hammond, Theresa Mayer. *American Paradise: German Travel Literature from Duden to Kisch*. Heidelberg: Carl Winter, 1980.

Hampel, Jürgen, Heidrun Mollenkopf, Ursula Weber and Wolfgang Zapf. 'Technik im Alltag von Familien'. In *Technik in Alltag und Arbeit: Beiträge der Tagung des Verbands Sozialwissenschaftliche Technikforschung*, edited by Burkart Lutz. Berlin: Edition Sigma, 1989.

———. *Alltagsmaschinen: Die Folgen der Technik in Alltag und Familie*. Berlin: Edition Sigma, 1991.

Hardach, Gerd. *Deutschland in der Weltwirtschaft, 1870–1970*. Frankfurt am Main: Campus, 1977.

——. *The First World War, 1914–1918*. Berkeley and Los Angeles: University of California Press, 1977.

—— 'Die Wirtschaft der fünfziger Jahre: Restauration und Wirtschaftswunder'. In *Die fünfziger Jahre: Beiträge zu Politik und Kultur*, edited by Dieter Bänsch. Tübingen: Gunter Narr, 1985.

Hardyment, Christina. *From Mangle to Microwave: The Mechanization of Household Work*. Cambridge: Polity Press, 1988.

Harsch, Donna. 'Public Continuity and Private Change? Women's Consciousness and Activity in Frankfurt, 1945–1955'. *Journal of Social History* 27 (fall 1993): 29–58.

Hausen, Karin. 'Große Wäsche. Technischer Fortschritt und sozialer Wandel in Deutschland vom 18. bis ins 20. Jahrhundert'. *Geschichte und Gesellschaft* 13 (1987): 273–303.

HaushaltsTräume: Ein Jahrhundert Technisierung und Rationalisierung im Haushalt. Königstein im Taunus: Karl Robert Langewiesche Nachfolger, 1990.

Hayden, Dolores. *The Grand Domestic Revolution: A History of Feminist Designs for American Homes, Neighborhoods, and Cities*. Cambridge: MIT Press, 1981.

Hebdige, Dick. *Hiding in the Light: On Images and Things*. London: Routledge, 1988.

Heineman, Elizabeth. '"Standing Alone": Single Women from Nazi Germany to the Federal Republic'. Dissertation, University of North Carolina, 1993.

——. 'The Hour of the Woman: Memories of Germany's "Crisis Years" and West German National Identity'. *American Historical Review* 101(2) (April 1996): 354–95.

——. 'Complete Families, Half Families, No Families at All: Female-Headed Households and the Reconstruction of the Family in the Early Federal Republic'. *Central European History* 29(1) (winter 1996): 19–60.

Hellmann, Ullrich. *Künstliche Kälte: Die Geschichte der Kühlung im Haushalt*. Gießen: Anabas-Verlag, 1990.

——. 'Ausgerechnet Bananen'. In *Oikos: Von der Feuerstelle zur Mikrowelle: Haushalt und Wohnen im Wandel,* edited by Michael Andritzky. Gießen: Anabas, 1992.

——. 'Der Keller in der Küche'. In *Technisiertes Familienleben: Blick zurück und nach vorn*, edited by Sibylle Meyer and Eva Schulze. Berlin: Edition Sigma, 1993.

Herf, Jeffrey. *Reactionary Modernism: Technology, Culture, and Politics in Weimar and the Third Reich.* Cambridge: Cambridge University Press, 1984.

Herlyn, Ulfert, Adelheid von Saldern and Wulf Tessin, eds. *Neubausiedlungen der 20er und 60er Jahre: Ein historisch-soziologischer Vergleich.* Frankfurt am Main: Campus, 1987.

Hobbensiefken, Günter. 'Statistik der Teilzahlungsfinanzierung'. In Wirtschaftsverband Teilzahlungsbanken e.V., *Handbuch der Teilzahlungswirtschaft,* pp. 257–96. Frankfurt am Main: Fritz Knapp, 1959.

Hockerts, Hans Günter. 'Metamorphosen des Wohlfahrtsstaats'. In *Zäsuren nach 1945: Essays zur Periodisierung der deutschen Nachkriegsgeschichte,* edited by Martin Broszat. Munich: R. Oldenbourg, 1990.

Höhn, Maria. 'Frau im Haus und Girl im *Spiegel*: Discourse on Women in the Interregnum Period of 1945–1949 and the Question of German Identity'. In *Central European History* 26(1) (1993): 57–90.

Hollstein, Walter. *Die Männer: Vorwärts oder zurück?* Stuttgart: Deutsche Verlags-Anstalt, 1990.

Huerkamp, Claudia. 'Jüdische Akademikerinnen in Deutschland, 1900–1938'. *Geschichte und Gesellschaft* 19 (July/Sept. 1993): 311–31.

Jantzen, Eva, and Merith Niehuss, eds. *Das Klassenbuch: Geschichte einer Frauengeneration.* Reinbek bei Hamburg: Rowohlt, 1997.

Jenkis, Helmut W. *Wohnungswirtschaft und Wohnungspolitik in beiden deutschen Staaten.* Hamburg: Hammonia, 1976.

Johnston, James P. *A Hundred Years of Eating: Food, Drink and the Daily Diet in Britain since the late Nineteenth Century.* Dublin: Gill & Macmillan, 1977.

Jungwirth, Nikolaus, and Gerhard Kromschröder. *Die Pubertät der Republik: Die 50er Jahre der Deutschen.* Reinbek bei Hamburg: Rowohlt, 1983.

Kanacher, Ursula. *Wohnstrukturen als Anzeiger gesellschaftlicher Strukturen: Eine Untersuchung zum Wandel der Wohnungsgrundrisse als Ausdruck gesellschaftlichen Wandels von 1850 bis 1975 aus der Sicht der Elias'schen Zivilisationstheorie.* Frankfurt am Main: R.G. Fischer, 1987.

Katona, George, Burkhard Strumpel and Ernest Zahn. *Aspirations and Affluence: Comparative Studies in the United States and Western Europe.* New York: McGraw-Hill, 1971.

Kettschau, Irmhild. 'Wieviel Arbeit macht ein Familienhaushalt? Zur Analyse von Inhalt, Umfang und Verteilung der Hausarbeit heute'. Dissertation, PH Ruhr, Dortmund, 1980.

Bibliography

Kittler, Gertraude. *Hausarbeit: Zur Geschichte einer 'Natur-Ressource'*. Munich: Verlag Frauenoffensive, 1980.

Kleßmann, Christoph. *Die doppelte Staatsgründung: Deutsche Geschichte 1945–1955*. Göttingen: Vandenhoeck & Ruprecht, 1982.

——. *Zwei Staaten, eine Nation: Deutsche Geschichte 1955-1970*. Göttingen: Vandenhoeck & Ruprecht, 1988.

——. 'Untergänge – Übergänge: Gesellschaftsgeschichtliche Brüche und Kontinuitätslinien vor und nach 1945'. In *Nicht nur Hitlers Krieg: Der Zweite Weltkrieg und die Deutschen*, edited by Christoph Kleßmann. Düsseldorf: Droste, 1989.

Koch, Ludwig. 'Das Haushaltsgeräte-Absatzpolitik in Elektrizitätsversorgungs-Unternehmen'. Dissertation, Munich, 1957.

Kolinsky, Eva. *Women in Contemporary Germany: Life, Work and Politics*, rev. edn. Providence: Berg, 1993.

König, René. *Materialien zur Soziologie der Familie*. Cologne: Kiepenheuer & Witsch, 1974.

Koonz, Claudia. *Mothers in the Fatherland: Women, the Family, and Nazi Politics*. New York: St. Martin's Press, 1987.

Kopp, Cornelia. *Richtig haushalten: Grundregeln durchdachter Hausarbeit*. Leipzig: Otto Beyer, 1933.

Krais, Beate. 'Gender and Symbolic Violence: Female Oppression in the Light of Pierre Bourdieu's Theory of Social Practice'. In *Bourdieu: Critical Perspectives*, edited by Craig Calhoun, Edward LiPuma, and Moishe Postone. Cambridge: Polity Press, 1993.

Krause, Joachim. 'Die Frankfurter Küche'. In *Oikos: Von der Feuerstelle zur Mikrowelle: Haushalt und Wohnen im Wandel*, edited by Michael Andritzky. Gießen: Anabas, 1992.

Krieg, Ilona. *Entwicklung der Familien- und Haushaltsstrukturen in zehn ehemals kleinbäuerlichen Dörfern der Bundesrepublik Deutschland: Ein Beitrag zum sozialen Wandel*. Bonn: Forschungsgesellschaft für Agrarpolitik und Agrarsoziologie e.V., 1975.

Kriegeskorte, Michael. *Werbung in Deutschland 1945-1965: Die Nachkriegszeit im Spiegel ihrer Anzeigen*. Cologne: DuMont, 1992.

Kuhn, Annette. 'Power and Powerlessness: Women after 1945, or the Continuity of the Ideology of Femininity'. *German History* 7 (April 1989): 35–46.

Kuhn, Bärbel. *Haus Frauen Arbeit 1915–1965: Erinnerungen aus fünfzig Jahren Haushaltsgeschichte*. St Ingbert: Röhrig, 1994.

Kühne, Thomas. '". . . aus diesem Krieg werden nicht nur harte Männer heimkehren": Kriegskameradschaft und Männlichkeit im 20. Jahrhundert'. In *Männergeschichte – Geschlechtergeschichte: Männlichkeit*

Bibliography

im Wandel der Moderne, edited by Thomas Kühne. Frankfurt am Main: Campus, 1996.

Lacey, Kate. *Feminine Frequencies: Gender, German Radio, and the Public Sphere, 1923–1945.* Ann Arbor: University of Michigan Press, 1996.

Lamousé, Annette. 'Family Roles of Women: A German Example'. *Journal of Marriage and the Family* 31 (1969): 145–53.

Langer-El Sayed, Ingrid. *Frau und Illustrierte im Kapitalismus.* Cologne: Pahl-Rugenstein, 1971.

'Die LDM (Leistungsgemeinschaft des deutschen Möbelhandels e. V.) stellt aus'. *Die Innenarchitektur* 1(5) (1954): 35–8.

Leiner, Wolfgang. *Geschichte der Elektrizitätswirtschaft in Württemberg.* Stuttgart: Energie-Versorgung Schwaben, 1985.

Lester, Rosemarie K. *Trivialneger: Das Bild des Schwarzen in westdeutschen Illustrierten.* Stuttgart: H.-D. Heinz, 1982.

Lieberman, Ben. 'Testing Peukert's Paradigm: The "Crisis of Classical Modernity" in the "New Frankfurt", 1925–1930'. *German Studies Review* 27 (May 1994): 287–303.

Lifshey, Earl. *The Housewares Story: A History of the American Housewares Industry.* Chicago: National Housewares Manufacturers Association, 1973.

Lippert, Elisabeth. *Hauswirtschaftliche Bildung in der Bundesrepublik Deutschland.* Bonn: Bundesministerium für Wirtschaft, 1966.

Loehlin, Jennifer. 'Consumers and the State: British and German Food Policy during the First World War'. Master's thesis, University of Texas at Austin, 1987.

Lorenz, Gabriela. *Lebensverhältnisse privater Haushalte in Europa: Sechs Länder im Zahlenvergleich.* Frankfurt am Main: Campus, 1991.

Lott, Sylvia. *Die Frauenzeitschriften von Hans Huffzky und John Jahr: Zur Geschichte der deutschen Frauenzeitschrift zwischen 1933 und 1970.* Berlin: Wissenschaftsverlag Volker Spiess, 1985.

Lott-Almstadt, Sylvia. *Brigitte 1886–1986: Die ersten hundert Jahre: Chronik einer Frauenzeitschrift.* Hamburg: Gruner & Jahr, 1986.

Lövgren, Britta. *Hemarbete som politik: Diskussioner om hemarbete, Sverige 1930-40-talen, och tillkomsten av Hemmens Forskningsinstitut.* Stockholm: Almqvist & Wiksell, 1993.

Lupton, Ellen. *Mechanical Brides: Women and Machines from Home to Office.* New York: Cooper-Hewitt National Museum of Design/ Princeton Architectural Press, 1993.

Lutz, Burkart, ed. *Technik und sozialer Wandel: Verhandlungen des 23. Deutschen Soziologentages, Hamburg 1986.* Frankfurt am Main: Campus, 1986.

——. *Technik in Alltag und Arbeit: Beiträge der Tagung des Verbands Sozialwissenschaftliche Technikforschung (Bonn, 29.–30. Mai 1989).* Berlin: Edition Sigma, 1989.

Maase, Kaspar. *BRAVO Amerika: Erkundungen zur Jugendkultur der Bundesrepublik in den fünfziger Jahren.* Hamburg: Junius, 1992.

McCracken, Ellen. *Decoding Women's Magazines: From Mademoiselle to Ms.* Houndmills, Basingstoke, Hampshire: Macmillan, 1993.

McRobbie, Angela. '*Jackie*: An Ideology of Adolescent Femininity'. In *Popular Culture: Past and Present,* edited by Bernard Waites, Tony Bennett and Graham Martin. London: Croom Helm, 1982.

Malos, Ellen, ed. *The Politics of Housework*. London: Allison & Busby, 1980.

Marchand, Roland. *Advertising the American Dream: Making Way for Modernity, 1920–1940.* Berkeley and Los Angeles: University of California Press, 1985.

Marschalck, Peter. 'Demographische Anmerkungen zur Rolle der Flüchtlinge und Vertriebenen in der westdeutschen Nachkriegsgeschichte'. In *Flüchtlinge und Vertriebene in der westdeutschen Nachkriegsgeschichte: Bilanzierung der Forschung und Perspektiven für die künftige Forschungsarbeit,* edited by Rainer Schulze, Doris von der Brelie-Lewien and Helga Grebing. Hildesheim: August Lax, 1987.

Martin, Martine. 'La Rationalisation du travail ménager en France dans l'entre-deux guerres'. *Culture technique* 3 (1980): 156–65.

——. 'Ménagère: une profession? Les dilemmes de l'entre-deux-guerres'. *Le Mouvement social* 140 (July–September 1987): 89–106.

May, Elaine Tyler. *Homeward Bound: American Families in the Cold War Era.* New York: Basic Books, 1988.

Mayer, Sigrid-Esther. 'Die Hauptursachen der tendenziellen Gestaltung der deutschen Lebenshaltung in der Nachkriegszeit (ab 1950)'. Dissertation, Göttingen, 1960.

Menge, Robert. 'Einzelhandel als Träger des Teilzahlungskredits'. In Wirtschaftsverband Teilzahlungsbanken e.V., *Handbuch der Teilzahlungswirtschaft,* pp. 79–81. Frankfurt am Main: Fritz Knapp, 1959.

——, 'Der Kundenkredit des Einzelhandels im Jahre 1963'. In *Die Teilzahlungswirtschaft* 12 (March 1965): 52.

Merkle, Judith A. *Management and Ideology: The Legacy of the International Scientific Management Movement.* Berkeley and Los Angeles: University of California Press, 1980.

Meyer, Sibylle. *Das Theater mit der Hausarbeit: Bürgerliche Repräsentation in der Familie der wilhelminischen Zeit.* Frankfurt am Main: Campus, 1982.

Bibliography

Meyer, Sibylle, and Eva Schulze. '"Alleine war's schwieriger und einfacher zugleich": Veränderung gesellschaftlicher Bewertung und individueller Erfahrung alleinstehender Frauen in Berlin 1943–1955'. In *Frauen in der Geschichte V: 'Das Schicksal Deutschlands liegt in der Hand seiner Frauen': Frauen in der deutschen Nachkriegsgeschichte*, edited by Anna-Elisabeth Freier and Annette Kuhn. Düsseldorf: Schwann, 1984.

——. '"Als wir wieder zusammen waren, ging der Krieg im Kleinen weiter": Frauen, Männer und Familien in Berlin der vierziger Jahre'. In *'Wir kriegen jetzt andere Zeiten': Auf der Suche nach der Erfahrung des Volkes in nachfaschistischen Ländern*, edited by Lutz Niethammer and Alexander von Plato. Berlin: J.H.W. Dietz Nachf., 1985

——. *Von Liebe sprach damals keiner: Familienalltag in der Nachkriegszeit*. Munich: C.H. Beck, 1985.

——. *Wie wir das alles geschafft haben: Alleinstehende Frauen berichten über ihr Leben nach 1945,* 3rd edn. Munich: C.H. Beck, 1985.

——. *Auswirkungen des II. Weltkriegs auf Familien: Zum Wandel der Familie in Deutschland*. Berlin: Technische Universität, 1989.

——. 'Fernseher contra Waschmaschine: Wie Familienstrukturen auf Technik wirken'. In *Familienbildung und Erwerbstätigkeit im demographischen Wandel: Proceedings der 23. Arbeitstagung der Deutschen Gesellschaft für Bevölkerungswissenschaft am 28. Februar-3. März 1989 in Bad Homburg v.d.H.*, edited by Gert Wagner, Notburga Ott and Hans-Joachim Hoffmann-Nowotny. Berlin: Springer-Verlag, 1989.

——. *Technikfolgen für Familien: Längsschnittanalyse und zukünftige Entwicklung. Technikfolgenabschätzung – Projektergebnisse*, vol. 5. Düsseldorf: Verein Deutscher Ingenieure – Technologiezentrum Physikalische Technologien, 1993.

——. 'Technisiertes Familienleben: Ergebnisse einer Längsschnittuntersuchung 1950–1990'. In *Technisiertes Familienleben: Blick zurück und nach vorn,* edited by Sibylle Meyer and Eva Schulze. Berlin: Edition Sigma, 1993.

——. 'Technology and Family: A Longitudinal Study on the Effects of Technology on the Family, Household, and Housing in the 20th Century'. Preliminary report. Berlin, n.d.

Meyer-Ehlers, Grete. *Wohnung und Familie: Ergebnisse einer Untersuchung im Auftrage des Bundesministers für Wohnungswesen und Städtebau*. Stuttgart: Deutsche Verlags-Anstalt, 1968.

——. *Raumprogramme und Bewohnererfahrungen: Planungsgrundlagen für den Wohnungsbau*. Stuttgart: Karl Krämer, 1971.

Mills, Sara, ed. *Gendering the Reader*. New York: Harvester Wheatsheaf, 1994.

Bibliography

Millum, Trevor. *Images of Women: Advertising in Women's Magazines.* Totowa, New Jersey: Rowman and Littlefield, 1975.

Möding, Nori. 'Die Stunde der Frauen? Frauen und Frauenorganisationen des bürgerlichen Lagers'. In *Von Stalingrad zur Währungsreform: Zur Sozialgeschichte des Umbruchs in Deutschland,* edited by Martin Broszat, Klaus D. Henke and Hans Woller. Munich: R. Oldenbourg, 1988.

Moeller, Robert G. 'Reconstructing the Family in Reconstruction Germany: Women and Social Policy in the Federal Republic, 1949–1955'. *Feminist Studies* 15 (spring 1989): 137–69.

——. *Protecting Motherhood: Women and the Family in the Politics of Postwar West Germany.* Berkeley and Los Angeles: University of California Press, 1993.

Mollenhauer, Hans P. *Von Omas Küche zur Fertigpackung: Aus der Kinderstube der Lebensmittelindustrie.* Gernsbach: Casimir Katz, 1988.

Møller, Hanne, Inger Stauning, Karen Syberg, Lisbeth Dehn Holgersen and Signe Arnfred. *Udsigten fra det kvindelige univers: En analyse af Eva .* Copenhagen: Røde Hane, 1972.

Mooser, Josef. 'Auflösung des proletarischen Milieus: Klassenbindung und Individualisierung in der Arbeiterschaft vom Kaiserreich bis in die Bundesrepublik Deutschland'. *Soziale Welt* 34(3) (1983): 270–306.

——. *Arbeiterleben in Deutschland 1900–1970.* Frankfurt am Main: Suhrkamp, 1984.

Morsey, Rudolf. *Die Bundesrepublik Deutschland.* Oldenbourg Grundriß der Geschichte 19. Munich: R. Oldenbourg, 1987.

Müller, Walter. 'Frauenerwerbstätigkeit im Lebenslauf'. In Walter Müller, Angelika Willms and Johann Handl, *Strukturwandel der Frauenarbeit 1880–1980.* Frankfurt am Main: Campus, 1983.

Müller, Walter, Angelika Willms and Johann Handl. *Strukturwandel der Frauenarbeit 1880–1980.* Frankfurt am Main: Campus, 1983.

Nave-Herz, Rosemarie, ed. *Wandel und Kontinuität der Familie in der Bundesrepublik Deutschland.* Stuttgart: Ferdinand Enke, 1988.

Nave-Herz, Rosemarie *et al. Familiäre Veränderungen seit 1950: Eine empirische Studie: Abschlußbericht, Teil I.* Oldenburg: Universität Oldenburg, Institut für Soziologie, n.d. [1985].

Niethammer, Lutz. 'Fragen – Antworten – Fragen: Methodische Erfahrungen und Erwägungen zur Oral History'. In *'Wir kriegen jetzt andere Zeiten': Auf der Suche nach der Erfahrung des Volkes in nachfaschistischen Ländern,* edited by Lutz Niethammer and Alexander von Plato. Bonn: J.H.W. Dietz Nachf., 1985.

Bibliography

Niethammer, Lutz, and Alexander von Plato, eds. '*Wir kriegen jetzt andere Zeiten': Auf der Suche nach der Erfahrung des Volkes in nachfaschistischen Ländern.* Berlin: J.H.W. Dietz Nachf., 1985.

Noelle, Elisabeth, and Erich Peter Neumann, eds. *The Germans: Public Opinion Polls 1947–1966.* Allensbach: Verlag für Demoskopie, 1967.

Nolan, Mary '"Housework Made Easy": The Taylorized Housewife in Weimar Germany's Rationalized Economy'. *Feminist Studies* 16 (fall 1990): 549–77.

———. *Visions of Modernity: American Business and the Modernization of Germany.* New York: Oxford University Press, 1994.

Oakley, Ann. *The Sociology of Housework.* New York: Pantheon, 1974.

Ockel, Karl. 'Zur volkswirtschaftlichen Problematik des Teilzahlungskredites: Eine vergleichende Untersuchung der Verhältnisse in den USA und der BRD unter besondere Berücksichtigung der Möglichkeiten einer Einflußnahme auf das Teilzahlungskreditgeschäft'. Dissertation, Frankfurt am Main, 1961.

Olney, Martha L. *Buy Now, Pay Later: Advertising, Credit, and Consumer Durables in the 1920s.* Chapel Hill: University of North Carolina Press, 1991.

Orland, Barbara. *Wäsche waschen: Technik- und Sozialgeschichte der häuslichen Wäschepflege.* Reinbek bei Hamburg: Rowohlt Taschenbuch Verlag, 1991.

———. 'Emanzipation durch Rationalisierung? Der "rationelle Haushalt" als Konzept institutionalisierter Frauenpolitik in der Weimarer Republik'. In Dagmar Reese, Eve Rosenhaft, Carola Sachse and Tilla Siegel, eds, *Rationale Beziehungen? Geschlechterverhältnisse im Rationalisierungsprozeß.* Frankfurt am Main: Suhrkamp, 1993.

Ortlieb, Heinz-Dietrich. 'Unsere Konsumgesellschaft: Glanz und Elend des deutschen Wirtschaftswunders'. In *Hamburger Jahrbuch für Wirtschafts- und Gesellschaftspolitik, Festausgabe für Eduard Heimann zum 70. Geburtstage*, edited by Heinz-Dietrich Ortlieb. Tübingen: J.C.B. Mohr (Paul Siebeck), 1959.

Pence, Katherine. 'Ambivalence toward "Americanization" of German Women as an Indication of Anxiety about Reconstruction of the West German State, 1945–1953'. Seminar paper, University of Michigan at Ann Arbor, 1991.

Peukert, Detlev J.K. *Inside Nazi Germany: Conformity, Opposition, and Racism in Everyday Life*, translated by Richard Deveson. New Haven: Yale University Press, 1987.

———. *The Weimar Republic: The Crisis of Classical Modernity*, translated by Richard Deveson. London: Allen Lane, 1991.

Bibliography

Pfeil, Elisabeth, ed. *Die Wohnwünsche der Bergarbeiter: Soziologische Erhebung, Deutung und Kritik der Wohnvorstellungen eines Berufes.* Tübingen: J.C.B. Mohr (Paul Siebeck), 1954.

Pfeil, Elisabeth. *Die Berufstätigkeit von Müttern: Eine empirisch-soziologische Erhebung an 900 Müttern aus vollständigen Familien.* Tübingen: J.C.B. Mohr, 1961.

Polm, Rita. '... *neben dem Mann die andere Hälfte eines Ganzen zu sein?!' Junge Frauen in der Nachkriegszeit.* Munich: Unrast, 1990.

Preuss-Lausitz, Ulf, *et al. Kriegskinder, Konsumkinder, Krisenkinder: Zur Sozialisationsgeschichte seit dem zweiten Weltkrieg.* Weinheim: Beltz, 1983.

Prinz, Michael, and Rainer Zitelmann, eds. *Nationalsozialismus und Modernisierung.* Darmstadt: Wissenschaftliche Buchgesellschaft, 1991.

Pross, Helge. *Gleichberechtigung im Beruf? Eine Untersuchung mit 7000 Arbeitnehmerinnen in der EWG.* Frankfurt am Main: Athenäum, 1973.

———. *Die Wirklichkeit der Hausfrau.* Reinbek bei Hamburg: Rowohlt, 1976.

Reagin, Nancy R. *A German Women's Movement: Class and Gender in Hanover, 1880–1933.* Chapel Hill: University of North Carolina Press, 1995.

Reese, Dagmar. *Straff, aber nicht stramm – herb, aber nicht derb: Zur Vergesellschaftung von Mädchen durch den Bund Deutscher Mädel im sozialkulturellen Vergleich zweier Milieus.* Weinheim: Beltz, 1989.

Reichling, Gerhard. 'Flucht und Vertreibung der Deutschen: Statistische Grundlagen und terminologische Probleme'. In *Flüchtlinge und Vertriebene in der westdeutschen Nachkriegsgeschichte: Bilanzierung der Forschung und Perspektiven für die künftige Forschungsarbeit,* edited by Rainer Schulze, Doris von der Brelie-Lewien and Helga Grebing. Hildesheim: August Lax, 1987.

Rerrich, Maria S. 'Veränderte Elternschaft: Entwicklungen in der familialen Arbeit mit Kindern seit 1950'. *Soziale Welt* 34 (1983): 420–49.

Roberts, Elizabeth. *Women and Families: An Oral History, 1940–1970.* Oxford: Blackwell, 1995.

Römer, Ruth. *Die Sprache der Anzeigenwerbung,* 3rd edn. Düsseldorf: Schwann, 1973.

Röpke, Wilhelm. *Vorgegessen Brot: Kritische Nachlese zur Diskussion über das Borgkaufwesen.* Cologne: Carl Heymanns Verlag, 1955.

Rosenbaum, Heidi. *Formen der Familie: Untersuchungen zum Zusammenhang von Familienverhältnissen, Sozialstruktur und sozialem Wandel in der deutschen Gesellschaft des 19. Jahrhunderts.* Frankfurt am Main: Suhrkamp, 1982.

Bibliography

Ruhl, Klaus-Jörg. 'Familie und Beruf: Weibliche Erwerbstätigkeit und katholische Kirche in den 50er Jahren'. *Aus Politik und Zeitgeschichte* 93 (23 April 1993): 30–8.

Ruppert, Wolfgang, ed. *Fahrrad, Auto, Fernsehschrank*. Frankfurt am Main: Fischer Taschenbuch Verlag, 1993.

Sandford, John. *The Mass Media of the German-Speaking Countries*. London: Oswald Wolff, 1976.

Schäfer, Hans Dieter. 'Amerikanismus im Dritten Reich'. In *Nationalsozialismus und Modernisierung*, edited by Michael Prinz and Rainer Zitelmann. Darmstadt: Wissenschaftliche Buchgesellschaft, 1991.

Schelsky, Helmut. *Wandlungen der deutschen Familie in der Gegenwart: Darstellung und Deutung einer empirisch-soziologischen Tatbestandsaufnahme*, 2nd edn. Stuttgart: Ferdinand Enke, 1954.

Schickling, Hella. *Ist die Hausfrau noch zu retten?* Munich: Delp, 1972.

Schildt, Axel, and Arnold Sywottek, eds. *Modernisierung im Wiederaufbau: Die westdeutsche Gesellschaft der 50er Jahre*. Bonn: J.H.W. Dietz Nachf., 1993.

Schissler, Hanna. 'Gender and Social Stability: The Restructuring of West German Society 1945 to 1955'. *German Historical Institute Bulletin* 6 (spring 1990): 21–4.

Schivelbusch, Wolfgang. *Disenchanted Night: The Industrialisation of Light in the Nineteenth Century*. Oxford: Berg, 1988.

Schmidt, Dorothea. 'Gesellschaftliche Bedingungen bei der Entwicklung der Wohnverhältnisse und Wohnwünsche in der BRD seit 1945'. Dissertation, Erlangen-Nuremberg, 1978.

Schmidt, Klaus-Dieter. *Strukturwandlungen des privaten Verbrauchs in der Bundesrepublik Deutschland, 1950–1985*. Kiel: Instutut für Weltwirtschaft, 1976.

Schmölders, Günter, with G. Scherhorn and G. Schmidtchen. *Der Umgang mit Geld im privaten Haushalt*. Berlin: Duncker & Humblot, 1969.

Schuberth, Klaus Herbert. *Konsumentenkredit und wirtschaftliche Entwicklung: Der Einfluß der Kreditfinanzierung des privaten Konsums auf die Struktur der Volkswirtschaft*. Spardorf: René F. Wilfer, 1988.

Schubnell, Hermann. 'Die Erwerbstätigkeit von Frauen und Müttern und die Betreuung ihrer Kinder'. *Wirtschaft und Statistik* 8 (August) 1964: 444–56.

Schwarzer, Alice. *So fing es an! Die neue Frauenbewegung*. Munich: Deutscher Taschenbuch Verlag, 1983.

Seeler, Angela. 'Ehe, Familie und andere Lebensformen in den Nachkriegsjahren im Spiegel der Frauenzeitschriften'. In *Frauen in der Geschichte V: 'Das Schicksal Deutschlands liegt in der Hand seiner*

Bibliography

Frauen': *Frauen in der deutschen Nachkriegsgeschichte*, edited by Anna-Elisabeth Freier and Annette Kuhn. Düsseldorf: Schwann, 1984.

Selle, Gert. *Die Geschichte des Design in Deutschland von 1870 bis heute: Entwicklung der industriellen Produktkultur.* Cologne: DuMont, 1978.

Sherayko, Gerard F. 'Selling the Modern: The New Consumerism in Weimar Germany'. Dissertation, Indiana, 1996.

Siebke, Jürgen. 'Die Nachfrage nach dauerhaften Konsumgütern und ihr Einfluß auf den Wirtschaftsablauf'. Dissertation, Bonn, 1965.

Siepmann, Eckhard, ed. *Bikini: Die fünfziger Jahre: Politik, Alltag, Opposition: Kalter Krieg und Capri-Sonne.* Reinbek bei Hamburg: Rowohlt, 1983.

Silbermann, Alphons. *Vom Wohnen der Deutschen.* Cologne: Westdeutscher Verlag, 1963.

Silberzahn-Jandt, Gudrun. *Wasch-Maschine: Zum Wandel von Frauenarbeit im Haushalt.* Marburg: Jonas-Verlag, 1991.

Simonton, Deborah. *A History of European Women's Work, 1700 to the Present.* London: Routledge, 1998.

Sorge, Martin K. *The Other Price of Hitler's War: German Military and Civilian Losses Resulting from World War II.* New York: Greenwood Press, 1986.

Speck, Otto. *Kinder erwerbstätiger Mütter.* Stuttgart: Ferdinand Enke, 1956.

Statistisches Bundesamt Wiesbaden. *Fachserie M: Preise, Löhne, Wirtschaftsrechnungen, Reihe 18: Einkommens- und Verbrauchsstichproben. Ausstattung privater Haushalte mit ausgewählten langlebigen Gebrauchsgütern 1962/63.* Stuttgart: W. Kohlhammer, 1964.

——. *Fachserie M: Preise, Löhne, Wirtschaftsrechnungen, Reihe 18: Einkommens- und Verbrauchsstichproben. Ausstattung privater Haushalte mit ausgewählten langlebigen Gebrauchsgütern 1969.* Stuttgart: W. Kohlhammer, 1970.

——. *Bevölkerung und Wirtschaft 1872–1972.* Stuttgart: W. Kohlhammer, 1972.

Stemler, Hildegard, and Erich Wiegand. 'Zur Entwicklung der Arbeitszeitgesetzgebung und der Arbeitszeit in Deutschland seit der Industrialisierung'. In *Wandel der Lebensbedingungen in Deutschland: Wohlfahrtsentwicklung seit der Industrialisierung*, edited by Erich Wiegand and Wolfgang Zapf. Frankfurt am Main: Campus, 1982.

Stephenson, Jill. *Women in Nazi Society.* London: Croom Helm, 1975.

Strasser, Susan. *Satisfaction Guaranteed: The Making of the American*

Mass Market. New York: Pantheon, 1989.

Teuteberg, Hans Jürgen. 'Studien zur Volksernährung unter sozial- und wirtschaftsgeschichtlichen Aspekten'. In *Der Wandel der Nahrungsgewohnheiten unter dem Einfluß der Industrialisierung*, edited by Hans Jürgen Teuteberg and Günter Wiegelmann, pp. 78–85. Göttingen: Vandenhoeck & Ruprecht, 1972.

——. 'Nahrungsmittelverzehr in Deutschland pro Kopf und Jahr 1850–1975'. *Archiv für Sozialgeschichte* 19 (1979): 331–88.

Thielmann, Georg. 'Die Entwicklung des Familienrechts im Bundesgebiet mit Berlin (West) seit 1949'. In Gesellschaft für Deutschlandforschung, Fachgruppe Rechtswissenschaft, *Das Familienrecht in beiden deutschen Staaten: Rechtsentwicklung, Rechtsvergleich, Kollisionsprobleme.* Cologne: Carl Heymanns Verlag, 1983.

Thrall, Charles A. 'The Conservative Use of Modern Household Technology'. *Technology and Culture* 23 (April 1982): 175–94.

Thurnwald, Hilde. *Gegenwartsprobleme Berliner Familien.* Berlin: Weidmann, 1948.

Tietz, Bruno. *Konsument und Einzelhandel: Strukturwandlungen in der Bundesrepublik Deutschland von 1960 bis 1985*, 2nd edn. Frankfurt am Main: Lorch-Verlag, 1973.

Tornieporth, Gerda. *Arbeitsplatz Haushalt: Zur Theorie und Ökologie der Hausarbeit.* Berlin: Dietrich Reimer, 1988.

Tröger, Annemarie. 'Die Dolchstoßlegende der Linken: Haben Frauen Hitler an die Macht gebracht?' In Gruppe Berliner Dozentinnen, *Frauen und Wissenschaft: Beiträge zur Berliner Sommeruniversität für Frauen, Juli 1976.* Berlin: Courage, 1977.

Tumpek-Kjellmark, Katharina. 'From Hitler's Widows to Adenauer's Brides: Towards a Construction of Gender and Memory in Postwar West Germany'. Dissertation, Cornell, 1994.

Ulshoefer, Helgard. *Mütter im Beruf: Die Situation erwerbstätiger Mütter in neun Industrieländern: Annotierte Bibliographie.* Weinheim: Beltz, 1969.

van Deenen, Bernd, and Christa Kossen-Knirim. *Landfrauen in Betrieb, Haushalt und Familie: Ergebnisse einer empirischen Untersuchung in acht Dörfern der Bundesrepublik Deutschland.* Bonn: Forschungsgesellschaft für Agrarpolitik und Agrarsoziologie e.V., 1981.

Vanek, Joann. 'Time spent in housework'. *Scientific American* 231 (November 1974): 116–20.

Von Ankum, Katharina, ed. *Women in the Metropolis: Gender and Modernity in Weimar Culture.* Berkeley and Los Angeles: University of California Press, 1997.

Bibliography

von Beyme, Klaus. *Der Wiederaufbau: Architektur und Städtebaupolitik in beiden deutschen Staaten*. Munich: R. Piper, 1987.

von Saldern, Adelheid. 'Victims or Perpetrators? Controversies about the Role of Women in the Nazi State'. In *Nazism and German Society, 1933-1945*, edited by David F. Crew. London: Routledge, 1994.

von Schweitzer, Rosemarie, and Helge Pross, eds. *Die Familienhaushalte im wirtschaftlichen und sozialen Wandel: Rationalverhalten, Technisierung, Funktionswandel der Privathaushalte und das Freizeitbudget der Frau*. Göttingen: Otto Schwarz, 1976.

von Simson, John. *Kanalisation und Städtehygiene im 19. Jahrhundert*. Düsseldorf: VDI-Verlag, 1983.

Wagner, Eva. *Technik für Frauen: Arbeitszusammenhang, Alltagserfahrungen und Perspektiven der Hausfrauen im Umgang mit technischen Artefakten*. Munich: Profil, 1991.

Wald, Renate. *Industriearbeiter privat*. Stuttgart: Ferdinand Enke, 1966.

Wandersleb, Hermann, ed. *Handwörterbuch des Städtebaues, Wohnungs- und Siedlungswesens*. Stuttgart: W. Kohlhammer, 1959.

Warhaftig, Myra. *Die Behinderung der Emanzipation der Frau durch die Wohnung und die Möglichkeit zur Überwindung*. Cologne: Pahl-Rugenstein, 1982.

Weismann, Anabella. *Froh erfülle Deine Pflicht: Die Entwicklung des Hausfrauenleitbildes im Spiegel trivialer Massenmedien in der Zeit zwischen Reichsgründung und Weltwirtschaftskrise*. Berlin: Schelzky & Jeep, 1988.

Werner, Brigitte Barbara. 'Sex in Advertising: A Cross-Cultural Content Analysis of US and West German Print Advertisements'. Master's thesis, University of Texas at Austin, 1989.

Werner, Françoise. 'Du ménage à l'art ménager: l'évolution du travail ménager et son écho dans la presse féminine française de 1919 à 1939'. *Le Mouvement social* 126 (January–March 1984): 61–87.

Weyrather, Irmgard. *Muttertag und Mutterkreuz: Der Kult um die 'deutsche Mutter' im Nationalsozialismus*. Frankfurt am Main: Fischer Taschenbuch Verlag, 1993.

Wildt, Michael. 'Das Ende der Bescheidenheit: Wirtschaftsrechnungen von Arbeitnehmerhaushalten in der Bundesrepublik Deutschland 1950–1963'. In *Arbeiter im 20. Jahrhundert*, edited by Klaus Tenfelde. Stuttgart: Klett-Cotta, 1991.

———. 'Konsum und Modernisierung in den fünfziger Jahren'. In *Zivilisation und Barbarei: Die widersprüchlichen Potentiale der Moderne*, edited by Frank Bajohr, Werner Johe and Uwe Lohalm. Hamburg: Hans Christians Verlag, 1991.

Bibliography

———. *Am Beginn der 'Konsumgesellschaft': Mangelerfahrung, Lebenshaltung, Wohlstandshoffnung in Westdeutschland in den fünfziger Jahren.* Hamburg: Ergebnisse, 1994.

———. 'Plurality of Taste: Food and Consumption in West Germany during the 1950s'. *History Workshop Journal* 39 (spring 1995): 23–41.

———. 'Technik, Kompetenz, Modernität: Amerika als zwiespältiges Vorbild für die Arbeit in der Küche, 1920–1960'. In *Amerikanisierung: Traum und Alptraum im Deutschland des 20. Jahrhunderts,* edited by Alf Lüdtke, Inge Marßolek and Adelheid von Saldern. Stuttgart: Franz Steiner, 1996.

Wilhening, Fritz. *Wohnraumgestaltung,* 2nd edn. Hamburg: Verlag Handwerk und Technik, 1967.

Willett, Ralph. *The Americanization of Germany, 1945–1949.* New York: Routledge, 1989.

Williamson, Judith. *Decoding Advertisements: Ideology and Meaning in Advertising.* London: Marion Boyars, 1978.

Willms, Angelika. 'Grundzüge der Entwicklung der Frauenarbeit von 1880 bis 1980'. In Walter Müller, Angelika Willms and Johann Handl, *Strukturwandel der Frauenarbeit 1880–1980.* Frankfurt am Main: Campus, 1983.

Winship, Janice. 'The Impossibility of *Best*: Enterprise Meets Domesticity in the Practical Women's Magazines of the 1980s'. In *Come On Down? Popular Media Culture in Post-war Britain,* edited by Dominic Strinati and Stephen Wagg. London: Routledge, 1992.

Wirtschaftsverband Teilzahlungsbanken e.V. *Handbuch der Teilzahlungswirtschaft.* Frankfurt am Main: Fritz Knapp, 1959.

Wurzbacher, Gerhard. *Leitbilder gegenwärtigen deutschen Familienlebens.* Stuttgart: Ferdinand Enke, 1952.

Zängl, Wolfgang. *Deutschlands Strom: Die Politik der Elektrifizierung von 1866 bis heute.* Frankfurt am Main: Campus, 1989.

Zapf, Wolfgang. *Lebensbedingungen in der Bundesrepublik: Sozialer Wandel und Wohlfahrtsentwicklung.* Frankfurt am Main: Campus, 1977.

Zapf, Wolfgang, Jürgen Hampel, Heidrun Mollenkopf and Ursula Weber. 'Technik im Alltag von Familien'. In *Technik in Alltag und Arbeit: Beiträge der Tagung des Verbands Sozialwissenschaftliche Technikforschung,* edited by Burkart Lutz. Berlin: Edition Sigma, 1989.

Zaretsky, Eli. *Capitalism, the Family, and Personal Life.* New York: Harper & Row, 1976.

Zuckerman, Mary Ellen. *Sources on the History of Women's Magazines, 1792–1960: An Annotated Bibliography.* New York: Greenwood Press, 1991.

Index

Index

Index

Index